Mastering Real Estate Mathematics

Sixth Edition

William L. Ventolo, Jr.
Ralph Tamper
Wellington J. Allaway

Real Estate
Education Company
a division of Dearborn Financial Publishing, Inc.

This publication is designed to provide accurate and authoritative information in regard to the subject matter covered. It is sold with the understanding that the publisher is not engaged in rendering legal, accounting, or other professional service. If legal advice or other expert assistance is required, the services of a competent professional person should be sought.

Publisher: Carol L. Luitjens
Development Editor: Cheryl D. Wilson
Project Editor: Debra M. Hall
Art and Design Manager: Lucy Jenkins
Cover Designer: DePinto Studios

97   10   9   8   7   6   5   4   3

In the interest of saving natural resources, the design of *Mastering Real Estate Mathematics* has been streamlined. The result is a shorter text we believe the reader will find more accessible and user-friendly.

Library of Congress Cataloging-in-Publication Data

Ventolo, William L.
      Mastering real estate mathematics : a self-instructional text / William L. Ventolo,
Jr., Ralph Tamper, Wellington J. Allaway,—6th ed.
         p.   cm.
      Includes bibliographical references and index,
      ISBN 0-7931-1142-0
      1. Business mathematics—Real estate business—Programmed instruction.
   I. Tamper, Ralph.   II. Allaway, Wellington J.   III. Title.
   HF5716.R4V46   1995
   333.33'01'51—dc20   95-24207
                                                                         CIP

CONTENTS

PREFACE

To survive in the real estate business, one must become comfortable and proficient with a variety of mathematical operations. As a real estate professional you will need to know how to compute taxes, expenses, income and the many other figures that underlie most transactions.

This text was written to assist you in developing a higher level of competence in working with the numbers and calculations used in the real estate business. Whether you are new or experienced in the applied use of mathematics, the information that follows will help you sharpen your skills by explaining the kinds of problems encountered during typical real estate activities. Read the explanations and directions carefully. Study the examples and work the practice problems by applying what has been illustrated in the instructional material. With a little patience, concentration and effort, you will become comfortable with the calculations that you need to do.

Great care has been taken to create a text that is accurate. Because practices are often regional, check the laws and procedures applicable to your area. This is particularly true regarding legal descriptions, ad valorem taxes and transfer taxes, prorations, financing and closing.

For their contributions in making this an accurate and reliable text, the authors would like to thank the following individuals for their advice and suggestions:

Cheryl E. Nance, Amarillo College, Amarillo, Texas
Larry Hogan, Fayetteville Technical Community College, Fayetteville, North Carolina
John Tirone, Oakland University, Rochester, Michigan
Helen C. Peemoeller, Berks Real Estate Institute, Reading, Pennsylvania
Tom Morton, North Lake College, Coppell, Texas
John Stovall, Jones Real Estate Colleges, Inc., Denver, Colorado
Mary Bohannon, Amarillo College, Amarillo, Texas
Gerald Cortesi, Triton College, River Grove, Illinois
James I. Wiedemer, Bellaire, Texas

For their assistance in the text's development, the authors wish to recognize:

Sarah Williamson, The Real Estate School, Houston, Texas
Glenda Jones, The Real Estate School, Houston, Texas
Don Shrum, The Real Estate School, Houston, Texas
Lynette K. Marks, instructional design consultant, Durham, North Carolina

ABOUT THE AUTHORS

William L. Ventolo, Jr., received his master's degree in psychology from the University of Pittsburgh. He is a former vice president of Development Systems Corporation and its subsidiary, Real Estate Education Company. Mr. Ventolo has developed and authored numerous industrial training programs and manuals, including a comprehensive dealership accounting correspondence course used by the Ford Motor Company. He has authored and co-authored many trade books and textbooks, including *Principles of Accounting, Fundamentals of Real Estate Appraisal, The Art of Real Estate Appraisal* and *The Complete Home Inspection Kit.* He also serves on the editorial board of the Real Estate Educators' Association Journal. Mr. Ventolo resides in Sarasota, Florida.

Ralph Tamper, DREI, GRI, is owner and director of The Real Estate School. A Life Member of the Texas Association of Real Estate Educators, he is also an instructor for the Texas Association of REALTORS® Graduate REALTORS® Institute. Mr. Tamper has served as a member of the advisory committee on mandatory continuing education to the Texas Real Estate Commission. He is in constant demand as a real estate seminar speaker and speaks throughout Texas on mandatory continuing education topics. Mr. Tamper is the author of numerous workbooks on real estate topics, including principles of real estate, agency, earnest money contract law and real estate practice. He has also authored *Texas Real Estate for the 1990's,* a text for Texas mandatory real estate education. Mr. Tamper resides in Houston, Texas.

Wellington J. Allaway was with the Northern Trust Company, Chicago, for 45 years. There he served as real estate manager and residential loan officer. Mr. Allaway's experience includes teaching various real estate courses, including mathematics, for the REALTORS® Institute of Illinois. In addition, he was an item writer for the American College Testing Service and Educational Testing Service. Mr. Allaway is the co-author of *Modern Real Estate Practice.* He resides in Lombard, Illinois.

INTRODUCTION:
How To Use This Book

BASIC MATH SKILLS

This textbook starts at a very basic math level. This is done deliberately in order to offer some relief to any persons who may experience anxiety in dealing with mathematical concepts. The early discussion of calculators in the Introduction is an effort to integrate a valuable math tool into the text, along with some basic math concepts. If calculators are new to you, these paragraphs should make their use easier.

This type of instructional book also may be new to you. The subject matter has been broken down into a series of numbered exercises. By following the exercises, you can teach yourself the mathematics involved in real estate transactions. Additionally, the text is designed to be augmented by classroom instruction.

The sequence of the exercises is important and designed to help you learn more efficiently. For that reason, you should not skip around in the book.

Almost every exercise presents a learning task that requires some response from you. You should have little difficulty arriving at each correct answer, provided you follow directions precisely, read the material and work through the book with care.

This kind of book also provides immediate feedback by giving you the answers to the questions asked. These answers have been placed at the end of each chapter. Immediate feedback is an important part of the learning process and will enable you to determine readily how your learning is progressing.

Do not look at the correct answer until *after* you have recorded your own answer. If you look before answering, you will only impair your own learning. If you make an error, be sure you know *why* before continuing.

Finally, this text is designed to be used as a workbook. Work through each problem by writing your computations in the spaces provided. This helps both you and your instructor when discussing the solutions.

Study Strategy

It seems appropriate to open our discussion of study strategy with a brief mention of an experience common among students of mathematics: math anxiety. Many people are intimidated by the anticipated difficulties of working math problems, to the point of becoming victims of stress. This book does not provide a psychological analysis of this matter. Rather, the authors have set forth some principles that will help students feel more comfortable with math.

Anxiety about one's ability to perform mathematical calculations is very common. Even college mathematics majors often dread math examinations! If this is so, how can this book effectively help people who have no special background in mathematics, who suddenly find that they need some basic math skills to pass a licensing examination or function more competently as real estate licensees?

In their article "Mastering Math Anxiety," Dr. William L. Boyd of Hardin Simmons University and Elizabeth A. Cox of Howard Payne University offer several ideas:

1. Math anxiety is not an indication of inability. It may be more an indication of excessive concern over possible embarrassment in front of our peers, our instructors, our clients or our customers.
2. Aptitude in math is not necessarily something we are born with. Our aptitude may reflect our attitude rather than our genes. The old saw, "If you think you can or if you think you can't, you're right," certainly applies in this situation. Through practice and study, we can build our skills and our confidence.
3. Self-image can affect our performance in many areas, including math. Make a determined effort to develop your competency in math. If others expect you to fail, don't fall to the level of their expectations! Rather, rise to the level of your potential through a little extra effort.
4. Learn to congratulate yourself on your successes. When you arrive at a correct solution, make a point of giving yourself the credit for your success.[1]

The following are study strategies that will work to your benefit:

1. Take time to carefully read and understand what is being asked. Consider the information given in the problem and decide how each portion relates to the solution. Careful and thoughtful reading will help you understand the problem.
2. Learn to discard those facts that have no bearing on the solution. You do this automatically in many areas of everyday life. Begin to practice this in math, also, by evaluating each bit of information.
3. Make a special effort to be neat. Sloppy figures carelessly jotted down are an invitation to error.
4. Develop a systematic approach to problem solving. Consider each aspect of the problem in its proper place and do not jump to conclusions. It is better to write down each step in the solution, no matter how trivial it seems, than to rely on performing a calculation "in your head."
5. Learn to restate the problem in your own words. By doing this, you can remove many obstacles to a solution. In fact, once you state the problem correctly, you need only perform the mechanics of the arithmetic accurately to arrive at the solution.
6. Form the habit of checking and double-checking your work. It is all too easy to make a mistake out of carelessness. If an error in calculation is not discovered, your solution will be flawed.
7. Request help when you need it. Don't hesitate to ask questions! Others who are puzzled by the same point as you may be reluctant to say so. If you ask the question, you and the entire class benefit.
8. Learn to question the "reasonableness" of the solution. If the answer you have calculated seems unlikely, perhaps it is! Your common sense can often reveal an error due to carelessness.
9. Become proficient with your calculator. The calculator's accuracy helps ensure your good results. But never rely on the machine to do it all! Learn to make your own estimate and compare this with the results of the calculator. If the calculator's answer does not seem plausible, clear the display and work the problem again, making sure you enter the figures and operations correctly. The calculator does not replace you! But it is a wonderful tool to enhance your professionalism.

1. William. L. Boyd and Elizabeth A. Cox, "Mastering Math Anxiety," *Real Estate Today* (March/April 1984): 41–43.

EXERCISES AND EXAMINATIONS

Each chapter concludes with Problems for Additional Practice, consisting of a series of multiple-choice questions patterned after those found in state licensing examinations. Answers to the problems appear at the end of each chapter.

At the end of this book, you will find Review Exam I, covering Chapters 2 through 8, and Review Exam II, covering Chapters 9 through 15.

Answers to all examination questions are in the Answer Key at the end of each exam. These solutions to the questions show the step-by-step mathematics.

LOCAL PRACTICES

Because this textbook is used nationally, some of the situations described may differ from practice in your local area. Therefore, your instructor may wish to skip certain portions of the textbook.

CALCULATORS

 The popularity of hand-held calculators has increased as their cost has decreased. The calculator is a wonderful tool that makes the real estate practitioner more efficient, accurate and productive. Choose a calculator and become familiar with it before you begin this course. Throughout the book, all examples and problem solutions use a simple four-function calculator rather than one of the more sophisticated models that have a percentage key or that perform financial, statistical and engineering functions. A four-function calculator adds, subtracts, multiplies and divides.

Most states permit license applicants to use silent, hand-held, battery-operated, nonprint calculators when taking a licensing exam.

Logic Functions

Calculators can be divided into general types by the form of logic they use. Chain logic and algebraic logic are the most common types. The difference between these two types of logic is illustrated as follows. Consider the calculation:

$$2 + 3 \times 4 = ?$$

If the numbers and arithmetic functions are entered into the chain logic calculator as shown above, the answer will be 20; on the algebraic logic calculator, the answer will be 14. The chain logic sees the data entered in the order that it is keyed in:

$$2 + 3 = 5, \text{ then}$$
$$5 \times 4 = 20,$$

whereas the algebraic logic follows the order of *M*ultiplication, *D*ivision, *A*ddition and then *S*ubtraction:

$$3 \times 4 = 12, \text{ then,}$$
$$12 + 2 = 14.$$

Some chain logic calculators use reverse polish notation, where there is no "=" key. In its place is an "ENTER" key. Certain Hewlett-Packard and Sharp calculator models also use reverse polish notation. Use the previous example of:

$$2 + 3 \times 4 = ?$$

Data on most calculators are entered using chain logic, just as the user would write it:

Press $\boxed{2}$

Press $\boxed{+}$

Press $\boxed{3}$

Press $\boxed{\times}$

Press $\boxed{4}$ Answer

Press $\boxed{=}$ $\boxed{20}$

The reverse polish notation keystrokes, however, are as follows:

$\boxed{2}$

$\boxed{\text{ENTER}}$

$\boxed{3}$

$\boxed{+}$

$\boxed{4}$ Answer

$\boxed{\times}$ $\boxed{20}$

Because most calculators use chain logic, the examples in this text are designed to fit that type. However, you should *thoroughly study the manual furnished with your calculator* for instructions on how to enter data.

Four-Function versus Multifunction Calculators

A basic four-function calculator will certainly be sufficient for this course, but if you plan to purchase a calculator, it is strongly recommended that you spend a few more dollars on one having financial functions, such as the BA Real Estate from Texas Instruments. This type of calculator can be easily identified by these additional keys:

$\boxed{n}$, $\boxed{i}$, $\boxed{\text{PMT}}$, $\boxed{\text{PV}}$, and $\boxed{\text{FV}}$,

where

$\boxed{\text{n}}$ is the number of interest compounding periods;

$\boxed{\text{i}}$ is the amount of interest per compounding period;

$\boxed{\text{PMT}}$ is the payment;

$\boxed{\text{PV}}$ is the present value; and

$\boxed{\text{FV}}$ is the future value.

Differences in Rounding

Calculators may display six, eight or ten digits, but regardless of the number, a calculator retains far more numbers than are displayed in a calculation. For example, if a calculator displays six digits, or single numbers, such as 123456, the calculator knows what follows the last digit, or single number, displayed. This last digit depends on whether the calculator "rounds" or "truncates." Consider an answer of 123456.7. This calculation displayed on a six-digit calculator will be 123457 for a calculator that rounds and 123456 for a calculator that truncates.

"Rounds" means that if the next digit not displayed is *less than* 5, the last digit to be displayed remains the same. However, if the next digit not displayed is *greater than* 5, the last digit to be displayed will be *increased* or *rounded up* to the next larger digit.

"Truncates" means that regardless of the value of the next digit not displayed, the calculator merely *cuts off the display,* or truncates, when its display capacity is full.

Whether your calculator rounds or truncates can make a difference in your answer when working with numbers having several digits. Therefore, if your answer in a complex calculation differs from your neighbor's by a few cents, do not worry about it. Furthermore, do not be concerned if your answers differ slightly from those in the book.

Greater calculator accuracy can be obtained if you *leave the answer on the display* and perform the next calculation by depressing additional keys rather than if you write down the answer, clear the calculator and reenter that number as the first step of the following calculation.

CALCULATOR PROBLEMS

CALCULATE

At this point, try solving some simple problems with your calculator to bolster your confidence. The keystrokes shown apply to any calculator except reverse polish notation models. Follow along with the steps shown for each if you need assistance.

1. Try adding 123 and 456.

First, turn on your calculator. If your calculator has a continuous memory, you may have to depress the "CLEAR" and the "CLEAR MEMORY" keys to be sure that no unwanted numbers are left in your calculator from a previous calculation.

Press	Display
1 then 2 then 3	123
+ (the plus, or addition, key)	123 (no change)
4 then 5 then 6	456
= (the equal sign key)	579 (the answer, or sum)

2. Now, try this multiplication problem: 123.45 times (or " × ") 6.789

Press	Display
1 then 2 then 3 then . then 4 then 5	123.45

Note: You *must* press the decimal point just as if it were a digit, or a single number. Otherwise, the answer will not include the decimal point and will be *incorrect*.

Press	Display
× (the multiplication, or times, key)	123.45 (no change)
6 then . then 7 then 8 then 9	6.789
= (equal sign)	838.1 (or 838.1020500)

3. Next, divide 56,789 by 1,234.

Press	Display
5 then 6 then 7 then 8 then 9	56,789 (Your calculator may not have the comma.)
÷ (the division key) (divided *by;* not into)	56,789
1 then 2 then 3 then 4	1,234
= (the equal sign key)	46.02 (or 46.02025932)

4. Finally, subtract .0123 from 4.56.

Press	Display
4 then . then 5 then 6	4.56

Note: Because of the way the problem was stated, you must enter the last number, 4.56, first. The calculator expects the number to be subtracted to be entered second.

Press	Display
− (the subtract, or minus, key)	4.56
. then 0 then 1 then 2 then 3	.0123

Note: You *must* press the zero key. Disregarding it will result in the wrong answer. Zeros are digits and parts of numbers; do not skip them.

Press	Display
= (equal sign key)	4.55 (or 4.547700000)

Remember the previous discussion of rounding.

Review of Basic Math Skills

Many students using this text-workbook may find themselves in a math class after several years of doing other things, and it is to this group that this text is primarily addressed. Some students also have built up a fear of math over the years. The exercises in this text will help eliminate those fears and give students sufficient knowledge and self-confidence not only to pass a licensing examination, but also to function adequately in the field of real estate listing and selling.

As you complete your work in this chapter, you will

- renew your acquaintance with units of measure and basic mathematical formulas;
- learn to use like units of measurement when setting up and solving problems; and
- come to understand the sequence of entering numbers in your calculator.

WARM-UP EXERCISES

Because readers will have varying amounts of knowledge and experience, the problems that follow will allow you to determine your familiarity with the material to be covered. Try all of the problems before checking your answers against the answer key at the end of the chapter. If you have no errors and have calculated the answers easily, you may need to spend very little time on the material in the chapter.

1. $(1 \times 2) + (3 \times 4) + (5 \times 6) - (4 \times 10) = ?$

    a. 40   c. 30

    b. 4   d. 2

2. $(1 + 2) \times (3 + 4) - 6 = ?$

    a. 3   c. 15

    b. 7   d. 6

3. (3 inches + 6 feet) × (9 inches + 27 feet) = ?

    a. 173.438   c. 6.25

    b. 27.75   d. 73,438

4. 16 acres + 87,120 square feet = ?

    a. 87,136   c. 78,408

    b. 87,120   d. 784,080

5. A rectangular warehouse 67 feet, 6 inches by 20 feet with a 10-foot roof height contains how many cubic yards of space?

    a. 13,500   c. 1,500

    b. 500   d. 15,000

Perhaps a brief review of things you learned when you were first taught math will help. One reason many people have trouble with number skills is that they do not practice neatness and legibility in working out problems. For example, it is easier to make a mistake in adding these numbers:

$$\begin{array}{r} \$12,345.67 \\ 89.10 \\ 5,432.08 \\ \underline{76543} \end{array}$$

than it is to add the same numbers when care has been given to neatness and legibility:

$$\begin{array}{r} \$12,345.67 \\ 89.10 \\ 5,432.08 \\ \underline{76,543.00} \end{array}$$

It is important to keep decimal points in a straight vertical line and write each digit of each number directly beneath the one above it.

ORDER OF OPERATIONS

Problems that feature multiple operations involve several calculations. Remember, *parentheses* are used to identify the calculation(s) to be completed first. Also, usually you *multiply* or *divide* before *adding* or *subtracting*.

EXAMPLE: (5 × 6) + (3 × 4) − (6 × 6) = ?

                    5 × 6 = 30   3 × 4 = 12   6 × 6 = 36

                            30 + 12 − 36 = 6

USING UNITS OF MEASUREMENT

Just as you cannot compare apples to oranges, numbers must be of the same kind or in the same form before you perform mathematical functions. To add these unlike things:

$$\frac{1}{2} + \frac{1}{3}$$

or

4 inches + 5 feet

or

6 acres + 7,890 square feet,

you must first put each into similar form, such as:

$$\frac{1}{2} = \frac{3}{6} \text{ and } \frac{1}{3} = \frac{2}{6}$$

$$\frac{3}{6} + \frac{2}{6} = \frac{5}{6}$$

or

$$4 \text{ inches} = \frac{4}{12} \text{ or } \frac{1}{3} \text{ foot}$$

$$\frac{1}{3} \text{ foot} + 5 \text{ feet} = 5\frac{1}{3} \text{ feet}$$

or

6 acres = 43,560 square feet × 6 = 261,360 square feet

261,360 square feet + 7,890 square feet = 269,250 square feet.

EXAMPLE: Suppose you measure your house for carpet and find that you need 1,125 square feet. However, the carpet store prices its merchandise per square *yard*. What will it cost if you choose carpet priced at $18 per square yard? First, you must change the units of measurement so they are alike. For simplicity, convert the 1,125 square feet to square yards. There are nine square feet in each square yard, so:

$$\frac{1,125 \text{ square feet}}{9 \text{ square feet/square yard}} = 125 \text{ square yards}$$

Now the units agree, so you can compute the price:

125 square yards × $18/square yard = $2,250

Convert *inches* to *feet* by dividing inches by 12.	**EXAMPLE:**	9 inches = $\dfrac{9}{12}$ = .75 feet
Convert *yards* to *feet* by multiplying yards by 3.	**EXAMPLE:**	39 yards × 3 = 117 feet
Convert *fractions* to *decimals* by dividing the top number (numerator) by the bottom number (denominator).	**EXAMPLE:**	$\dfrac{3}{4}$ = .75
Convert *percentages* to *decimals* by moving the decimal point two places to the left and adding zeros as necessary.	**EXAMPLE:**	22.5% = .225 80% = .80 3.4% = .034
Convert *square feet* to *square yards* by dividing square feet by 9.	**EXAMPLE:**	$\dfrac{1{,}125 \text{ square feet}}{9}$ = 125 square yards
Convert *cubic feet* to *cubic yards* by dividing cubic feet by 27.	**EXAMPLE:**	$\dfrac{486}{27}$ = 18 cubic yards

BALANCING EQUATIONS

When you progress into simple equations, remember that the "=" (equals) sign means *absolutely* that. You would not write:

$$1 + 2 = 3 + 4$$

because 3 does *not* equal 7. It is *not* an equality or an equation. It is an inequality because it is out of *balance*. In order for the equation to balance, the numbers on the left-hand side of the "=" must actually equal the numbers on the right-hand side. If you think of an equation as a child's see-saw, or a balance scale, you recognize that both sides must have the same weight at the same point or the system will tilt and not balance. Therefore, if you wish to consider the preceding example as an equation (where both sides are equal), you must either add something to the left side or subtract something from the right side:

$$1 + 2 = 3 + 4 \qquad \text{No}$$
$$3 = 7 \qquad \text{No}$$
$$\text{but}$$
$$3 + 4 = 7 \qquad \text{Yes}$$
$$\text{or}$$
$$3 = 7 - 3 - 1 \qquad \text{Yes}$$

If two numbers are related by addition (+), you can break that relationship by subtraction (−); if they are related by multiplication (×), you can break that relationship by division (÷). To illustrate:

$$5 + 6 = 7 + x$$
$$11 = 7 + x$$

The 7 is joined to x (the unknown number) by addition; therefore, you must use subtraction to balance the equation. In solving this problem, separate the knowns from the unknowns. You know all but the x. Recalling the illustration of the scale, if you subtract 7 from the right-hand side of the equal sign, the equation will be out of balance unless you also subtract 7 from the left-hand side:

$$
\begin{aligned}
11 &= 7 + x \\
\underline{-7} \quad &\underline{-7} \leftarrow \text{ subtracted from both sides} \\
4 &= 0 + x \\
4 &= x
\end{aligned}
$$

Sometimes, it is the simplest things that we forget over the years. For instance:

$$(7 - 7) \times 8 = ?$$

Here, you must first perform the operation indicated within the parentheses. In this case, that result is zero. To finish the calculation, zero times any other number is zero.

Also remember, a number divided by itself always equals one. So that:

$$\frac{1}{1} = 1 \text{ or } \frac{486}{486} = 1$$

You can also treat units of measurement or algebraic letters the same way. For example:

$$\frac{\text{feet}}{\text{feet}} = 1$$

$$\frac{\text{acres}}{\text{acres}} = 1$$

$$\frac{x}{x} = 1$$

$$\frac{LW}{LW} = 1$$

Having obtained the answer 1 from any of these operations, if you then multiply that 1 by any other number, unit of measurement or algebraic symbol, the answer is that same number, unit of measurement or algebraic symbol:

$$
\begin{aligned}
1 \times 23 &= 23 \\
1 \times \text{foot} &= \text{foot} \\
1 \times y &= y \\
1 \times \text{Anything} &= \text{Anything}
\end{aligned}
$$

Also, it is important to recall that you cannot divide a number by zero. However, if you divide a number by 1, you have not changed the value of the original number.

Please do not become anxious or nervous because these rules are treated so sparingly. Remember, this is merely a very basic review of things you may already know. The purpose of this chapter is to stir your memory, as well as to introduce briefly some of the material to be covered in following chapters.

Finally, in this text, you will encounter two basic types of exercises. These include number problems—which are already set up in the proper format, such as 123 + 456 = ?—and word, or stated, problems. To gain proficiency in solving word problems, which are similar to real-world situations, begin by analyzing each problem. Learn to recognize certain "function indicators," or key words that indicate whether you should add, subtract, multiply or divide.

Addition indicators:	plus, more than, sum, increase, and
Subtraction indicators:	minus, less than, decrease, difference, take away
Multiplication indicators:	of, times, factor, product
Division indicators:	quotient, fraction, reciprocal

Units of Measure

Linear measure	12 inches = 1 foot
	36 inches = 3 feet = 1 yard
	5,280 feet = 1,760 yards = 1 mile
Square measure	144 square inches = 1 square foot
	1,296 square inches = 9 square feet = 1 square yard
	To convert square feet to square yards, divide square feet by 9.
	To convert square yards to square feet, multiply square yards by 9.
Cubic measure	1,728 cubic inches = 1 cubic foot
	46,656 cubic inches = 27 cubic feet = 1 cubic yard
	To convert cubic feet to cubic yards, divide cubic feet by 27.
	To convert cubic yards to cubic feet, multiply cubic yards by 27.
Circular measure	360 degrees = a circle
	60 minute = 1 degree
	60 seconds = 1 minute
Surveyor's measure	43,560 square feet = 1 acre
	640 acres = 1 square mile = 1 section
	36 sections = a township
	1 township = 36 square miles

Basic Formulas

For calculating *area*	Length (in feet) × Width (in feet) = Square feet
	To convert square feet to square yards, divide square feet by 9.
For calculating *volume*	Length (in feet) × Width (in feet) × Height (in feet) = Cubic feet
	To convert cubic feet to cubic yards, divide cubic feet by 27.
For calculating *part, total* or *rate** (percent)	Total × Rate (percent) = Part
	Part ÷ Rate (percent) = Total
	Part ÷ Total = Rate (percent)

*Rate may be expressed as a percent or a decimal equivalent. This will be more thoroughly discussed in Chapter 2.

PROBLEMS FOR ADDITIONAL PRACTICE

When you have solved these problems, check your answers against the answers that follow.

1. 12 feet + 18 inches + 15 yards = ? feet

a. 45   c. 231
b. 58.5   d. 270

2. $(8 \times 9) - (6 \times 7) + (4 \div 2) \times (3 - 1) = ?$

a. 64   c. 56
b. 118   d. 48

3. How many cubic feet are in a carton measuring 6 feet, 8 inches by 3 yards by $4\frac{1}{2}$ inches?

a. 91.8   c. 9.005
b. 90.005   d. 22.5

4. How many square yards of carpet will it take to cover a living room 18 feet by 20 feet and a dining room 15 feet by 12 feet?

a. 540   c. 20
b. 60   d. 180

5. What is the total square footage of the following three contiguous tracts of land?
   Tract one is 3 sections.
   Tract two is 10 acres.
   Tract three is 130,680 square feet.

a. 696,960   c. 83,678,760
b. 84,201,480   d. 566,388

6. What is $\frac{2}{3}$ plus $\frac{1}{2}$ plus $\frac{5}{8}$ plus $\frac{3}{4}$?

a. .647   c. $2\frac{1}{2}$

b. 2.542   d. $\frac{11}{17}$

7. How many square feet are in a lot that measures 75 feet across the front and is 150 feet deep?

a. 11,250   c. .259 acre
b. 450   d. 1,250

8. If a property sold for $125,000, what total commission would the seller pay at $5\frac{1}{2}$ percent?

a. $6,000   c. $7,500
b. $6,250   d. $6,875

9. Sam Seller owns 2 acres of commercially zoned property. If he sells it for $8.25 per square foot, what is the selling price?

a. $79,860

b. $6,468,660

c. $26,626.11

d. $718,740

10. How many acres are there in 653,400 square feet?

a. 24

b. 15

c. 29.6

d. 150.207

ANSWER KEY

SOLUTIONS: WARM-UP EXERCISES

1. (b): $1 \times 2 = 2$ $3 \times 4 = 12$ $5 \times 6 = 30$ $4 \times 10 = 40$
$2 + 12 + 30 - 40 = 4$

2. (c): $1 + 2 = 3$ $3 + 4 = 7$
$3 \times 7 - 6 = 15$

3. (a): $3 \div 12 = .25$ $.25 + 6 = 6.25$ feet
$9 \div 12 = .75$ $.75 + 27 = 27.75$ feet
6.25 feet $\times 27.75$ feet $= 173.438$ square feet

4. (d): 16 acres $\times$ 43,560 square feet $= 696,960$ square feet
696,960 square feet $+$ 87,120 square feet $= 784,080$ square feet

5. (b): 6 inches $= .5$ foot
67.5 feet $\times$ 20 feet $\times$ 10 feet $= 13,500$ cubic feet
13,500 cubic feet $\div 27 = 500$ cubic yards

SOLUTIONS: PROBLEMS FOR ADDITIONAL PRACTICE

1. (b): 18 inches $\div 12 = 1.5$ feet
15 yards $\times 3 = 45$ feet
12 feet $+ 1.5$ feet $+ 45$ feet $= 58.5$ feet

2. (a): $8 \times 9 = 72$ $6 \times 7 = 42$ $4 \div 2 = 2$ $3 - 1 = 2$
$72 - 42 + 2 \times 2 = 64$

3. (d): 8 inches $\div 12 = .667$ feet; $.667$ feet $+ 6$ feet $= 6.667$ feet
3 yards $\times 3 = 9$ feet
4.5 inches $\div 12 = .375$ feet
6.667 feet $\times 9$ feet $\times .375$ feet $= 22.5$ cubic feet

4. (b): 18 feet × 20 feet = 360 square feet
15 feet × 12 feet = 180 square feet
360 square feet + 180 square feet = 540 square feet
540 square feet ÷ 9 = 60 square yards

5. (b): 3 sections × 640 acres × 43,560 square feet = 83,635,200 square feet
10 acres × 43,560 square feet = 435,600 square feet
83,635,200 square feet + 435,600 square feet + 130,680 square feet = 84,201,480 square feet

6. (b): 2 ÷ 3 = .667   1 ÷ 2 = .50   5 ÷ 8 = .625   3 ÷ 4 = .75
.667 + .50 + .625 + .75 = 2.542

7. (a): 75 feet × 150 feet = 11,250 square feet

8. (d): 5.5% = .055
.055 × $125,000 = $6,875

9. (d): 2 acres × 43,560 square feet = 87,120 square feet
87,120 square feet × $8.25 = $718,740

10. (b): 653,400 square feet ÷ 43,560 square feet = 15 acres

Fractions, Decimals and Percentages

Most of the math you will encounter in real estate will require that you be comfortable with fractions, decimals and percentages. When you have completed your work in Chapter 2, you will be able to

- accurately convert percentages and fractions to decimals;
- apply the basic formulas for problem solving for part, total or rate (percentage); and
- use the following diagram as a tool in solving total, rate and part problems:

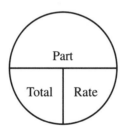

WARM-UP EXERCISES

Because readers will have varying amounts of knowledge and experience, the problems that follow will allow you to determine your familiarity with the material to be covered. Try all of the problems before checking your answers against the answer key at the end of the chapter.

1. Mr. Jones was one of five equal owners of an apartment building. The building was recently sold for $2.5 million, of which 2% was deducted for fees. How much money did Mr. Jones receive?

   a. $2,450,000
   b. $50,000

   c. $490,000
   d. $400,000

2. If Mr. Jones originally paid $400,000 for his share in the above building, what percentage of profit did he realize when it sold?

   a. 22.5%
   b. 20%

   c. 18.37%
   d. 1.225%

3. A property listed for $85,500 and sold for 90% of the list price. What was the sales price of this property

    a. $95,000   c. $8,550

    b. $85,500   d. $76,950

4. Mrs. Johnston's home sold for $61,320, which was 84% of the list price. What was the list price of this property?

    a. $71,131   c. $51,509

    b. $73,000   d. $112,829

5. Sammy Salesperson is calculating his share of the commission on a property he listed at $186,500 and that subsequently sold for $175,000. What will be the amount of his check if the seller is charged a 7% fee and if Sammy's broker pays him 60% of the commission remaining after paying the buyer's broker 40% of the total commission charged?

    a. $4,700   c. $4,410

    b. $2,940   d. $7,833

CALCULATE

At the outset of this chapter, a word about calculators is important. Some calculators have a "%" key, which requires fewer keystrokes to calculate percentages. However, due to the various ways of entering data on different calculators, this text will use decimals in all problems and solutions.

A *part* of the *total* can be expressed as a:

Fraction

    EXAMPLE: 25 is $\frac{1}{4}$ of 100

Decimal

    EXAMPLE: 25 is .25 of 100

Percentage

    EXAMPLE: 25 is 25% of 100

To convert a *fraction* to a *decimal*, divide the fraction's top number (numerator) by its bottom number (denominator).

    EXAMPLE: $\frac{7}{8}$

                        $7 \div 8 = .875$

To convert a *percentage* to a *decimal,* move the decimal two places to the left and drop the percent sign. If necessary, add zeros.

    EXAMPLE: 75% = .75

                       3.5% = .035

CONVERTING FRACTIONS TO DECIMALS

Proper Fractions

A proper fraction is one whose numerator is less than its denominator. It is a part of the total, and its value is *always* less than 1.

EXAMPLES: $\dfrac{1}{2}$ $\dfrac{1}{4}$ $\dfrac{1}{5}$ $\dfrac{5}{19}$ $\dfrac{7}{100}$

```
┌─────────────────────────────────┐
│            FRACTION             │
│                                 │
│   1   ←──────── numerator       │
│  ───                            │
│   2   ←──────── denominator     │
│                                 │
└─────────────────────────────────┘
```

The *numerator* (top number of a fraction) indicates how many parts there are in the fractional amount.

The *denominator* (bottom number of a fraction) indicates how many parts make up the whole.

The fraction $\dfrac{1}{2}$ means 1 part of the total that is made up of 2 equal parts.

The fraction $\dfrac{3}{4}$ means 3 parts of the total that is made up of 4 equal parts.

The figure 35% means 35 parts out of the 100 parts that make up the total. It can also be written as the fraction $\dfrac{35}{100}$ or as the decimal .35.

1. Convert the following fractions to decimals.

    a. $\dfrac{1}{5}$ c. $\dfrac{5}{100}$

    b. $\dfrac{1}{2}$ d. $\dfrac{97}{100}$

The answers for chapter problems are located at the end of each chapter.

Improper Fractions

An improper fraction is one whose numerator is equal to or greater than its denominator. The value of an improper fraction is *more* than 1.

EXAMPLES: $\dfrac{5}{4}$ $\dfrac{10}{9}$ $\dfrac{81}{71}$

To change an improper fraction to a whole number, divide the numerator by the denominator. Any part left over will be shown as a decimal.

EXAMPLE: Change $\dfrac{8}{5}$ to a whole number.

$$\dfrac{8}{5} = 1.6$$

2. Change the following improper fractions to whole numbers.

a. $\dfrac{5}{4}$

c. $\dfrac{16}{5}$

b. $\dfrac{9}{2}$

d. $\dfrac{26}{9}$

Mixed Numbers

A mixed number (a whole number and a fraction), such as $1\dfrac{3}{4}$, can be changed by converting the fraction to a decimal (divide the top number by the bottom number) and adding back the whole number.

EXAMPLE: $1\dfrac{3}{4}$

$3 \div 4 = .75$

$.75 + 1 = 1.75$

3. Change the following mixed numbers to whole numbers plus decimal equivalents.

a. $2\dfrac{1}{4}$

c. $8\dfrac{1}{4}$

b. $3\dfrac{2}{3}$

d. $1\dfrac{5}{6}$

4. Convert the following fractions to decimals.

a. $\dfrac{8}{5}$

e. $\dfrac{52}{10}$

i. $9\dfrac{3}{4}$

b. $\dfrac{9}{10}$

f. $\dfrac{3}{12}$

j. $108\dfrac{6}{10}$

c. $6\dfrac{7}{8}$

g. $\dfrac{81}{71}$

d. $\dfrac{34}{100}$

h. $\dfrac{13}{3}$

PERCENTAGES

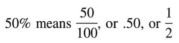

> Percent (%) means per hundred or per hundred parts.
> "per" means "by the"
> "cent" means "100"

For example, 50% means 50 parts out of a total of 100 parts (100 parts equal 1 whole), and 100% means all 100 of the 100 total parts, or 1 whole unit. Throughout this book, we shall refer to 100% as the total.

$$50\% \text{ means } \frac{50}{100}, \text{ or } .50, \text{ or } \frac{1}{2}$$

$$100\% \text{ means } \frac{100}{100}, \text{ or } 1.00, \text{ or } 1$$

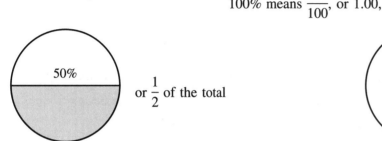

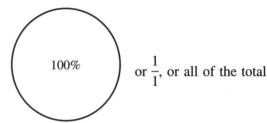

CONVERTING DECIMALS TO PERCENTAGES

To change a decimal into a percentage, move the decimal point two places to the *right* and add the "%" sign. Therefore, you can change the number .50 to a percentage by moving the decimal point (.) two places or two digits to the right and adding the percent symbol (%). By moving the decimal point two places to the right, you actually *multiply* .50 by 100, to equal 50. When you add the percent symbol, you *divide* the 50 by 100 according to the definition of percent, so that .50 equals 50%. Thus, the actual value hasn't changed at all, or you are back where you started.

Any percentage that is less than 100% means a part or fraction of 100% or the entire unit. For example, because 99% means 99 parts out of 100 parts, it is less than the total.

EXAMPLES: .10 = 10%
  1.00 = 100%
  .98 = 98%
  .987 = 98.7%

5. Change the following decimals to percentages.

a. .37   d. .10000

b. .09   e. .7095

c. .080   f. .01010

CONVERTING PERCENTAGES TO DECIMALS

This process is the reverse of the one you just completed. To change a percentage to a decimal, move the decimal point two places to the *left* and drop the "%" sign.

All numbers have a decimal point, although it is usually not shown when only zeros follow it.

EXAMPLES: 99 is really 99.0
6 is really 6.0
$1 is the same as $1.00

So, percentages can be readily converted to decimals.

EXAMPLES: 99% = 99.0% = .990 = .99
6% = 6.0% = .060 = .06
5% = 5.0% = .050 = .05
70% = 70.0% = .700 = .70

Note: Adding zeros to the *right* of a decimal point after the last figure does not change the value of the number.

6. Change the following percentages to decimals.

a. 1%   c. 75.5%

b. 65%   d. 2.1%

7. Complete the following chart.

	Simple Fraction	Decimal	Percent
a.			75%
b.	$\frac{1}{10}$		
c.		.80	
d.	$\frac{1}{8}$		
e.	$\frac{3}{10}$		
f.			67%
g.		.56	

ADDING DECIMALS

Decimals are added like whole numbers. When you add longhand, decimal points *must* be lined up under each other as shown in the examples.

EXAMPLES:

300	.3	.891
5	.005	.05
+590	+.59	+.063
895	.895	1.004

8. Add the following decimals.

a. .05
   .2
+.695

b. .983
   .006
+.32

SUBTRACTING DECIMALS

Decimals are subtracted like whole numbers. Again, line up the decimal points.

EXAMPLES:

861	.861	.549
−190	−.190	−.32
671	.671	.229

9. Practice adding and subtracting the following decimals.

a. $.23 + .051 + .6$

c. $.588 − .007$

b. $.941 − .6$

d. $.741 + .005 + .72$

MULTIPLYING DECIMALS

Decimal numbers are multiplied like whole numbers. When entering decimal numbers in your calculator, be sure to enter the decimal point in the proper place. Obviously, a misplaced decimal point will yield an incorrect answer.

10. Practice multiplying the following decimals.

a. $.100 \times 3$

b. $4.006 \times .51$

c. $.035 \times .012$

DIVIDING DECIMALS

You may divide a whole number by a decimal number.

EXAMPLE: $6 \div .50 = 12$

You may divide a decimal number by a whole number.

EXAMPLE: $.50 \div 6 = .083$

When dividing, always enter into your calculator the number to be divided, then push the "÷" key before entering the number by which you are dividing (the divisor).

11. Practice dividing the following decimals.

   a. $2 \div .08$ b. $.36 \div 3$ c. $.15 \div 5$

PERCENTAGE PROBLEMS

Percentage problems usually involve three elements: the rate (percent), the total and the part.

EXAMPLE: 5%   of   200   is   10
                  ↑   ↑   ↑
                 rate   total   part

A problem involving percentages is really a multiplication problem. To solve the problem in the example below, first convert the percentage to a decimal, then multiply.

EXAMPLE: What is 25% of 300?
               $25\% = .25$
               $300 \times .25 = 75$

A generalized formula for solving percentage problems follows:

$$\text{Total} \times \text{Rate (percent)} = \text{Part}$$
(or, Rate × Total = Part; the order of multiplication is not important)

To solve a percentage problem, you must know the value of two of the elements of this formula. The value that you must find is called the *unknown* (most often shown in the formula as *x*).

EXAMPLE: Mr. Jones has purchased a secondhand stereo unit at 45% of the original cost, which was $150. What did Mr. Jones pay for the unit?

$$Rate \times Total = Part$$
$$45\% \times \$150 = Part$$
$$.45 \times \$150 = \$67.50$$

12. If Ms. Smith spent 60% of her total savings of $3,000, how much did she spend? What formula will you use to solve the problem?

FORMULAS

When working with problems involving percentages or decimal equivalents, use one of the formulas discussed below.

When you know the total (which always equals 100%) and you know the rate (percent) and you are looking for the part, use the following formula:

$$Total \times Rate \ (percent) = Part$$

When you know the part and the total and you are looking for the rate, use the following formula:

$$Part \div Total = Rate$$

When you know the part and the rate and you are looking for the total, use the following formula:

$$Part \div Rate = Total$$

Many math students have found it helpful to use a circle as an aid in solving for the answer. The part always goes in the top section; the total goes in the lower left section, and the rate (perhaps expressed as a percentage or a decimal equivalent) goes in the lower right section. Enter the two known numbers in their proper places and solve for the unknown by either dividing or multiplying. If your known numbers include one above and one below the horizontal line, divide the top number by the bottom number to solve for the unknown. If your known numbers are side by side, separated by the vertical line, multiply.

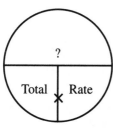

Total × Rate = Part

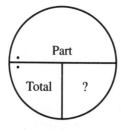

Part ÷ Total = Rate

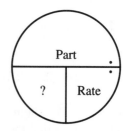

Part ÷ Rate = Total

EXAMPLE: An acre contains 43,560 square feet. How many square feet are in 20% of an acre?

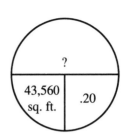

20% = .20
43,560 square feet (total) × .20 (rate) = 8,712 square feet (part)

EXAMPLE: What percentage of an acre does 17,424 square feet represent?

17,424 square feet (part) ÷ 43,560 square feet (total) = .40 (rate)

Remember, if you want to express the rate as a percentage, you must move the decimal point two places to the right and add the "%" sign. Therefore, in the above example, .40 equals 40%.

EXAMPLE: 17,424 square feet is 40% of an acre. How many square feet are in an acre?

40% = .40
17,424 square feet (part) ÷ .40 (rate) = 43,560 square feet (total)

Always remember the following information:

- You can find any one of the three elements if you know the other two.
- The long horizontal line separates the circle into division areas.
- The short vertical line separates the circle into multiplication areas.

Knowing this, you can cover the portion of the circle that contains the unknown (or what you are looking for), then perform the indicated multiplication or division.

Applying this to the previous example in which you found 20% of 43,560, the part was the unknown. If you cover up the portion of the circle labeled "Part," you are left with "Total" and "Rate," separated by a multiplication function.

However, in the example in which you determined 17,424 square feet to be 40% of an acre, you looked for the rate. By covering up this part of the circle, you leave "Part" and "Total" separated by a division function.

This shortcut can be used to solve many types of problems, including the following.

EXAMPLE: If 30% of the 1,500 houses in your area have 4 bedrooms, how many houses have 4 bedrooms?

We know:

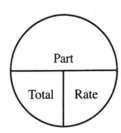

Rate = 30%, or .30
Total = 1,500

Cover "Part."

Total × Rate = ?
1,500 × .30 = 450

13. If 20% (or 500) of the houses in your area are less than 5 years old, how many houses are there in your area?

14. Which of the following values is missing from this problem: 6 is 12% of what number

    a. Total

    b. Part

    c. Rate

    d. None of the above

EXAMPLE: 30 is 50% of what number?

The suggested problem-solving sequence is as follows:

Step 1. Read the problem carefully.

Step 2. Analyze the problem, pick out the important factors and put those factors into a simplified question.

Step 3. State the formula. $\dfrac{\text{Part}}{\text{Rate}} = \text{Total}$

Step 4. Substitute values. $\dfrac{30}{.50} = \text{Total}$

Step 5. Solve the problem. $\dfrac{30}{.50} = 60$

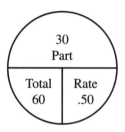

15. 1,500 is 300% of what number?

Step 1. Read the problem.

Step 2. Analyze the problem.

Step 3. State the formula.

Step 4. Substitute values.

Step 5. Solve the problem.

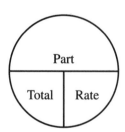

16. Try to solve the following problem without referring back to material in this chapter: $125 is 20% of what dollar amount?

EXAMPLE: What percentage of 56 is 14?

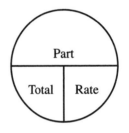

Note that the rate element is missing. By covering "Rate" in the circle to the right, you know to divide the part by the total:

$$\frac{\text{Part}}{\text{Total}} = \text{Rate}$$

Next, substitute the values from the problem for those elements in the new formula:

$$\frac{14}{56} = \text{Rate}$$

Then divide:

$$\frac{14}{56} = .25$$

Finally, convert the decimal to a percentage:

$$.25 = 25\%$$

EXAMPLE: What percentage of 87 is 17?

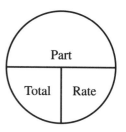

Step 1. Read the problem.

Step 2. Analyze the problem.

Step 3. State the formula. $\dfrac{Part}{Total} = Rate$

Step 4. Substitute values. $\dfrac{17}{87} = Rate$

Step 5. Solve the problem. $\dfrac{17}{87} = .195$

Step 6. Convert the decimal to a percentage. $.195 = 19.5\%$

17. What percentage of 95 is 18?

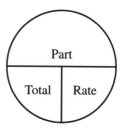

Remember: This diagram will help you remember the formulas for part, total and rate.

Because *part* is over *rate,* make a fraction of these two elements when looking for a *total.*

$$\dfrac{Part}{Rate} = Total$$

Because *part* is over *total,* make a fraction of these two elements when looking for a *rate.*

$$\dfrac{Part}{Total} = Rate$$

Because *rate* and *total* are both in the lower part of the diagram, multiply these two elements when looking for a *part.*

$$Total \times Rate = Part$$

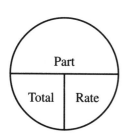

    Now try some problems related to the real estate field, using what you've learned about rates (percentages), fractions and decimals.

18. A house is assessed at 42% of market value, which is $50,000. What is its assessed value?

    a. What is the unknown value?

    b. State the formula.

    c. Solve the problem.

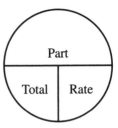

19. A house sold for $81,000, which was 90% of the original price. What was the original list price?

    a. What is the unknown value?

    b. State the formula.

    c. Solve the problem.

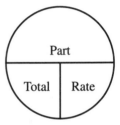

20. A property has an assessed value of $15,000. If the assessment is 34% of market value, what is the market value?

    a. What is the unknown value?

    b. State the formula.

    c. Solve the problem. Round off your answer to the nearest hundred dollars.

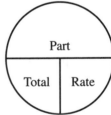

PERCENTAGE OF CHANGE

If you hear that houses in your area have increased in value 8% during the past year, and you know that the average price of houses sold last year was $60,000, what is the average price of houses sold today?

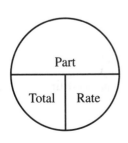

This is a two-step problem. First, find the part. You know the total and rate, so:

$$\$60,000 \times .08 = \$4,800$$

Add the $4,800 increase to last year's average price of $60,000, giving this year's average price of $64,800 (or $60,000 × 1.08 = $64,800).

Consider a similar problem from a different starting point: If the average price of houses today is $70,000 compared to $60,000 one year ago, what is the percentage of change?

First, find the *amount* of change: $70,000 − $60,000 = $10,000. Next, use the circle aid to find the *rate* of change:

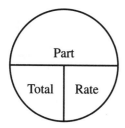

10,000 (part) ÷ $60,000 (total) = .167, or 16.7% (rate)

Or remember this general formula:

$$\frac{\text{New value} - \text{Old value}}{\text{Old value}} = \text{Rate (percent) of change}$$

21. If there were 800 foreclosures this year and 700 last year, what is the percentage of change?

Suppose that this year's foreclosures numbered 700 and last year's equaled 800. What is the percentage of change?

New value = 700
Old value = 800
Difference <100> (negative number)

<100> (part) ÷ 800 (total) = <.125> (rate), or <12.5%>

This means the change occurred in a downward, or negative, direction.

In summary, remember that fractions, decimals and percentages are all interrelated.

REMEMBER!

To convert a *fraction* to a *decimal,* divide the top number by the bottom number.

To convert a *percentage* to a *decimal,* move the decimal two places to the left and drop the "%" sign.

To convert a *decimal* to a *percentage,* move the decimal two places to the right and add the "%" sign.

To solve problems, always *convert fractions* and *percentages* to *decimals.*

Use the circle aid to assist you in solving for an unknown number.

Total × Rate = Part

Part ÷ Rate = Total

Part ÷ Total = Rate

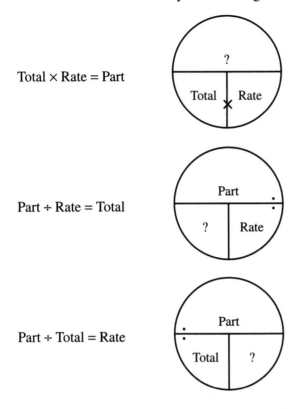

In real estate practice, you will use these formulas in many situations. The following circles show some of the more common ones.

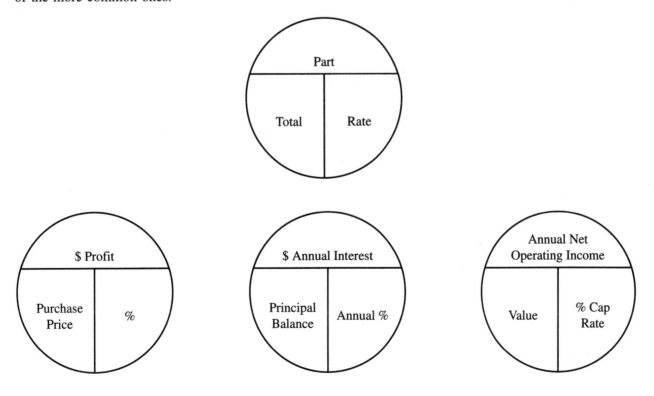

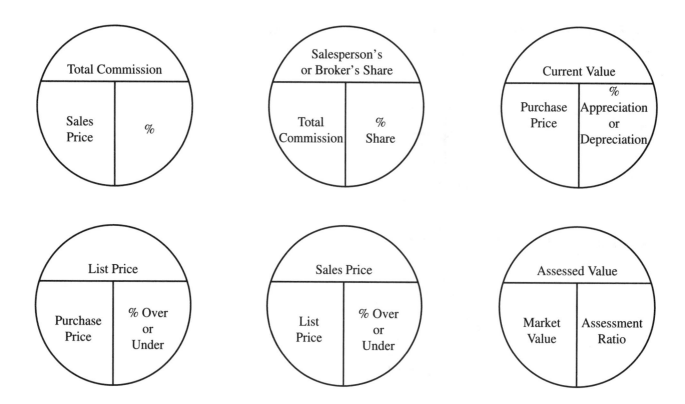

You have now completed Chapter 2. If you feel you understand the material in this chapter, work the Problems for Additional Practice that follow. After working the problems, you may find that you are unsure about certain points. Review those points before continuing with the next chapter.

PROBLEMS FOR ADDITIONAL PRACTICE

When you have finished these problems, check your answers against those at the end of the chapter. If you miss any of the problems, review this chapter before going on to Chapter 3.

1. Convert the following to decimals.

   a. 3.875%

   b. $\dfrac{20}{10}$

   c. $\dfrac{1}{6}$

   d. 5%

   e. 348%

2. A house listed for $55,000 and sold for 90% of the list price What was the sales price of the house?

   a. $61,111

   b. $49,500

   c. $59,950

   d. $60,500

3. Mr. Tomas's house sold for $40,000, which was 92% of the list price. What did the house list for? Round off your answer to the nearest hundred dollars.

a. $43,200   c. $43,000
b. $36,800   d. $43,500

4. Mrs. Burns purchased her house for $80,000. She sold it for $90,000. What percentage profit did she make on her investment?

a. 11.1%   c. 10%
b. 12.5%   d. 110%

5. Salesperson Rose Accetta is computing her share of the commission on a $46,500 sale. The full commission rate is 7%, and the salesperson's share is 60%, which is

a. $1,974.   c. $1,935.
b. $1,953.   d. $1,997.

6. The assessed value of a residence is 22% of the market value of $39,000, which is

a. $7,800.   c. $8,580.
b. $8,700.   d. $8,850.

7. The office in which you work sold 128 homes last year. You sold 29 of these. Your sales are what percentage of the total sales?

a. 21.7%   c. 46.07%
b. 44.13%   d. 22.7%

8. What percentage of $800 is $420?

a. 1.90%   c. 19%
b. 52.5%   d. 5.25%

9. Erik Smith received a proceeds check at closing for $67,500. His home sold for $75,000. What percentage of the sales price did Smith receive?

a. 90%   c. 99%
b. 11.1%   d. 94%

10. A house is assessed at 53% of market value. What is the assessed value of that property if it has a market value of $125,000?

a. $235,849   c. $66,250
b. $191,250   d. $53,000

11. What percentage of 125,000 is 18,750?

a. 6.67%   c. 85%
b. 15%   d. 1.7%

12. Which of the following formulas is *incorrect?*

  a. Part × Rate = Total   c. Part ÷ Total = Rate
  b. Rate × Total = Part   d. Part ÷ Rate = Total

13. Carolyn Grisho bought a lot for $10,000 and sold it several years later for $18,000. Her percentage of profit is

  a. 180%.   c. 44%.
  b. 80%.   d. 100%.

14. One-sixth is equal to what percent?

  a. 8.25%   c. 1.65%
  b. 12.5%   d. 16.7%

15. What is the decimal equivalent of $3\frac{3}{4}$?

  a. .375   c. 3.75
  b. 37.5   d. .0375

ANSWER KEY

SOLUTIONS: WARM-UP EXERCISES

1. (c): $\frac{1}{5} = .20$

  $2,500,000 × .02 = \$50,000$
  $\$2,500,000 − \$50,000 = \$2,450,000$
  $\$2,450,000 × .20 = \$490,000$

2. (a): $\$490,000 − \$400,000 = \$90,000$
  $\$90,000 ÷ \$400,000 = .225$, or 22.5%

3. (d): $\$85,500 × .90 = \$76,950$

4. (b): $\$61,320 ÷ .84 = \$73,000$

5. (c): $\$175,000 × .07 = \$12,250$
  $100\% − 40\% = 60\%$
  $\$12,250 × .60 = \$7,350$
  $\$7,350 × .60 = \$4,410$

SOLUTIONS: CHAPTER PROBLEMS

1. a. $\dfrac{1}{5} = .20$ c. $\dfrac{5}{100} = .05$

    b. $\dfrac{1}{2} = .50$ d. $\dfrac{97}{100} = .97$

2. a. $\dfrac{5}{4} = 1.25$ c. $\dfrac{16}{5} = 3.20$

    b. $\dfrac{9}{2} = 4.50$ d. $\dfrac{26}{9} = 2.889$

3. a. $1 \div 4 = .25$
       $.25 + 2 = 2.25$
   b. $2 \div 3 = .667$
       $.667 + 3 = 3.667$
                   c. $1 \div 4 = .25$
                       $.25 + 8 = 8.25$
                   d. $5 \div 6 = .833$
                       $.833 + 1 = 1.833$

4. a. $8 \div 5 = 1.60$
   b. $9 \div 10 = .90$
   c. $7 \div 8 = .875$
       $.875 + 6 = 6.875$
   d. $34 \div 100 = .34$
   e. $52 \div 10 = 5.20$
   f. $3 \div 12 = .25$

   g. $81 \div 71 = 1.141$
   h. $13 \div 3 = 4.333$
   i. $3 \div 4 = .75$
      $.75 + 9 = 9.75$
   j. $6 \div 10 = .60$
      $.60 + 108 = 108.60$

5. a. $.37 = 37\%$
   b. $.09 = 9\%$
   c. $.080 = 8\%$

   d. $.10000 = 10\%$
   e. $.7095 = 70.95\%$
   f. $.01010 = 1.01\%$

6. a. $1\% = .01$
   b. $65\% = .65$

   c. $75.5\% = .755$
   d. $2.1\% = .021$

7.

	Simple Fraction	Decimal	Percent
a.	$\dfrac{75}{100} = \dfrac{3}{4}$	.75	75%
b.	$\dfrac{1}{10}$	.10	10%
c.	$\dfrac{80}{100} = \dfrac{4}{5}$	.80	80%
d.	$\dfrac{1}{8}$	.125	12.5%
e.	$\dfrac{3}{10}$	.30	30%
f.	$\dfrac{67}{100}$	.67	67%
g.	$\dfrac{56}{100} = \dfrac{14}{25}$	.56	56%

8. a. $.05 + .2 + .695 = .945$
b. $.983 + .006 + .32 = 1.309$

9. a. $.23 + .051 + .6 = .881$ c. $.588 - .007 = .581$
b. $.941 - .6 = .341$ d. $.741 + .005 + .72 = 1.466$

10. a. $.100 \times 3 = .3$
b. $4.006 \times .51 = 2.04306$
c. $.035 \times .012 = .00042$

11. a. $2 \div .08 = 25$
b. $.36 \div 3 = .12$
c. $.15 \div 5 = .03$

12. Total $\times$ Rate $=$ Part
$\$3,000 \times .60 = \$1,800$

13. 500 (part) $\div$ .20 (rate) $= 2,500$ houses (total)

14. (a): Total. The part is 6 and the rate is 12%. Therefore, 6 divided by .12 equals 50.

15. Step 3 Part $\div$ Rate $=$ Total
Step 4 1,500 (part) $\div$ 3 (rate) $=$ Total
Step 5 1,500 (part) $\div$ 3 (rate) $= 500$ (total)

16. Part $\div$ Rate $=$ Total
$20\% = .20$
$\$125 \div .20 = \$625$

17. Part $\div$ Total $=$ Rate
$18 \div 95 = .189473684$ or 18.9%

18. a. Part
b. Total $\times$ Rate $=$ Part
c. $\$50,000 \times .42 = \$21,000$

19. a. Total
b. Part $\div$ Rate $=$ Total
c. $90\% = .90$
$\$81,000 \div .90 = \$90,000$

20. a. Total
b. Part $\div$ Rate $=$ Total
c. $34\% = .34$
$\$15,000 \div .34 = \$44,117.65$ or $\$44,100$ (rounded)

21. $800 - 700 = 100$
$100 \div 700 = .143$ or 14.3%

SOLUTIONS: PROBLEMS FOR ADDITIONAL PRACTICE

1. a. 3.875% = .03875

  b. $\dfrac{20}{10} = 2$

  c. $\dfrac{1}{6} = .167$

  d. 5% = .05

  e. 348% = 3.48

2. (b): .90 × $55,000 = $49,500

3. (d): $40,000 ÷ .92 = $43,478.26 or $43,500 (rounded)

4. (b): $90,000 − $80,000 = $10,000
$10,000 ÷ $80,000 = .125 or 12.5%

5. (b): 46,500 × .07 = $3,255
3,255 × .60 = $1,953

6. (c): $39,000 × .22 = $8,580

7. (d): 29 ÷ 128 = .227 or 22.7%

8. (b): $420 ÷ $800 = .525 or 52.5%

9. (a): $67,500 ÷ $75,000 = .90 or 90%

10. (c): $125,000 × .53 = $66,250

11. (b): 18,750 ÷ 125,000 = .15 or 15%

12. (a)

13. (b): $18,000 − $10,000 = $8,000
$8,000 ÷ $10,000 = .80 or 80%

14. (d): 1 ÷ 6 = .167 or 16.7%

15. (c): 3 ÷ 4 = .75
.75 + 3 = 3.75

Commission

This chapter will help you apply what you have learned about percentages and decimals to the specific task of calculating real estate commissions. When you complete your work in Chapter 3, you will be able to

- accurately compute the total commission on a given sales price;
- calculate the listing broker's and salesperson's shares; and
- calculate the sales price when given the commission paid and the commission rate.

Because readers will have varying amounts of knowledge and experience, the problems that follow will allow you to determine your familiarity with the material to be covered. Try all of the problems before checking your answers against the answer key at the end of the chapter.

1. What is the dollar amount of a 7% commission charged on a $100,000 sale?

   a. $7,000
   b. $6,000
   c. $3,500
   d. $3,000

2. What is the total commission charged on the sale of a $503,500 property if the fee is 7% of the first $100,000, 6% of the next $200,000 and $4\frac{1}{2}$% of the balance?

   a. $9,157.50
   b. $28,157.50
   c. $27,157.50
   d. $22,657.50

3. A house sold for $75,000. The total commission received by the broker was $5,000. What was the rate of commission?

   a. 6%
   b. 6.67%
   c. 7%
   d. 6.5%

4. The listing broker negotiated a $7\frac{1}{2}$% commission with Mr. and Mrs. Watts. If the house is sold by another broker for $120,000, what amount of commission does the selling salesperson receive if the listing broker pays 60% to the selling broker, who then pays 70% to the salesperson?

   a. $3,024
   b. $3,528

   c. $4,410
   d. $3,780

5. Susan Salesperson received a commission check for $3,000, which was her share of the commission for listing the Johnston home. The total commission charged by her company was 7% of the sales price. Her broker paid the selling broker 45% of the total fee and paid Susan 60% of the portion retained by her broker. What was the sales price of the house?

   a. $100,000.00
   b. $129,870.14

   c. $ 85,714.29
   d. $158,730.16

PROBLEM-SOLVING STRATEGY

This chapter begins with a look at how to solve *word* problems. Here's the strategy you should use:

Step 1. Read the problem carefully.

Step 2. Analyze the problem, pick out the important factors and put those factors into a simplified question, disregarding unimportant factors.

Step 3. Choose the proper formula for the problem.

Step 4. Substitute numbers for the known elements of the formula.

Step 5. Solve the problem.

If you use this strategy throughout this chapter and wherever it applies in this book, you'll have an easier time with word problems. Remember, word problems are simply everyday situations described in writing.

EXAMPLE: Consider an example that applies the step-by-step strategy to a problem involving a broker's commission.

Step 1. Read the following problem carefully:

   A house sold for $62,300. The selling broker received a 7% commission on the sale. What amount did the broker receive?

Step 2. Analyze the problem, pick out the important factors and put those factors into a simplified question.

   What is 7% of $62,300?

Step 3. Choose the proper formula for the problem from the following:

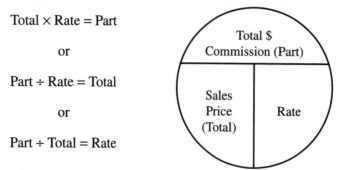

Total × Rate = Part

or

Part ÷ Rate = Total

or

Part ÷ Total = Rate

The correct formula for this problem is:

Total × Rate = Part
or
Sales price × Commission rate = Total commission

Step 4. Substitute numbers for the known elements of the formula.

7% = .07
$62,300 (total) × .07 (rate) = Part

Step 5. Solve the problem.

$62,300 (total) × .07 (rate) = $4,361 (part)

Note: The steps and the solution would be the same if irrelevant factors such as the date of sale, amount of closing costs and type of financing had been included. Learn to sift out these unimportant factors so you will not be confused by them.

EXAMPLE: Now apply this strategy to another commission problem. Be careful—this one's a bit different. When you are finished, check your answer below.

Step. 1. Read the following problem carefully:

The selling broker received the entire commission of $1,662 on a real estate transaction. What was the selling price of the property if his rate of commission was 6%?

Step 2. Analyze the problem, pick out the important factors and put those factors into a simplified question.

Step 3. Choose the proper formula for the problem. (If you need to, refer to the formulas shown on the preceding page.)

Step 4. Substitute numbers for the known elements of the formula.

Step 5. Solve the problem.

The answers are as follows:

Step 2. $1,662 is 6% of what amount?

Step 3. Part ÷ Rate = Total

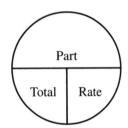

Step 4. 6% = .06
$1,662 (part) ÷ .06 (rate) = Total

Step 5. $1,662 (part) ÷ .06 (rate) = $27,700 (total)

1. Complete the following formulas. Try not to refer back to material in the book.

a. _____ × _____ = Part

b. _____ ÷ _____ = Total

c. _____ ÷ _____ = Rate

2. Miss Martin received $9,080 for a parcel of real estate after the broker deducted a 5% commission and $40 for advertising expenses. How much did the real estate sell for?

a. Analyze the problem and state it in simplified terms.

b. What value are you looking for (what is the unknown)?

c. What formula will you use?

Let's take a further look at the last problem. First of all, you know that the real estate sold for:

$$\$9,080 + \$40 + 5\% \text{ commission } (5\% \text{ of the total})$$

Therefore, you must add:

$$
\begin{array}{r}
\$9,080 \\
+\ 40 \\
\hline
\$9,120
\end{array}
$$

Thus, $9,120 plus the 5% commission equals the total.

What percentage of the total is $9,120? The total, or the sales price, must equal 100%, so:

$$
\begin{array}{r}
100\% \\
-\ 5\% \\
\hline
95\%
\end{array}
$$

Therefore, you can say that $9,120 is 95% of the total sales price. Or, in question form:

$$\$9,120 \text{ is } 95\% \text{ of what amount?}$$

Because you must solve for the total, the correct formula is:

$$\frac{\text{Part}}{\text{Rate}} = \text{Total}$$

3. Now substitute numbers for the known elements of the formula and solve the problem.

4. Using the figures in problem 3 and the problem-solving strategy, find the amount of the broker's commission.

   a. Analyze the problem, pick out the important factors and put those factors into a simplified question.

   b. Choose the proper formula. (Try not to refer back to material in the book.)

   c. Substitute numbers for the known elements of the formula.

   d. Solve the problem.

5. Apply the problem-solving strategy to the following problem:

A house sold for $75,000. The total commission received by the broker was $4,500. What was the rate of commission?

a. Step 1.

b. Step 2.

c. Step 3.

d. Step 4.

e. Step 5.

SPLITTING COMMISSIONS

Broker and Salesperson

When commissions are divided between a broker and his or her salesperson, the total commission is calculated first, then the broker's and the salesperson's shares are determined.

Remember, any time a commission is split between a broker and a salesperson, multiple calculations will be involved.

Proceed as follows:

1. Calculate the total commission.

$$\text{Sales price (total)} \times \text{Rate} = \text{Total commission (part)}$$

2. Split the total commission between brokers if more than one is involved. (This step is deleted on an "in-house" sale.)
3. Split the broker's (company's) share between the broker and the salesperson.

$$\text{Total commission} \times \text{Salesperson's share (\%)} = \text{Salesperson's commission}$$

6. The following problem deals with splitting commissions. Apply the problem-solving strategy and think through the steps as you go along. If you need to, write each step down in the space provided.

Property was sold for $5,800. The salesperson involved in the transaction received 40% of the 6% broker's commission. How much money did the salesperson receive?

7. Analyze and restate this problem:

   Mr. Johnson's house sold for $55,000 and the total commission was 6% of that amount. The broker received three-fourths of the commission and the salesperson received one-fourth. How much was the salesperson's commission?

8. Here's another type of commission problem. Follow the steps you've learned to solve it:

   What was the selling price of a house if the salesperson received $3,000 as her half of the 6% commission charged by the broker?

9. The 6% commission charged by a broker for selling a house was divided as follows: 10% to the salesperson getting the listing and one-half of the balance to the salesperson making the sale. What was the selling salesperson's commission if the sales price was $40,000?

10. List the five steps involved in the problem-solving strategy and the three equations you've used in solving commission problems.

   a. Step 1.

   b. Step 2.

c. Step 3.

d. Step 4.

e. Step 5.

More than One Broker

Frequently, a real estate transaction involves more than one broker. Broker A's salesperson might list the property and Broker B's salesperson might sell it. The amount of commission that Broker A charges the seller is a matter of negotiation between those two parties, and the division of the commission between the two brokers is subject to negotiation by the two brokers. The manner in which each listing broker shares his or her portion of the commission with each salesperson is decided by each broker.

11. Consider the sale of a $100,000 house that involved two brokers. The listing broker negotiated a $6\frac{1}{2}\%$ commission with the seller, then agreed to pay the selling broker 55% of the total commission. The listing salesperson received 25% of his broker's commission and the selling salesperson received 30% of his broker's commission. How much did each receive?

Your problem analysis should reveal five steps to obtain the solution. Work in an orderly fashion.

12. A house sold for $85,000 and the commission was 7.25%. The broker paid a franchise fee of 5.5% of the total commission plus a multiple-listing service transaction fee of $\frac{1}{4}$ of 1% of the total commission. Of the remainder, the agent received 55% of the office net commission and paid a $20 computer use fee to the broker on the transaction. How much did the office and the salesperson receive?

Your problem analysis should reveal seven steps to obtain the solution.

Charging Graduated Commission Rates

In many markets, brokers will charge different rates on different portions of the sales price. When this is done, you simply calculate the commission on each portion and add your answers.

EXAMPLE: A broker charges 6% on the first $100,000 of the sales price, 4.5% on the next $100,000 and 2% on the balance exceeding $200,000. What is the total commission charged on a property selling for $436,500?

$$
\begin{array}{r}
\$436,500 \text{ sales price} \\
-\$100,000 \times .\ 06 = \$\ 6,000 \\
\underline{-\$100,000} \times .045 = \$\ 4,500 \\
\$236,500 \times .\ 02 = \underline{\$\ 4,730} \\
\$15,230 \text{ total commission}
\end{array}
$$

PROBLEMS FOR ADDITIONAL PRACTICE

When you have finished these problems, check your answers against those at the end of the chapter. If you miss any of the problems, review this chapter before going on to Chapter 4.

1. A 6% commission was charged by the broker for the sale of a house that sold for $50,000. The commission was divided as follows: 10% to the salesperson getting the listing, one-half of the balance to the salesperson making the sale and the remainder to the broker. What was the amount of commission earned by the salesperson making the sale?

    a. $3,000

    b. $300

    c. $1,350

    d. $1,500

2. What was the selling price of a house if the salesperson received $1,000 as her half of the 5% commission charged by the broker?

    a. $40,000

    b. $20,000

    c. $80,000

    d. $10,000

3. Mr. Brinner's house sold for $85,000 and the total commission was 6.5% of that amount. The broker received three-fourths of that amount and the salesperson received one-fourth. How much was the broker's commission?

    a. $5,525.00

    b. $1,381.25

    c. $3,847.50

    d. $4,143.75

4. Salesperson Mike Scherer received $787.50 as his half of his broker's 7% commission on a sale. The sale price was

    a. $45,000.

    b. $22,500.

    c. $22,000.

    d. $25,000.

5. Two cooperating brokers split equally the 6% commission on a sale. Broker A paid her salesperson $1,620 as his 60% of broker A's share. The sale price of the property was

a. $27,000.

c. $63,000.

b. $54,000.

d. $90,000.

6. A broker paid his salesperson $3,600, the agreed upon three-fifths share of a 6% commission. For what amount did the property sell?

a. $100,000

c. $150,000

b. $120,000

d. $80,000

7. A salesperson received $2,250 as his 50% of the commission on a $75,000 sale. The full commission was computed at the rate of

a. 5%.

c. 6%.

b. 5.5%.

d. 6.5%.

8. What was the sales price of a property whose owner paid a $6,000 commission at a 6% rate?

a. $360

c. $100,000

b. $36,000

d. $136,000

9. On the sale of a house, broker Audrey Kirch earns 7% of the first $50,000 and 3% of any amount exceeding $50,000. What was the selling price of a house if her total commission was $4,475?

a. $44,750

c. $32,500

b. $89,500

d. $82,500

10. A broker was paid a 6% commission on the first $100,000 of a house that sold for $150,000. If the total commission was $8,500, what was the percentage of commission paid on the balance?

a. 5%

c. 1.7%

b. 5.7%

d. 2.5%

11. John Bellows earns an 8% commission on the first $75,000 of sales for the month and 3% on all sales exceeding that amount. If Mr. Bellows sold houses totaling $162,100 for the month, how much more would he have earned at a straight 6% commission?

a. $1,113

c. $9,726

b. $810.50

d. $2,613

12. The brokerage fee on a house that listed for $90,000 is 6%. What is the commission loss to the broker if the actual sales price of the house was 10% less than the list price?

a. $4,860

c. $5,400

b. $3,600

d. $540

13. Salesperson George Sutter sells a house for $84,500. The listing broker receives 50% of the 6% commission. How much does the salesperson receive if he gets 40% of the commission due the selling broker?

a. $2,028

c. $2,535

b. $1,014

d. $5,070

14. Alice Listor took a listing for her company, ABC Realty, that sold for $82,500. Betty Bought, who works for First Realty, produced the purchasers. The brokers have agreed to divide the 7% commission equally and Alice will receive 55% of her broker's share, which is

    a. $2,887.50.   c. $1,588.13.

    b. $5,775.00.   d. $1,229.38.

15. What commission rate was charged if Barry received $4,800, which represents 60% of the total commission charged to the seller on a $100,000 sales price?

    a. 6%   c. 7%

    b. 5.75%   d. 8%

ANSWER KEY

SOLUTIONS: WARM-UP EXERCISES

1. (a): $100,000 \times .07 = $7,000

2. (b): $100,000 \times .07 = $7,000
$200,000 \times .06 = $12,000
$503,500 - $300,000 = $203,500
$203,500 \times .045 = $9,157.50
$7,000 + $12,000 + $9,157.50 = $28,157.50

3. (b): $5,000 \div $75,000 = .0667 or 6.67%

4. (d): $120,000 \times .075 = $9,000
$9,000 \times .60 = $5,400
$5,400 \times .70 = $3,780

5. (b): $3,000 \div .60 = $5,000
$5,000 \div .55 = $9,090.91
$9,090.91 \div .07 = $129,870.14

SOLUTIONS: CHAPTER PROBLEMS

1. a. Total × Rate = Part
    b. Part ÷ Rate = Total
    c. Part ÷ Total = Rate

2. a. $9,080 plus $40 is 95% of what amount?

   b. You are looking for the total.

   c. $\dfrac{\text{Part}}{\text{Rate}} = \text{Total}$

3. 95% = .95

   $9,120 ÷ .95 = $9,600

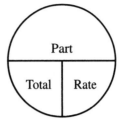

4. a. What is 5% of $9,600?

   b. Rate × Total = Part

   c. 5% × $9,600 = Part

   d. .05 × $9,600 = $480

5. Step 1. Read the problem carefully.

   Step 2. Analyze, pick out the important factors and restate the problem.

   $4,500 is what percentage of $75,000?

   Step 3. Choose the correct formula.

   $$\dfrac{\text{Part}}{\text{Total}} = \text{Rate}$$

   Step 4. Substitute.

   $$\dfrac{\$4,500}{\$75,000} = \text{Rate}$$

   Step 5. Solve.

   $$\dfrac{\$4,500}{\$75,000} = .06,\ \text{or } 6\%$$

6. Analysis and restatement: This problem has two parts:

   Part 1. What is 6% of $5,800?
   Part 2. What is 40% of that figure?

Formula: Part 1. Total × Rate = Part
   Part 2. Total × Rate = Part

Substitution and solution:
   Part 1. 6% × $5,800 = Part
   6% = .06
   .06 × $5,800 = $348 total commission
   Part 2. 40% × $348 = Part
   40% = .40
   .40 × $348 = $139.20 salesperson's share of the commission

7. Analysis and restatement: This problem has two parts:

Part 1. What is 6% of $55,000?

Part 2. One-fourth $= \dfrac{1}{4} = .25$ or 25%

What is 25% of the figure found in Part 1?

Formula: Part 1. Rate × Total = Part
Part 2. Rate × Total = Part

Substitution and solution:
Part 1. 6% × $55,000 = Part
6% = .06
.06 × $55,000 = $3,300 total commission
Part 2. 25% × $3,300 = Part
25% = .25
.25 × $3,300 = Part = $825 salesperson's commission

8. Analysis and restatement: $3,000 is one-half of the total commission, so $3,000 plus $3,000 equals $6,000, which is the total commission. $6,000 is 6% of what amount?

If you missed this step, correct your solution before you read the rest of the answer.

Formula: Part ÷ Rate = Total

Substitution and solution: $6,000 ÷ 6% = Total
6% = .06
$6,000 ÷ .06 = $100,000

9. Analysis and restatement: This problem has three parts:

Part 1. What is 6% of $40,000?
Part 2. What is the selling salesperson's percentage of the total commission?
Part 3. What is the selling salesperson's commission?

Formula: Part 1. Total × Rate = Part
Part 2. Total × Rate = Part
Part 3. Total × Rate = Part

Substitution and solution:
Part 1. $40,000 × 6% = Part
6% = .06
$40,000 × .06 = $2,400 total broker's commission
Part 2. $2,400 = 100% of the commission. The salesperson getting the listing receives 10%. This leaves 90% to be split evenly between the broker and the salesperson. One-half of 90% is 45%, the salesperson's percentage of the total commission.
Part 3. $2,400 × 45% = Part
45% = .45
$2,400 × .45 = $1,080 salesperson's commission

10. a. Read the problem carefully.
 b. Analyze the problem, pick out the important factors and put those factors into a simplified question.
 c. Choose the proper formula for the problem.
 d. Substitute numbers for the known elements of the formula.
 e. Solve the problem.

Total × Rate = Part
Part ÷ Rate = Total
Part ÷ Total = Rate

11. Step 1. 6.5% = .065
$100,000 × .065 = $6,500 total commission

Step 2. 45% = .45
$6,500 × .45 = $2,925 to listing broker

Step 3. 55% = .55
$6,500 × .55 = $3,575 to selling broker

Step 4. 25% = .25
$2,925 × .25 = $731.25 to listing salesperson

Step 5. 30% = .30
$3,575 × .30 = $1,072.50 to selling salesperson

12. Step 1. 7.25% = .0725
$85,000 × .0725 = $6,162.50 total commission

Step 2. 5.5% = .055
$6,162.50 × .055 = $338.94 franchise fee

Step 3. .25% = .0025
$6,162.50 × .0025 = $15.41 MLS fee

Step 4. $6,162.50 − $338.94 − $15.41 = $5,808.15 office net commission

Step 5. 55% = .55
$5,808.15 × .55 = $3,194.48 salesperson's gross commission

Step 6. $3,194.48 − $20 computer fee = $3,174.48 salesperson's net commission

Step 7. $5,808.15 − $3,174.48 = $2,633.67

SOLUTIONS: PROBLEMS FOR ADDITIONAL PRACTICE

1. (c): 6% = .06
$50,000 × .06 = $3,000
100% − 10% = 90% or .90
.90 × .50 = .45
$3,000 × .45 = $1,350

2. (a): 50% = .50
$1,000 ÷ .50 = $2,000
5% = .05
$2,000 ÷ .05 = $40,000

3. (d): 6.5% = .065
$85,000 × .065 = $5,525
75% = .75
$5,525 × .75 = $4,143.75

4. (b): 50% = .50
$787.50 ÷ .50 = $1,575
7% = .07
$1,575 ÷ .07 = $22,500

5. (d): 60% = .60
$1,620 ÷ .60 = $2,700
50% = .50
$2,700 ÷ .50 = $5,400
6% = .06
$5,400 ÷ .06 = $90,000

6. (a): three-fifths = .60
$3,600 ÷ .60 = $6,000
$6,000 ÷ .06 = $100,000

7. (c): 50% = .50
$2,250 ÷ .50 = $4,500
$4,500 ÷ $75,000 = .06 or 6%

8. (c): 6% = .06
$6,000 ÷ .06 = $100,000

9. (d): 7% = .07
$50,000 × .07 = $3,500
$4,475 − $3,500 = $975
3% = .03
$975 ÷ .03 = $32,500
$50,000 + $32,500 = $82,500

10. (a): 6% = .06
$100,000 × .06 = $6,000
$8,500 − $6,000 = $2,500
$150,000 − $100,000 = $50,000
$2,500 ÷ $50,000 = .05 or 5%

11. (a): 8% = .08
$75,000 × .08 = $6,000
$162,100 − $75,000 = $87,100
3% = .03
$87,100 × .03 = $2,613
$6,000 + $2,613 = $8,613
6% = .06
$162,100 × .06 = $9,726
$9,726 − $8,613 = $1,113

12. (d): 10% = .10
$90,000 × .10 = $9,000
6% = .06
$9,000 × .06 = $540

13. (b): 6% = .06
$84,500 × .06 = $5,070
50% = .50
$5,070 × .50 = $2,535
40% = .40
$2,535 × .40 = $1,014

14. (c): 7% = .07
$82,500 × .07 = $5,775
50% = .50
$5,775 × .50 = $2,887.50
55% = .55
$2,887.50 × .55 = $1,588.13

15. (d): 60% = .60
$4,800 ÷ .60 = $8,000
$8,000 ÷ $100,000 = .08 or 8%

CHAPTER

Sales Price, List Price and Net Price Problems

In this chapter, you will continue your work with the three basic formulas involving total, rate and part. You will apply what you have learned in previous chapters to solve for sales price, list price and net price in various real estate settings. When you have completed your work, you will be able to

- help a seller price his or her property to recover the seller's investment and achieve the profit margin he or she seeks and
- mathematically help a seller establish the correct asking price to give the seller his or her desired net, to cover expenses and to pay the broker.

WARM-UP EXERCISES

Because readers will have varying amounts of knowledge and experience, the problems that follow will allow you to determine your familiarity with the material to be covered. Try all of the problems before checking your answers against the answer key at the end of the chapter.

1. A house sold for $54,000, which was 90% of the list price. What did the house list for?

    a. $48,600   c. $59,400

    b. $60,000   d. $50,670

2. In the above problem, if the broker deducted a 6% commission and the house was originally purchased for $38,070, what rate of profit did the seller realize?

    a. 6.4%   c. 38.5%

    b. 41.8%   d. 33.3%

3. At what price must a property sell to give the seller a net of $60,000 after paying the broker a 6% commission, paying off a $480 lien and paying closing costs of $850?

a. $64,930.00

c. $65,244.68

b. $65,009.80

d. $65,159.78

4. For how much must you sell a property (you paid $125,000) if you want to net a 15% profit and pay your broker a 7% commission for selling the property?

a. $154,569.89

c. $153,812.50

b. $152,375.00

d. $143,750.00

5. If you sold a property for $154,569.89, paid the broker 7% and realized a profit of 15%, what did you pay for the property?

a. $120,000

c. $125,000

b. $123,000

d. $125,615

Following is the basic equation you've been working with:

$$\text{Total} \times \text{Rate} = \text{Part}$$

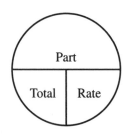

In Chapter 3, total, part and rate *usually* meant:

Total	Total sales price
Part	Commission amount
Rate	Commission percentage

However, in this chapter, which deals with list price, gross sales price and net sales price, the three components of this basic formula will *generally* mean:

Total	Gross selling price (what the buyer pays for the real estate)
Part	Net amount (what the seller receives for the property—gross price minus expenses, commission, etc.)
Rate	100% minus deductions (expenses, commission, etc.)

Seller net ÷ Sales price = Rate
Seller net ÷ Rate = Sales price
Sales price × Rate = Seller net

List price ÷ Cost = Rate
List price ÷ Rate = Cost
Cost × Rate = List price

List price ÷ Selling price = Rate
List price ÷ Rate = Selling price
Selling price × Rate = List price

Sales price ÷ Cost = Rate
Sales price ÷ Rate = Cost
Cost × Rate = Sales price

If you have any difficulty understanding the problems in this chapter, review Chapter 2.

1. What are the formulas for solving for total and rate if:

$$\text{Total} \times \text{Rate} = \text{Part}$$

a. _____ ÷ _____ = Total

b. _____ ÷ _____ = Rate

You will use the same problem-solving strategy presented in Chapter 3, as well as the same basic formulas.

Step 1. Read the problem carefully.

Step 2. Analyze the problem, pick out the important factors and put those factors into a simplified question, disregarding unimportant factors.

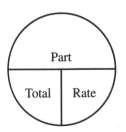

Step 3. Choose the proper formula for the problem.

Step 4. Substitute numbers for the known elements of the formula.

Step 5. Solve the problem.

If you use this strategy throughout this chapter, and wherever it applies in this book, you'll have an easier time solving word problems.

EXAMPLE: Now apply the problem-solving strategy to a typical real estate problem.

Step 1. Read the following problem carefully:

> A house sold for $61,625, which was 85% of the original list price. At what price was the house originally listed?

Step 2. Analyze the problem, pick out the important factors and put those factors into a simplified question.

$61,625 is 85% of what amount?

Step 3. Choose the proper formula for the problem.

$$\frac{\text{Part}}{\text{Rate}} = \text{Total}$$

Step 4. Substitute numbers for the known elements of the formula.

$$\frac{\$61,625}{85\%} = \text{Total}$$

Step 5. Solve the problem.

$$\frac{\$61,625}{.85} = \$72,500$$

2. To prove the answer for the preceding example, ask whether $61,625 is really 85% of $72,500 (in other words, what is 85% of $72,500?).

Complete the proof for this problem.

3. Now apply the problem-solving strategy to the following problem:

The net amount received by Kenneth Plummer for his house after the broker had deducted a sales commission of 6% was $55,648. What was the selling price? (Because net sales proceeds and commission rates are known, find the gross sales price.)

The gross sales price is the total, or 100%. If the broker receives 6% of the sales price, the seller will *net* the remainder of 100%, which is 94% (100% − 6% = 94%).

a. Analyze and restate the problem.

b. Choose the proper formula.

c. Substitute.

d. Solve.

Remember, the selling price, or *gross* selling price, is the agreed upon total price to be paid by the purchaser. After the broker deducts the sales commission and expenses from this amount, the seller will be entitled to the *net* amount of the selling proceeds.

4. Prove your answer for problem 3.

5. Solve the following problem. Work it out step by step, as you've learned:

Ms. Cornelius paid $75,500 for a house. She now wants to sell it and net a 20% profit after paying the broker's commission. She gave the broker the listing at 5%. What would the selling price have to be?

6. Calculate the amount of the broker's commission on the sale of the property described in problem 5, assuming Ms. Cornelius received her required selling price.

7. If you bought a house for $64,000, which was 20% less than the list price, what percentage of profit would you net on your investment if you sold the house for 10% more than the original list price? What would your profit amount to in dollars?

8. A house listed for $54,000. The seller received $48,450 net after the broker deducted $2,550 for her 5% commission. What was the selling price of this house?

NET PRICE

Frequently, a seller will tell the broker or salesperson that the seller wants to net a certain amount from the sale of his or her property. The broker or salesperson must then estimate the total costs to be paid by the seller and determine whether the resulting list price is within the market value range. (**Note:** Net listings are prohibited in many states and discouraged in most others.)

EXAMPLE: If a seller wants to net $80,000 from a property without a mortgage, what will be the list price if the commission is 7% and the seller's closing costs are 4% of the sales price?

First, you must total the expenses:

          7% commission
        +4% closing costs
        11% total sales expenses

If the seller is to net $80,000, that amount must equal the list price less the sales expenses, or:

          List price − Sales expenses = Net

The list price equals 100% and the sales expenses equal 11%; therefore, the $80,000 net price must equal 89% (100% − 11%) of the list price. To express this mathematically:

          $80,000 = 89% of list price

Apply this formula:

$$\frac{\text{Part}}{\text{Rate}} = \text{Total}$$

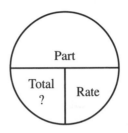

Substitute numbers:

$$\frac{\$80,000}{.89} = \text{Total}$$

Solve:

$$\frac{\$80,000}{.89} = \$89,887.64$$

Proof: Step 1. $89,887.64 list price
              ×   .07 commission rate
              $ 6,292.13 commission

         Step 2. $89,887.64 list price
              ×   .04 other closing costs rate
              $ 3,595.51 other closing costs

         Step 3. $ 6,292.13 commission
              + 3,595.51 other closing costs
              $ 9,887.64 total sales expenses

         Step 4. $89,887.64 list price
              − 9,887.64 total sales expenses
              $80,000.00 seller's net

The most common error made in this type of problem is for the salesperson to multiply the seller's net by the total sales expense rate, add this amount to the seller's net and call this figure the list price. Let's see how this error would affect the calculations for this property:

Step 1. $80,000 seller's net
        ×   .11 total sales expense rate
        $ 8,800 total sales expenses

Step 2. $80,000 seller's net
        +8,800 total sales expenses
        $88,800 list price

Now, for the proof of error:

Step 1. $88,800 list price
        ×   .11 total sales expense rate
        $ 9,768 total sales expenses

Step 2. $88,800 list price
        −9,768 total sales expenses
        $79,032 seller's net

    Notice that the seller's net indicated in the proof is $79,032—$968 *less* than the seller wants. Understandably, the seller will be distressed. Who do you suppose the seller might expect to pay for this error?

RATE (PERCENTAGE) OF PROFIT

Another problem encountered in the field by a salesperson is the situation described in the example below.

EXAMPLE: If a person buys a house for 20% less than the list price, then sells it for the original list price, what rate of profit is realized?

    First, let's examine two diagrams and visualize them as two rulers, one five inches long and one four inches long:

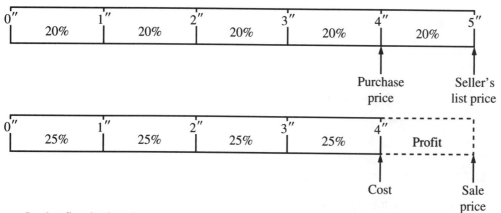

    In the five-inch ruler, each of the one-inch increments, or divisions, represents 20% of the entire length of five inches to total 100% of the list price. Because the buyer paid 20% less than the seller's list price, the purchase price can be represented graphically as being at the four-inch mark on the five-inch ruler:

100% − 20% = 80%, or the four-inch mark

The buyer now owns the house, so his 80% price now represents 100% of his "owning" price or cost. This can be represented graphically as a four-inch ruler. His percentage of profit upon resale is calculated on his cost or his purchase price. When the house is resold for the original list price, this lengthens the four-inch ruler by an amount sufficient to make the ruler the original length of five inches. Therefore, this graphically displays the original list price:

1. Each inch on the five-inch ruler represents $\frac{1}{5}$ (20%) of the total length of this ruler, yet
2. Each inch is the same absolute length regardless of which of the two rulers is used, but
3. Each inch on the four-inch ruler represents $\frac{1}{4}$ (25%) of the total length of this ruler.

By examining both diagrams, you can deduce the answer to the problem: 25%. In percentages, it depends on where you *start,* and that starting point is called the total. Therefore, the percentage of *profit must be based on what the person paid for the house,* not on the list price.

However, the percentage of *reduction must be based on the list price.* It all depends on the starting point, the total. If you are still not clear at this point, you may wish to refer back to Chapter 2 and reread "Percentage of Change."

Now, let's suppose that the list price was $100,000 and that the buyer paid 20% less and resold at list price. What was the percentage of profit? First, find the buyer's cost, or price:

Step 1. 100% asking price − 20% = 80% purchase price

Step 2.

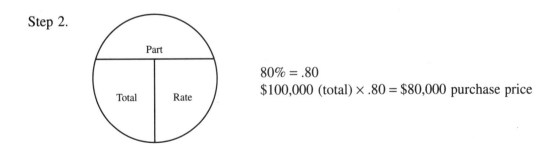

80% = .80
$100,000 (total) × .80 = $80,000 purchase price

If the property is resold by the new owner at the original asking price, what percentage (rate) of profit would he realize?

Step 3. $100,000   original asking price

        <u>−80,000</u>   current owner's purchase price

      $ 20,000   profit

Step 4.

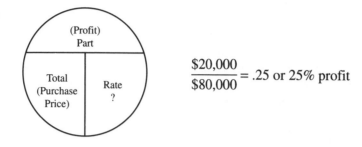

$$\frac{\$20,000}{\$80,000} = .25 \text{ or } 25\% \text{ profit}$$

Remember, the total is always the amount the current owner paid for the property, not what was asked.

9. Beryl Stewart bought a house for $150,000 and resold it for $200,000. What rate of profit did he realize?

RATE (PERCENTAGE) OF LOSS

The rate of loss is calculated exactly the same as the profit except that the order of the numbers is reversed. In each case, the rate of profit *or* loss is figured in relation to the *original* number or amount.

     Rate of loss (depreciation) will be explored in detail in Chapter 6.

PROBLEMS FOR ADDITIONAL PRACTICE

When you have finished these problems, check your answers against those at the end of the chapter. If you miss any of the problems, review this chapter before going on to Chapter 5.

1. Jay's house sold for $62,250, which was 75% of the list price. What did the house list for?

    a. $77,812.50   c. $83,000.00

    b. $74,700.00   d. $81,250.00

2. Mrs. Tomas received a net of $73,320 for her house after the broker deducted a 6% commission. What was the gross sales price of this house?

    a. $77,720   c. $77,179

    b. $69,654   d. $78,000

3. The Harrington family wishes to sell its house at a 14% net profit. The Harringtons purchased the house for $37,000. What would the sales price have to be to give the Harringtons a 14% profit after they pay the selling broker a 5% commission on the sales price?

   a. $44,400   c. $44,289
   b. $47,360   d. $40,936

4. A seller received $51,700 after her broker deducted the agreed upon 6% commission. The sales price was

   a. $50,000.   c. $55,000.
   b. $60,000.   d. $57,000.

5. When the sale on the Morgan house was closed, the broker withheld the seller's title expense of $250, after deducting his $6\frac{1}{2}$% commission of $5,200, and delivered to the seller a net check for

   a. $74,550.   c. $84,350.
   b. $75,000.   d. $71,750.

6. A house sold for $75,200, which was 94% of the listing price of

   a. $78,875.   c. $79,712.
   b. $78,125.   d. $80,000.

7. The owners want to make a 15% profit on the sale of their house after paying a 6% broker's fee. Their cost was $40,000. What will their sales price have to be?

   a. $46,000   c. $48,936
   b. $42,936   d. $49,836

8. Indicate the net amount received by the seller from a sale in which the broker received a 6% commission of $3,480 and the seller's other expenses were $175 for the title insurance fee and $95 for the transfer tax and recording fee.

   a. $54,520   c. $54,250
   b. $55,250   d. $57,730

9. Jenny Banks bought a house for $48,000 with the intention of remodeling it, then selling it in two years for $78,000. How much can Jenny spend on remodeling if taxes are $1,200 each year, the commission rate is 6% of the intended selling price and the profit she requires is $12,000?

   a. $12,120   c. $10,920
   b. $13,320   d. $12,720

10. Joan and Bob Thatcher bought an 80-acre tract for $1,980 per acre. Taxes, insurance and other expenses amounted to $12,400 per year. At the end of four years, the property was sold for a net price of $1\frac{3}{4}$ times its original cost. What was the net profit on the sale of the property?

   a. $118,800   c. $227,600
   b. $69,200   d. $32,000

11. Five years ago, an investor bought four lots for $10,000 each. A house was built on one of the lots at a cost of $60,000. The lot with the house recently sold for $100,000 and the remaining vacant lots sold for $2\frac{1}{2}$ times their original cost. The percentage of gross profit was

    a. 42.8%.
    b. 57.1%.

    c. 175%.
    d. 75%.

12. If you bought a house for the list price less 20% and sold the house for the list price, what percentage of profit would you make?

    a. 25%
    b. 20%

    c. 80%
    d. 125%

13. A house listed for $60,000. The seller received $50,760 net after the broker deducted $3,240 for his commission. What rate of commission was the seller charged?

    a. 5.4%
    b. 5%

    c. 5.5%
    d. 6%

14. You bought a home for $50,000, which was 20% less than the list price, and you sold the house for 10% more than the original list price. The list price was

    a. $66,000.
    b. $60,000.

    c. $68,750.
    d. $62,500.

15. You bought a house for 15% less than the list price and sold it for the list price one month later. Your percentage of profit was

    a. 85%.
    b. 82.4%.

    c. 15%.
    d. 17.6%.

ANSWER KEY

SOLUTIONS: WARM-UP EXERCISES

1. (b): $54,000 ÷ .90 = $60,000

2. (d): $54,000 × .94 = $50,760
    $50,760 − $38,070 = $12,690
    $12,690 ÷ $38,070 = .333 or 33.3%

3. (c): $60,000 + $480 + $850 = $61,330
    $61,330 ÷ .94 = $65,244.68

4. (a): Original cost = 1
    Desired profit = 15% or .15
    Desired seller net = 1 + .15 or 1.15
    $125,000 × 1.15 = $143,750
    $143,750 ÷ .93 = $154,569.89

5. (c): $154,569.89 × .93 = $143,749.9977 or
    $143,750 (rounded)
    $143,750 ÷ 1.15 = $125,000

SOLUTIONS: CHAPTER PROBLEMS

1. a. Part ÷ Rate = Total
   b. Part ÷ Total = Rate

2. $72,500 × .85 = $61,625

3. a. $55,648 is 94% of what number?
   b. Part ÷ Rate = Total
   c. $55,648 ÷ .94 = Total
   d. $55,648 ÷ .94 = $59,200

4. $59,200 × .94 = $55,648
            or
   $59,200 × .06 = $3,552.00
   $59,200 − $3,552 = $55,648

5. $75,500 × .20 = $15,100
   $75,500 + $15,100 = $90,600
   100% − 5% = 95% or .95
   $90,600 ÷ .95 = $95,368.42

6. $95,368.42 × .05 = $4,768.42

7. $64,000 ÷ .80 = $80,000
   $80,000 × 1.10 = $88,000
   $88,000 − $64,000 = $24,000
   $24,000 ÷ $64,000 = .375 or 37.5%

8. $48,450 + $2,550 = $51,000
            or
   $48,450 ÷ .95 = $51,000
            or
   $2,550 ÷ .05 = $51,000

9. $200,000 − $150,000 = $50,000
   $50,000 ÷ $150,000 = .333 or 33.3%

SOLUTIONS: PROBLEMS FOR ADDITIONAL PRACTICE

1. (c): $62,250 ÷ .75 = $83,000

2. (d): $73,320 ÷ .94 = $78,000

3. (a): $37,000 × 1.14 = $42,180
   $42,180 ÷ .95 = $44,400

4. (c): $51,700 ÷ .94 = $55,000

5. (a): $5,200 ÷ .065 = $80,000
   $80,000 − $5,200 − $250 = $74,550

6. (d): $75,200 ÷ .94 = $80,000

7. (c): $40,000 × 1.15 = $46,000
   $46,000 ÷ .94 = $48,936 (rounded)

8. (c): $3,480 ÷ .06 = $58,000
   $58,000 − $3,480 − $175 − $95 = $54,250

9. (c): $1,200 × 2 = $2,400
   $78,000 × .06 = $4,680
   $78,000 − $2,400 − $4,680 − $12,000 −
   $48,000 = $10,920

10. (b): 80 acres × $1,980 = $158,400
   $12,400 × 4 = $49,600
   $158,400 × 1.75 = $277,200
   $277,200 − $158,400 − $49,600 = $69,200

11. (d): $10,000 × 4 = $40,000
   $40,000 + $60,000 = $100,000
   $30,000 × 2.5 = $75,000
   $100,000 + $75,000 = $175,000
   $175,000 − $100,000 = $75,000
   $75,000 ÷ $100,000 = .75 or 75%

12. (a): 100% × .80 = 80%
   80% ÷ 100% = .25 or 25%
            or
   100 − 80 = 20
   20 ÷ 80 = .25 or 25%

13. (d): $50,760 + $3,240 = $54,000
   $3,240 ÷ $54,000 = .06 or 6%

14. (d): $50,000 ÷ .80 = $62,500

15. (d): 100 × .85 = 85
   100 − 85 = 15
   15 ÷ 85 = .17647 or 17.6%

Area and Volume

Land is frequently sold by the front foot or by the square foot of land area. Building materials are sold by the square foot, square yard or cubic yard. In most areas, improved real estate is sold or leased by the square foot. It is imperative that real estate practitioners be able to accurately measure and calculate linear, square and cubic measure.

At the conclusion of your work in this chapter, you will be able to accurately calculate

- the front feet of a lot;
- square feet and square yards; and
- cubic feet and cubic yards.

Because readers will have varying amounts of knowledge and experience, the problems that follow will allow you to determine your familiarity with the material to be covered. Try all of the problems before checking your answers against the answer key at the end of the chapter.

1. Compute the area of each lettered division of the following figure:

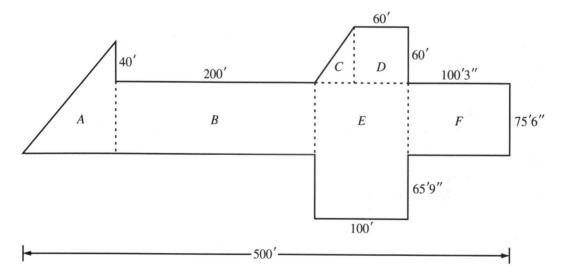

2. Each lettered division of the figure in question 1 represents a lot that is for sale. Mr. Jorgenson is considering buying all of them. At $6 per square foot, how much would all six lots cost him?

a. $276,926.64

b. $262,526.64

c. $193,526.64

d. $284,126.64

3. Mr. Bower is the broker for the property shown in question 1. Mr. Simmons would like to buy lot E, which sells by itself for $6.50 per square foot. Mr. Bower receives a 7% commission. If this sale goes through, how much will Mr. Bower's commission be?

a. $91,112.50

b. $84,750.00

c. $6,426.88

d. $5,466.75

4. The owner of lot B (shown in question 1) proposes to build an office-showroom building that is 40 feet high, 30 feet wide and 45 feet long. If the bid is $97,200, what is the cost of this building per cubic foot?

a. $1.80

b. $1.50

c. $7.20

d. $4.50

5. If the owner builds the building described in question 4 on lot B, what will be property (land and building) cost per square foot of building area? (Remember, the land was purchased at $6 per square foot.)

a. $150.00

b. $144.46

c. $139.11

d. $72.00

6. What would it cost to build a patio 6 inches thick that covers an area 20 feet by 18 feet if concrete costs $40 per cubic yard and finishing costs are $1.80 per square foot?

a. $914.67

b. $960.00

c. $648.00

d. $1,448.00

Before attempting to calculate area or volume problems, it is important to do the following:

1. Convert all dimensions to feet.

EXAMPLE: 8 feet, 6 inches becomes 8.5 feet

To convert *inches* to *feet,* divide the inches by 12.

$$\frac{6 \text{ inches}}{12 \text{ inches}} = .50 \text{ feet}$$

2. Become familiar with the information that follows:

LINEAR MEASURE = A LINE

12 inches = 1 foot
3 feet = 1 yard
1 link = 7.92 inches
1 vara = 33.333 inches
1 rod = 16.5 feet = 5.5 yards
1 mile = 5,280 feet = 320 rods
1 chain = 66 feet = 4 rods = 100 links

SQUARE MEASURE = AREA

Length (L) × Width (W) = Area (A) (in square unit measurements)

12″ × 12″ = 144 square inches = 1 square foot
3′ × 3′ = 9 square feet = 1 square yard

To convert *square yards* to *square feet,* multiply square yards by 9.
To convert *square feet* to *square yards,* divide square feet by 9.

1 acre = 43,560 square feet

To convert *acres* to *square feet,* multiply acres by 43,560.
To convert *square feet* to *acres,* divide square feet by 43,560.

1 section = 640 acres

To convert *sections* to *acres,* multiply sections by 640.
To convert *acres* to *sections,* divide acres by 640.

CUBIC MEASURE = VOLUME

Length (L) × Width (W) × Height (H) = Volume (V) (in cubic unit measurements)

12″ × 12″ × 12″ = 1,728 cubic inches = 1 cubic foot
3′ × 3′ × 3′ = 27 cubic feet = 1 cubic yard

To convert *cubic yards* to *cubic feet,* multiply cubic yards by 27.
To convert *cubic feet* to *cubic yards,* divide cubic feet by 27.

LINEAR

Front Feet (inches or yards)

In certain situations, the price of a tract of land may be priced by the front foot. Typically, this occurs where the tract "fronts" onto or faces something quite desirable so that the frontage is the a major element of value. This is true because it is the *frontage* of a tract that provides access to something of value, such as a main street, a river or a lake. This avenue of access then becomes quite valuable, so much so that it assumes the pricing burden of the entire tract.

For example, consider a tract of land facing (or fronting on) Eagle Mountain Lake:

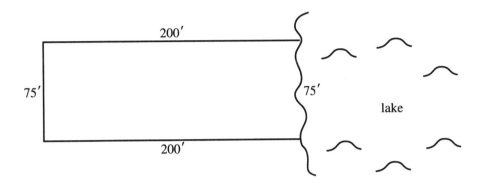

Because lakefront lots are so desirable, these lots are priced at $1,200 per front foot, while nonfronting lots are priced at $3 per square foot.

Therefore, the lakefront lot shown above would be valued at $90,000 (75 feet × $1,200 = $90,000), while a lot of equal size not fronting on the lake would be valued at half as much, or $45,000 (75 feet × 200 feet = 15,000 square feet; 15,000 square feet × $3 = $45,000).

1. Eagle Mountain Lake regulates the length of piers. A pier cannot exceed 80% of the lot's frontage on the water. How many feet long may a pier be constructed?

2. What would be the cost of the above pier at $12 per linear foot?

When the dimensions of a lot are given, front feet are always listed first. Thus, a lot 60 feet by 125 feet would have 60 front feet.

To calculate the price per front foot, divide the sales price by the number of front feet:

Sales price ÷ Front feet = Price per front foot

EXAMPLE: If a lot 60 feet by 125 feet sold for $168,000, how much was its selling price per front foot?

$168,000 ÷ 60 feet = $2,800 per front foot

3. A property on Market Street is valued at $62,500. What is its value per front foot if it has a frontage of 35 feet?

Linear—Perimeter

The cost of constructing fences will usually be quoted as × $s per linear foot. Fences are frequently installed on the property lines or perimeter of the property to enclose an area. The perimeter is simply the total linear feet of the sides that enclose an area.

EXAMPLE: Herchel purchased a tract of land that he wants to enclose with a fence. The tract is 960 feet by 2,200 feet. The desired fence can be purchased at $2.10 per linear foot.

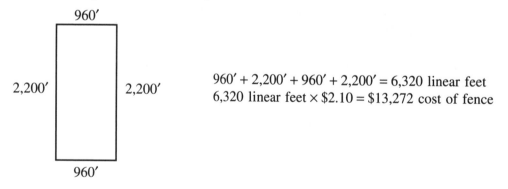

960′ + 2,200′ + 960′ + 2,200′ = 6,320 linear feet
6,320 linear feet × $2.10 = $13,272 cost of fence

AREA

Square Feet (inches or yards)

It is imperative that every real estate professional be able to calculate square footage and area accurately because

- commercial real estate is leased at dollars per square foot;
- vacant lots are sold at dollars per square foot when not sold at dollars per front foot; and
- homes are sold at dollars per square foot.

Before you start working area problems, let's review some basics about shapes and measurements.

> The space inside a two-dimensional shape is called its *area*.

A *right angle* is the angle formed by one-fourth of a circle. Because a full circle is 360 degrees, and one-fourth of 360 degrees is 90 degrees, a right angle is a 90-degree angle.

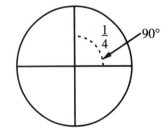

A *rectangle* is a closed figure with four sides that are at right angles to one another. In other words, each angle in a rectangle is 90 degrees.

4. A *square* is a special type of rectangle. Which statement below best describes a square (illustrated at the right)?

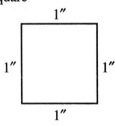

   a. All sides of a square are of equal length.
   b. Only the opposite sides of a square are of equal length.
   c. Squares are rectangles with four sides of equal length.
   d. Rectangles are squares.
   e. Squares are rectangles with equal angles.

5. Which of the following figures is(are) square(s)? Which is(are) rectangle(s)?

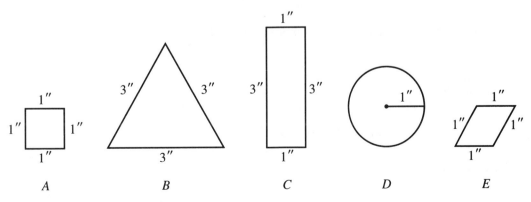

In math, the word *square* may be defined as a

- shape with four sides of equal length and each angle containing 90 degrees;
- unit for measuring the area of various shapes; or
- multiple of a number by or times itself.

EXAMPLE: The number 9 is the "square" of 3 because if you multiply 3×3, the answer is 9.

Units of measurement can be treated in the same manner as numbers, and a clear understanding of this fact greatly simplifies math. For example, if 3 times 3 equals 9, which is the square of 3, then yards multiplied by yards equals square yards. Or, to illustrate this example further:

$$3 \text{ yards} \times 3 \text{ yards} = ?$$

Step 1. Multiply the numbers together:

$$3 \times 3 = 9$$

Step 2. Multiply the units of measurement together:

$$\text{Yards} \times \text{Yards} = \text{Square yards}$$

Now let's look at some *square units.*

A square whose four sides equal one inch each is a *square inch* or one inch square. Likewise, one square mile is one mile on each of the four sides, or one mile square, which amounts to 640 acres.

EXAMPLE:

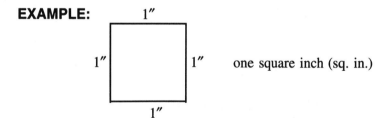

one square inch (sq. in.)

A square whose four sides equal one foot each is a *square foot.*

EXAMPLE:

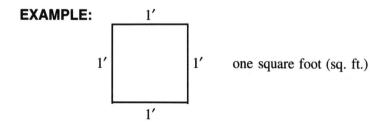

one square foot (sq. ft.)

To calculate the area inside a shape, measure the number of *square units* inside the shape. One way to find the number of square units is to place the shape on a larger number of square units and count the number of square units inside the shape.

6. Count the number of square inches inside the square below.

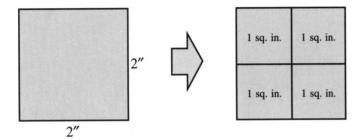

What is the area of this square?

7. Count the number of square inches inside the rectangle below.

What is the area of this rectangle?

Area of Squares and Rectangles

Because counting squares is cumbersome, use the following formula to compute the area of any rectangle:

$$\text{Length} \times \text{Width} = \text{Area}$$
$$\text{or}$$
$$L \times W = A$$

Check your figures in questions 6 and 7, applying this formula. The formula should give you the same answers that counting squares did.

$$2'' \times 2'' = 4 \text{ square inches} \qquad 1'' \times 3'' = 3 \text{ square inches}$$

8. Compute the area of the following rectangle, using the formula $L \times W = A$:

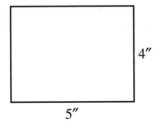

Your answer to Exercise 8 should have been 20 square inches.

Remember, when inches are multiplied by inches, the answer must be in square inches. Likewise, recalling our previous discussion:

$$\text{Feet} \times \text{Feet} = \text{Square feet}$$

9. What is the area of the rectangle below?

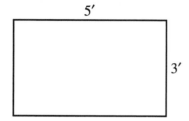

10. What is the area of the square below?

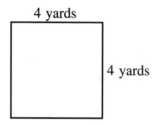

Now you can apply what you have learned about the area of a rectangle to a practical real estate problem.

11. Mr. Shrum leases a parking lot that measures 80 feet by 150 feet. How much rent must he pay each year if the lot rents for $1.30 per square foot per year?

Conversion—Using Like Measures for Area

When an area is computed, all of the dimensions used must be given in the same *kind of unit.* When you found areas in problems 6 and 7 by counting square units, all of the units you counted were of the same kind— inches. When you use a formula to find an area, you must also use units of the same kind for each element of the formula, with the answer as square units of that kind. So inches must be multiplied by inches to arrive at square inches, feet must be multiplied by feet to arrive at square feet and yards must be multiplied by yards to arrive at square yards.

If the two dimensions you want to multiply are in different units of measure, you must convert one to the other.

It is best to convert all units to feet; therefore, you will

- multiply *yards* by 3 to get *feet* and
- divide *inches* by 12 to get *feet.*

12. Convert and solve the following:

   a. $36'' \times 3' = \underline{\ ?\ }$ square feet

       $\underline{\quad} \times 3' = \underline{\quad}$ square feet

   b. $15'' \times 1.5' = \underline{\ ?\ }$ square feet

       $\underline{\quad} \times 1.5' = \underline{\quad}$ square feet

   c. $72'' \times 7' = \underline{\ ?\ }$ square feet

       $\underline{\quad} \times 7' = \underline{\quad}$ square feet

   d. 6 yards $\times 5' = \underline{\ ?\ }$ square feet

       $\underline{\qquad} \times 5' = \underline{\quad}$ square feet

   e. 17 yards $\times 24'' = \underline{\ ?\ }$ square feet

       $\underline{\qquad} \times \underline{\quad} = \underline{\quad}$ square feet

It is best to calculate square feet, then convert to square inches or square yards:

- ■ To convert *square feet* to *square inches,* multiply the square feet by 144 square inches ($12'' \times 12''$).
- ■ To convert *square feet* to *square yards,* divide the square yards by 9 square feet ($3' \times 3'$).

Convert the answers in problem 12 to square inches, then to square yards.

13. a. $\underline{\quad 9 \quad}$ square feet $\times \underline{\quad 144 \quad} = \underline{\quad 1{,}296 \quad}$ square inches

   b. $\underline{\qquad\qquad}$ square feet $\times \underline{\qquad\qquad} = \underline{\qquad\qquad}$ square inches

   c. $\underline{\qquad\qquad}$ square feet $\times \underline{\qquad\qquad} = \underline{\qquad\qquad}$ square inches

   d. $\underline{\qquad\qquad}$ square feet $\times \underline{\qquad\qquad} = \underline{\qquad\qquad}$ square inches

   e. $\underline{\qquad\qquad}$ square feet $\times \underline{\qquad\qquad} = \underline{\qquad\qquad}$ square inches

14. a. $\underline{\quad 9 \quad}$ square feet $\div \underline{\quad 9 \quad} = \underline{\quad 1 \quad}$ square yards

   b. $\underline{\qquad\qquad}$ square feet $\div \underline{\qquad\qquad} = \underline{\qquad\qquad}$ square yards

   c. $\underline{\qquad\qquad}$ square feet $\div \underline{\qquad\qquad} = \underline{\qquad\qquad}$ square yards

   d. $\underline{\qquad\qquad}$ square feet $\div \underline{\qquad\qquad} = \underline{\qquad\qquad}$ square yards

   e. $\underline{\qquad\qquad}$ square feet $\div \underline{\qquad\qquad} = \underline{\qquad\qquad}$ square yards

15. Mr. Milgren's house is on a lot that is 90 feet by 720 inches. What is the area of his lot?

   Note: In the real estate business, lot sizes are generally calculated in square feet rather than square inches.

16. Compute the area of the lot below in square feet.

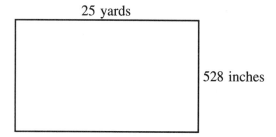

25 yards

528 inches

17. A broker sold a lot with 66 feet and 9 inches of street frontage and a depth of 150 feet to an alley. The sale price was $4 per square foot. Compute the amount the broker received from this sale if her commission rate was 6%.

18. You have contracted to build a sidewalk in front of your house. It is to be 5 feet wide by 27 feet and 6 inches long. If the contractor charges $200 per square yard, how much will the sidewalk cost you?

Area of Triangles

 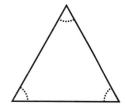 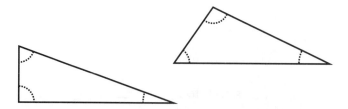

> A *triangle* is a closed figure with three straight sides and three angles. *Tri* means three.

The square-inch figure at the right has been cut in half by a straight line drawn through the opposite corners, to make two equal triangles.

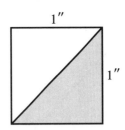

19. How many square inches are in the shaded part of the above square?

20. How many square inches are contained in the triangle below when it is placed on a square-inch grid?

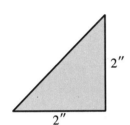 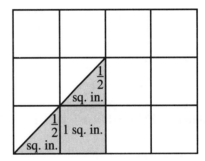

21. What is the area of the triangle below?

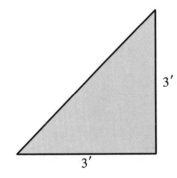 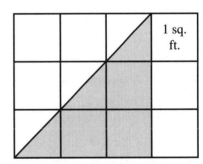

As before, the square-unit grid is cumbersome for computing large areas. It is more convenient to use the following formula for finding the area of a triangle:

$$\frac{1}{2}(\text{Base} \times \text{Height}) = \text{Area of a triangle}$$

$$\frac{1}{2}(BH) = A \, \Delta$$

or

$$\frac{B \times H}{2} = \text{Area of a triangle}$$

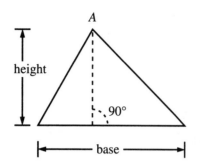
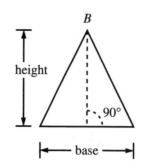
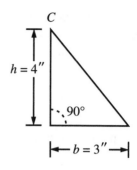

The *base* is the side on which the triangle sits.

The *height* is the straight line distance from the top of the uppermost angle to the base. The height line must form a 90-degree angle to the base.

22. Compute the area of triangle *C*.

23. The diagram below shows a lakefront lot. Compute its area.

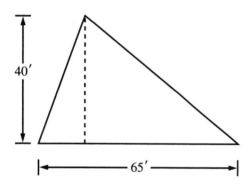

24. Mr. Wier has purchased the following lot at $4.75 per square foot. His broker received a 10% commission on the sale. How much was the broker's commission?

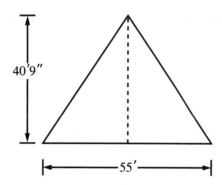

Area of Irregular Closed Figures

25. Use the following drawing of two neighboring lots to answer the questions below.

    a. What is the area of lot *A*?
    b. What is the area of lot *B*?
    c. What is the total area of both lots?

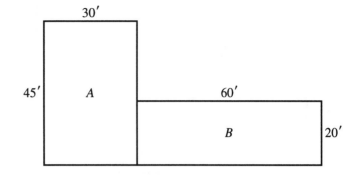

26. Make two rectangles by drawing one straight line inside the figure below.

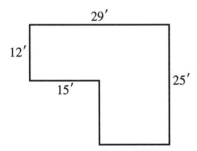

27. Using the measurements given in problem 26, compute the total area of the figure. (Find the area of each rectangle and add them.)

    The area of an irregular figure can be found by dividing it into regular figures, computing the area of each regular figure and adding all the areas together to obtain the total area.

28. Divide the following figure into rectangles and calculate its square footage.

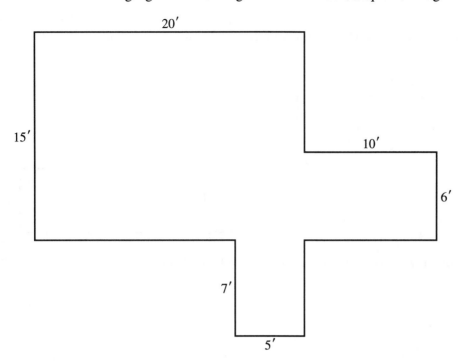

Sometimes it is easier to square off a figure and subtract the missing pieces than it is to try to divide it. To demonstrate, let's look at two ways to calculate the square footage of the following figure.

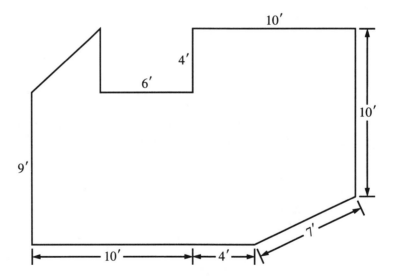

One way is to divide it into rectangles and triangles and calculate the square feet in each, then add the areas to arrive at the total square feet.

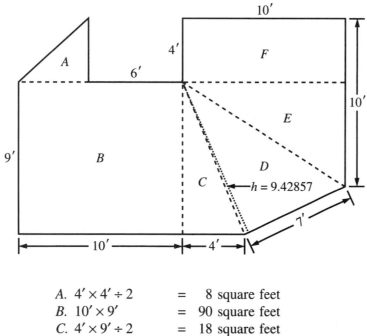

A. $4' \times 4' \div 2$ = 8 square feet
B. $10' \times 9'$ = 90 square feet
C. $4' \times 9' \div 2$ = 18 square feet
D. $7' \times 9.42857' \div 2$ = 33 square feet (rounded)
E. $10' \times 6' \div 2$ = 30 square feet.
F. $10' \times 4'$ = 40 square feet
　　　　　　Total　219 square feet

An easier way to calculate the total area is to (1) square off the figure, (2) calculate the square footage of the squared-off figure and (3) calculate the square footage of and subtract the missing pieces.

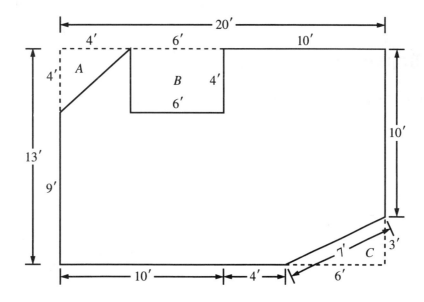

The missing pieces are identified as A, B and C in the above figure.

The total figure is 20′ × 13′ = 260   square feet
Less: *A.* 4′ × 4′ ÷ 2   = <8> square feet
      B. 6′ × 4′   = <24> square feet
      C. 6′ × 3′ ÷ 2   =   <9> square feet
Total   219   square feet

In your real estate practice, most of your area calculations will be related to the square footage of a lot or house. When calculating the square feet of living area (heated and air conditioned area) in a house, use the following five steps:

1. Sketch the foundation.
2. Measure and record the dimensions of all outside walls, remembering to convert inches to the decimal equivalent of a foot.
3. Square off your sketch and identify the missing areas of living space. These include the attached garage, patios, breezeways, porches, and so on.
4. Calculate the total square feet.
5. Subtract the missing areas.

29. Calculate the living area of the house shown here.

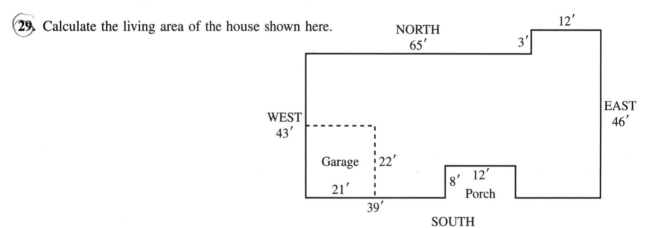

Area of Trapezoids

The shape of the figure in the following exercise is called a trapezoid. You can compute its area by applying the formula

$$\frac{a+b}{2} \times h = A$$

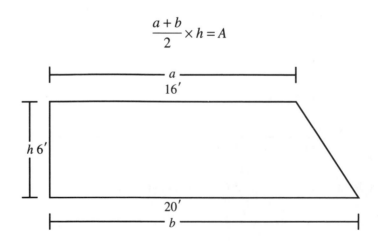

Substituting, we have:

Step 1. $\dfrac{16' + 20'}{2} \times 6' = A$

Step 2. $\dfrac{36'}{2} \times 6' = A$

Step 3. $18' \times 6' = A$

Step 4. 108 square feet $= A$

You can also divide a trapezoid into a rectangle and a triangle.

EXAMPLE:

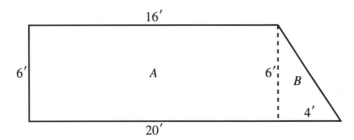

$$A. \ 16' \times 6' \ \ = \ \ 96 \text{ square feet}$$
$$B. \ 4' \times 6' \div 2 = \ \underline{\ 12\ } \text{ square feet}$$
$$\text{Total} \quad 108 \text{ square feet}$$

VOLUME

Cubic Feet (inches or yards)

When a shape encloses a space, the shape has *volume*.

> The space that a three-dimensional object occupies is called its *volume*.

Technically speaking, each shape with three dimensions can also be measured in terms of its surface area. For example, a bedroom has volume because it has three dimensions—length, width and height; however, *one wall* can be measured as a *surface area,* or length times height equals area.

30. a. Which of the following shapes have volume?

 b. Which have only area?

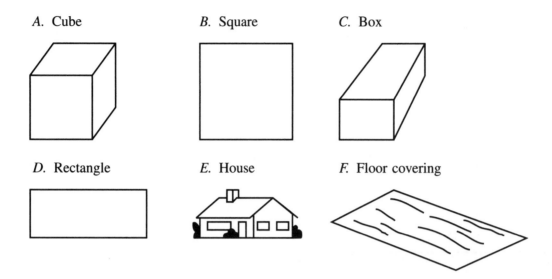

A. Cube   *B.* Square   *C.* Box

D. Rectangle   *E.* House   *F.* Floor covering

 Flat shapes—squares, rectangles, triangles and so on—do *not* have volume. Flat shapes have two dimensions (length and width or height) and shapes with volume have three dimensions (length, width and height).

Cubic Units

A *cube* is made up of six squares. Look at the six sides of the following cube:

 top   bottom   sides of the cube

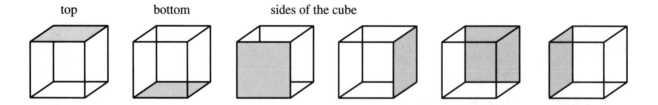

Volume is measured in *cubic* units. Look at the following cube:

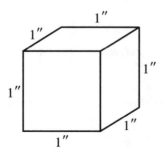

Each side measures one inch. The figure represents *1 cubic inch,* abbreviated *cu. in.* Just as yards times yards equals square yards, a multiple of three units of space equals cubic units, or:

Inches × Inches × Inches = Cubic inches

31. How many cubic inches are there in the following figure?

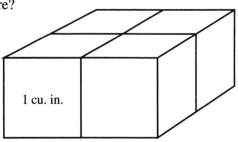

The following figure represents 1 *cubic foot,* abbreviated cu. ft.:

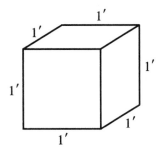

32. How many cubic feet are represented by the following figure?

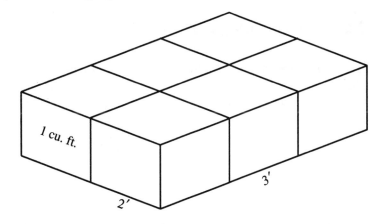

Volume of Box Shapes

Use the following formula for computing volume:

$$L \text{ (length)} \times W \text{ (width)} \times H \text{ (height)} = V \text{ (volume)}$$

33. Find the volume of each of the boxes below.

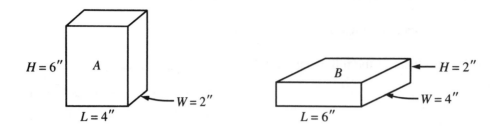

34. How many cubic feet of dirt must be excavated to dig a hole 5 feet long, 4 feet wide and 4 feet deep? (Depth is the equivalent of height.)

35. A building cost $90,000. It is 50 feet long, 35 feet wide and 40 feet high, including the basement. What was the cost of this building per cubic foot?

Volume of Triangular Prisms

To compute the volume of a three-dimensional triangular figure, called a *prism* (e.g., an A-frame house), use the following formula:

$$\frac{1}{2}(b \times h \times w) = V \text{ (volume)}$$

EXAMPLE: To compute the volume of the following house:

A. Divide the house into shapes, prism and cube.

Prism

Cube

B. Find the volume of the prism.

$$V = \frac{1}{2}(b \times h \times w)$$

$$= \frac{1}{2}(25' \times 10' \times 40')$$

$$= \frac{1}{2}(10,000 \text{ cubic feet}) = 5,000 \text{ cubic feet}$$

C. Find the volume of the cube.

$$V = L \times W \times H$$

$$= 25' \times 40' \times 12' = 12,000 \text{ cubic feet}$$

D. Find the total volumes of the prism and the cube.

5,000 cubic feet + 12,000 cubic feet = 17,000 cubic feet

36. The Williamson family has purchased a two-story house for $123,500. The house is 35 feet long and 20 feet wide and the first story is 10 feet high. The second story is A-shaped, with a roof 8 feet high at the tallest point. How many cubic feet of space does the house contain? What was its cost per cubic foot?

37. How many cubic yards of space are there in a flat-roofed house 27 feet long, 18 feet wide and 9 feet high?

38. What is the cost of pouring a concrete driveway 20 feet wide, 80 feet long and 4 inches thick if concrete costs $60 per cubic yard and the finishing costs $2.28 per square foot, including setting the forms and furnishing the steel?

39. What will it cost to excavate a basement 9 feet deep for a ranch-style house 65 feet by 45 feet if the cost of excavation is $4.50 per cubic yard?

PROBLEMS FOR ADDITIONAL PRACTICE

When you have finished these problems, check your answers at the end of the chapter. If you miss any of the problems, review this chapter before going on to chapter 6.

Using the diagram below, answer the first five questions:

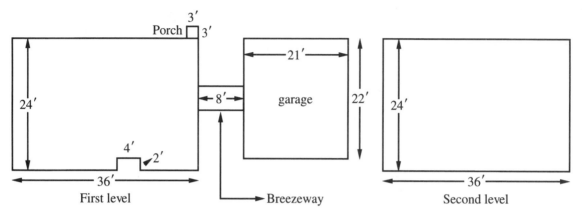

1. The total square feet of living area on the first floor of this house is

   a. 864.

   b. 856.

   c. 905.

   d. 873.

2. The total square feet of living area in the entire house is

   a. 1,761.

   b. 1,796.

   c. 1,769.

   d. 1,720.

3. At $18 per square foot, what would it cost to build the garage?

   a. $8,780

   b. $7,548

   c. $8,316

   d. $8,696

4. At $53 per square foot, what was the cost of building the *house* if the porch cost $1,800 and the breezeway cost $2,850 to construct?

   a. $91,160

   b. $95,810

   c. $92,960

   d. $94,010

5. If the house and garage sit on a lot 75 feet by 150 feet that cost $4 per square foot, what was the total cost to buy the lot and to build the house and garage?

   a. $137,960

   b. $140,810

   c. $146,276

   d. $149,126

6. The following building costs $48 per cubic yard. What is the total cost of this building?

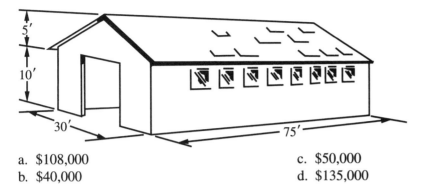

a. $108,000

b. $40,000

c. $50,000

d. $135,000

7. The area of a rectangle that is 5 feet by 17 feet is

a. 22 feet.

b. 85 square feet.

c. 44 square feet.

d. 44 linear feet.

8. Lloyd Hampton owned a tract of land 150 feet wide and 700 feet long, with the 150 feet fronting on an east-west road. Hampton sold the northern 300 feet of this tract. The remaining land was leased to a neighbor at the annual rate of $500 an acre (an acre is 43,560 square feet). The neighbor's approximate yearly rent is

a. $666.66.

b. $515.50.

c. $688.50.

d. $650.00.

9. A west Texas broker sold a triangular tract of land for $1,750 an acre. What is the amount of his commission at 8% if the land had a base length of 1,200 feet and the height of the triangle measured 700 feet?

a. $1,156.80

b. $1,349.60

c. $16,870

d. $1,012.20

10. A seller owned a rectangular 10-acre tract of land with a frontage of 726 feet along the south side of a paved road. After selling the southern half of this tract, the owner fenced the remaining land at a cost of $2.50 per running, or linear, foot. The fence cost

a. $2,652.

b. $4,576.

c. $5,130.

d. $2,565.

11. A U-shaped barn consists of two rectangles 30 feet by 75 feet and a connecting section 20 feet by 50 feet. The approximate cost of a concrete floor 4 inches thick, at the rate of $36 per cubic yard, is

a. $44,000.

b. $2,222.

c. $2,442.

d. $1,444.

12. A building has been razed to make parking spaces and the basement area must be filled with earth and solid fill. The hole is 35 feet wide by 79 feet long and is 6 feet deep. What is the approximate amount of cubic yards of fill required?

a. 614

b. 2,765

c. 5,530

d. 18,590

13. What is the cost of $\frac{2}{5}$ of 174,240 square feet of land if the price per acre is $1,500?

    a. $2,400   c. $1,500

    b. $6,000   d. $1,200

14. A 60 foot by 175 foot lot has a 35 foot by 70 foot right triangle alley easement on one corner. The square feet of usable area is

    a. 8,050.   c. 9,275.

    b. 10,395.   d. 10,500.

15. What is the square footage of the living area of the house shown in the illustration below?

    a. 2,750   c. 3,486

    b. 3,531   d. 3,738

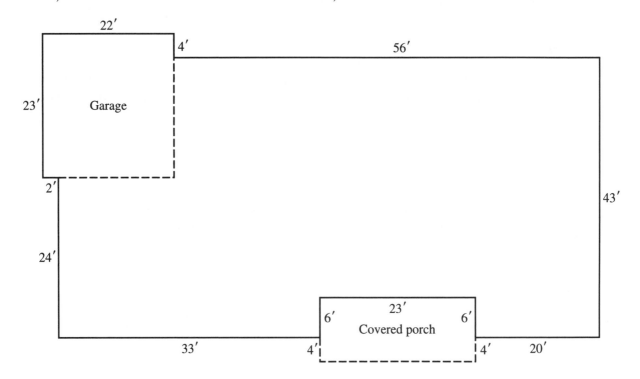

ANSWER KEY

SOLUTIONS: WARM-UP EXERCISES

1. A. $115.5 \times 99.75 \div 2 = 5{,}760.56$ square feet
    B. $200 \times 75.5 = 15{,}100$ square feet
    C. $40 \times 60 \div 2 = 1{,}200$ square feet
    D. $60 \times 60 = 3{,}600$ square feet
    E. $100 \times 141.25 = 14{,}125$ square feet
    F. $100.25 \times 75.5 = \underline{7{,}568.88}$ square feet
          Total $47{,}354.44$ square feet

2. (d): 47,354.44 square feet $\times$ $6 = $284,126.64

3. (c): 14,125 square feet $\times$ $6.50 = $91,812.50
      $91,812.50 \times .07 = $6,426.88

4. (a): $45' \times 30' \times 40' = 54{,}000$ cubic feet
      $97,200 \div 54{,}000$ cubic feet $= $1.80 per cubic foot

5. (c): 15,100 square feet × $6 = $ 90,600 land cost
                                        + 97,200 building cost
                                        $187,800 total cost

    45 × 30 = 1,350 square feet
    $187,800 ÷ 1,350 square feet = $139.11 per square foot

6. (a): 6″ ÷ 12″ = .5′
    20′ × 18′ × .5′ = 180 cubic feet
    180 cubic feet ÷ 27 = 6.667 cubic yards
    6.667 cubic yards × $40 = $266.67
    20′ × 18′ = 360 square feet
    360 square feet × $1.80 = $648
    $266.67 + $648 = $914.67

SOLUTIONS: CHAPTER PROBLEMS

1. 75′ × .80 = 60′

2. 60′ × $12 = $720

3. $62,500 ÷ 35′ = $1,785.71

4. (c): Squares are rectangles with four sides of equal length.

5. Figure A is a square.
    Figures A and C are rectangles. Remember, a square is a rectangle with four sides of equal length.

6. 4 square inches

7. 3 square inches

8. 5″ × 4″ = 20 square inches

9. 5′ × 3′ = 15 square feet

10. 4 yards × 4 yards = 16 square yards

11. 80′ × 150′ = 12,000 square feet
    12,000 square feet × $1.30 = $15,600

12. a. 36″ ÷ 12 = 3′   d. 6 yards × 3 = 18′
            3′ × 3′ = 9 square feet   18′ × 5′ = 90 square feet
        b. 15″ ÷ 12 = 1.25′   e. 17 yards × 3 = 51′
            1.25′ × 1.5′ = 1.875 square feet   24″ ÷ 12 = 2′
        c. 72″ ÷ 12 = 6′   51′ × 2′ = 102 square feet
            6′ × 7′ = 42 square feet

13. a.   9   square feet × 144 =   1,296 square inches
        b.   1.875   square feet × 144 =   270 square inches
        c.   42   square feet × 144 =   6,048 square inches
        d.   90   square feet × 144 = 12,960 square inches
        e.   102   square feet × 144 = 14,688 square inches

14. a.   9   square feet ÷ 9 = 1   square yards
    b.   1.875 square feet ÷ 9 = .2083 square yards
    c.   42   square feet ÷ 9 = 4.667 square yards
    d.   90   square feet ÷ 9 = 10   square yards
    e. 102   square feet ÷ 9 = 11.333 square yards

15. 720″ ÷ 12 = 60′
    90′ × 60′ = 5,400 square feet

16. 25 yards × 3 = 75′
    528″ ÷ 12 = 44′
    75′ × 44′ = 3,300 square feet

17. 9″ ÷ 12 = .75′
    .75′ + 66′ = 66.75′
    66.75′ × 150′ = 10,012.50 square feet
    10,012.50 square feet × $4 = $40,050
    $40,050 × .06 = $2,403

18. 6″ ÷ 12 = .5′
    .5′ + 27′ = 27.5′
    27.5′ × 5′ = 137.50 square feet
    137.50 square feet ÷ 9 = 15.278 square yards
    15.278 square yards × $200 = $3,056 (rounded)

19. 1″ × 1″ ÷ 2 = .5 square inch

20. 2″ × 2″ ÷ 2 = 2 square inches

21. 3′ × 3′ ÷ 2 = 4.5 square feet

22. 3″ × 4″ ÷ 2 = 6 square inches

23. 65′ × 40′ ÷ 2 = 1,300 square feet

24. 9″ ÷ 12 = .75′
    .75′ + 40′ = 40.75′
    55′ × 40.75′ = 2,241.25 square feet
    2,241.25 square feet ÷ 2 = 1,120.625 square feet
    1,120.625 square feet × $4.75 = $5,322.97
    $5,322.97 × .10 = $532.30

25. a. 30′ × 45′   = 1,350 square feet
    b. 60′ × 20′   = <u>1,200</u> square feet
    c. 1350 square feet + 1200 square feet = 2,550 square feet

26.

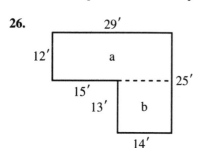   or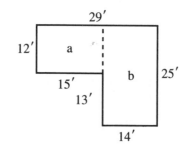

27. a. $29' \times 12' = 348$ square feet   or $15' \times 12' = 180$ square feet
     b. $14' \times 13' = \underline{182}$ square feet $14' \times 25' = \underline{350}$ square feet
        Total   530 square feet   Total   530 square feet

28. a. $20' \times 15' = 300$ square feet
     b. $5' \times 7' = 35$ square feet
     c. $10' \times 6' = \underline{60}$ square feet
        Total   395 square feet

29.

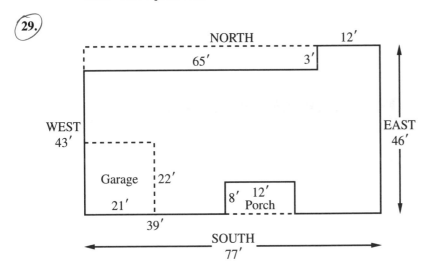

$77' \times 46'$ $= 3,542$ square feet
Less: $65' \times 3' \; = <195>$ square feet
       $21' \times 22' = <462>$ square feet
       $8' \times 12' = \underline{< \; 96>}$ square feet
         Total   2,789   square feet

30. a. *A.* cube   *C.* box   *E.* house
     b. *B.* square   *D.* rectangle   *F.* floor covering

31. 4 cubic inches

32. 6 cubic feet

33. *A.* $4'' \times 2'' \times 6'' = 48$ cubic inches
     B. $6'' \times 4'' \times 2'' = 48$ cubic inches

34. $5' \times 4' \times 4' = 80$ cubic feet

35. $50' \times 35' \times 40' = 70,000$ cubic feet
     $\$90,000 \div 70,000$ cubic feet $= \$1.29$ (rounded)

36. $35' \times 20' \times 10' \quad = 7,000$ cubic feet
     $35' \times 20' \times 8' \div 2 = \underline{2,800}$ cubic feet
            Total   9,800 cubic feet
     $\$123,500 \div 9,800$ cubic feet $= \$12.60$ per cubic foot

37. $27' \times 18' \times 9' = 4,374$ cubic feet
     $4,374$ cubic feet $\div 27 = 162$ cubic yards

38. $4'' \div 12 = .333'$
$80' \times 20' \times .333' = 532.8$ cubic feet
532.8 cubic feet $\div 27 = 19.733$ cubic yards
19.733 cubic yards $\times \$60 = \$1,183.98$
$80' \times 20' = 1,600$ square feet
$1,600 \times \$2.28 = \$3,648$
$\$1,183.98 + \$3,648 = \$4,831.98$

39. $65' \times 45' \times 9' = 26,325$ cubic feet
$26,325$ cubic feet $\div 27 = 975$ cubic yards
975 cubic yards $\times \$4.50 = \$4,387.50$

SOLUTIONS: PROBLEMS FOR ADDITIONAL PRACTICE

First level. $36' \times 24' = 864$ square feet
$\qquad\qquad 864$ square feet $- (2' \times 4') = 856$ square feet
Second level. $36' \times 24' = 864$ square feet
Garage. $21' \times 22' = 462$ square feet

1. (b): 856 square feet

2. (d): 856 square feet + 864 square feet = 1,720 square feet

3. (c): 462 square feet $\times \$18 = \$8,316$

4. (b): 1,720 square feet $\times \$53 = \$91,160$
$\$91,160 + \$1,800 + \$2,850 = \$95,810$

5. (d): $75' \times 150' = 11,250$ square feet
$11,250$ square feet $\times \$4 = \$45,000$
$\$95,810 + \$8,316 + \$45,000 = \$149,126$

6. (c): $75' \times 30' \times 10' = 22,500$ cubic feet
$75' \times 30' \times 5' \div 2 = 5,625$ cubic feet
$22,500$ cubic feet $+ 5,625$ cubic feet $= 28,125$ cubic feet
$28,125$ cubic feet $\div 27 = 1,041.667$ cubic yards
$1,041.667$ cubic yards $\times \$48 = \$50,000$

7. (b): $5' \times 17' = 85$ square feet

8. (c): $150' \times 700' = 105,000$ square feet
$150' \times 300' = 45,000$ square feet
$105,000$ square feet $- 45,000$ square feet $= 60,000$ square feet
$60,000$ square feet $\div 43,560$ square feet $= 1.377$ acres
1.377 acres $\times \$500 = \$688.50$

9. (b): $1,200' \times 700' \div 2 = 420,000$ square feet
$420,000$ square feet $\div 43,560$ square feet $= 9.64$ acres
9.64 acres $\times \$1,750 = \$16,870$
$\$16,870 \times .08 = \$1,349.60$

10. (c): 10 acres × 43,560 square feet = 435,600 square feet
435,600 square feet ÷ 726′ = 600′
600′ ÷ 2 = 300′
726′ + 300′ + 726′ + 300′ = 2,052′
2,052′ × $2.50 = $5,130

11. (c): 30′ × 75′ = 2,250 square feet
2,250 square feet × 2 = 4,500 square feet
20′ × 50′ = 1,000 square feet
4,500 square feet + 1,000 square feet = 5,500 square feet
4″ ÷ 12 = .333′
5,500 square feet × .333′ = 1,831.5 cubic feet
1,831.5 cubic feet ÷ 27 = 67.833 cubic yards
67.833 cubic yards × $36 = $2,441.99, or $2,442 (rounded)

12. (a): 35′ × 79′ × 6′ = 16,590 cubic feet
16,590 cubic feet ÷ 27 = 614.444 cubic yards, or 614 (rounded)

13. (a): 2 ÷ 5 = .40
.40 × 174,240 square feet = 69,696 square feet
69,696 square feet ÷ 43,560 square feet = 1.6 acres
1.6 acres × $1,500 = $2,400

14. (c): 60′ × 175′ = 10,500 square feet
35′ × 70′ ÷ 2 = 1,225 square feet
10,500 square feet − 1,225 square feet = 9,275 square feet

15. (a):

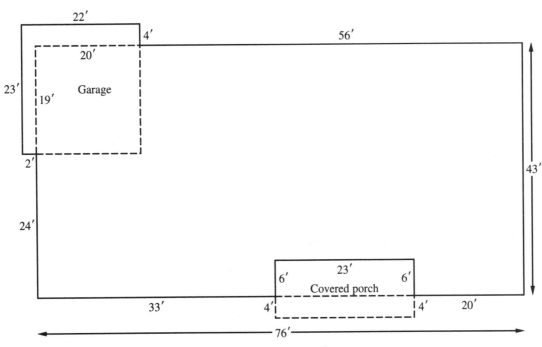

House. 76′ × 43′ = 3,268 square feet
Garage. 20′ × 19′ = 380 square feet
Porch. 23′ × 6′ = 138 square feet

3,268 square feet − 380 square feet − 138 square feet = 2,750 square feet

Depreciation

This chapter covers some of the more basic uses of depreciation. Because the use and the definition of depreciation are subject to federal and state laws, Internal Revenue Service (IRS) regulations and Tax Court rulings, the reader is urged to consult legal counsel regarding any points of law. Any careless discussion of "depreciation" can lead an unsuspecting seller or buyer into tax consequences that may be unfavorable. The material presented in this chapter is intentionally very general in content. This is because of frequent and sometimes major changes in the tax laws. Do not be concerned about the generalizations. Instead, learn the concepts and methods so that you can apply them to whatever tax laws may be in effect. Remember, this textbook is an introduction to real estate math and not a text on taxation.

After working through the material in this chapter, you will be able to

- accurately calculate straight-line depreciation and
- calculate depreciation, using the IRS cost recovery tables for residential and nonresidential properties.

WARM-UP EXERCISES

Because readers will have varying amounts of knowledge and experience, the problems that follow will allow you to determine your familiarity with the material to be covered. Try all of the problems before checking your answers against the answer key at the end of the chapter.

1. If Bobbye paid $75,000 for a rental property with a 30-year life, how much straight-line depreciation can she take each year if the lot is worth $15,000?

   a. $2,500   c. $2,000
   b. $500   d. $3,000

2. In problem 1, how much depreciation will accumulate in five years?

   a. $10,000   c. $15,000
   b. $2,500   d. $12,500

3. Jeny bought new printing equipment for $70,000, paying $10,000 cash and obtaining a loan for the remainder. If she depreciates the equipment over a 12-year term, how much depreciation will accrue the first year, calculating straight-line depreciation?

a. $5,000.00

b. $5,833.33

c. $833.33

d. $6,666.67

4. Charles Johnson purchased a property six years ago for $70,000. At the time of purchase, the lot was valued at $15,000. If, during his six years of ownership, the lot has appreciated at 4% per year straight-line and the improvements have depreciated at 2.5% per year, what is the current value of the improvements?

a. $59,500

b. $8,250

c. $61,750

d. $46,750

5. What is the current value of the property described in the problem above?

a. $65,350

b. $61,750

c. $73,600

d. $51,400

USES OF DEPRECIATION

The term *depreciation* has several shades of meaning, according to its application. The real estate salesperson is likely to encounter all of these uses. Generally, depreciation is used in appraising, tax reporting and accounting.

Depreciation in Appraisal

Depreciation is used in the cost approach method for appraising real property. Basically, it measures the amount by which the value of property diminishes owing to physical wasting away. This use of depreciation will not be discussed further here because it is covered more completely in Chapter 7.

Depreciation for Income Tax Purposes

Depreciation may be used as a deduction on federal or state individual or corporate income taxes. As is the case for appraisal, depreciation for tax purposes applies only to buildings and improvements—such as parking lot surfaces, fences, utility lines and orchards—and *not* to land. Certain qualifying items of personal property used in a trade or business also may be depreciated. Some examples include furniture, equipment and vehicles. The length or term of depreciation is determined by tax law and IRS regulations.

Depreciation in Accounting—Bookkeeping Function

In accounting practices, depreciation may be calculated as a bookkeeping function. It is used in determining the profit and loss of a business establishment. Depreciation is listed as an expense, even though no *actual* expense for that item was incurred. If a business still makes payments on the item being depreciated, those payments and the amount of depreciation have no relationship to one another. The payment depends on the amount and length of a loan or note, and its interest rate, while depreciation depends on the economic, or useful, life of the item for bookkeeping purposes.

Note that the purpose of depreciation, when used in tax calculation or bookkeeping, is to allow an owner to recover the initial cost of the item being depreciated. The *depreciated value,* or *book value,* has no bearing on the *market value* (the price a willing buyer would pay) of the item being depreciated. For example, through inflation, the typical building has a market value considerably greater than its depreciated value. (If a building is sold for more than its depreciated value, the excess is taxable under various laws and regulations.)

STRAIGHT-LINE METHOD

The straight-line method of depreciation will be used in the following calculations. This method involves an equal amount of depreciation to be deducted on an annual basis. Note: The term *economic life,* which is used in the following example, refers to that period of time during which the article can be expected to provide an economic benefit.

EXAMPLE: Under the straight-line method, an air conditioner that cost $10,000 and has an economic life of ten years can be depreciated at $1,000 per year for ten years. By the end of the ten-year period, the entire $10,000 would have been recovered. To determine the annual depreciation amount, divide the initial cost of an item by its economic life, or:

Initial cost ÷ Economic life = Annual depreciation amount

Now you try it by working the following exercise.

1. Jeanette bought new display counters and furniture for her craft shop. The entire cost was $4,000. If she depreciates it over a period of seven years, how much depreciation can Jeanette take, or use, each year?

Using the same information, you can prepare a depreciation chart for the seven-year term, showing how the annual depreciation affects the book value of Jeanette's shop furnishings.

Year	Annual Depreciation	Book Value
New		$4,000.00
1	$571.43	3,428.57
2	571.43	2,857.14
3	571.43	2,285.71
4	571.43	1,714.28
5	571.43	1,142.85
6	571.43	571.42
7	571.42	-0-

EXAMPLE: Susan bought a rental house for $55,000 by paying $5,000 cash and obtaining a mortgage loan for $50,000, to be repaid over a 30-year term. The tax assessor values the lot at $10,000. If Susan depreciates the house over a 27.5-year period, how much depreciation can she take, or use, each year?

First, you must sort out the nonessentials and disregard them. For example, the cash invested, the loan amount and the length of the loan have no bearing on this problem. Also, remember that the lot, or the land, cannot be depreciated because, theoretically, it does not deteriorate in value. Therefore, the value of the lot must be subtracted from the total cost of the property.

$55,000 total cost of property
−10,000 value of lot
$45,000 value of building to be depreciated

Next, the depreciation period is 27.5 years, which is not related in any way to the length of the loan. Therefore, the value of the building must be divided by the number of years that the depreciation is to be taken.

$45,000 ÷ 27.5 = $1,636.36 annual depreciation

In the real world of tax laws and regulations, Susan would go to the IRS cost recovery chart (the tax code refers to depreciation as cost recovery) for residential property and apply the appropriate factor to the original value of the building.

The following charts give the appropriate factors for calculating depreciation deductions for federal tax purposes. Use the residential chart (27.5 years) for all property used as dwelling units and use the non-residential chart (39 years) for all other investment property. Apartment buildings are residential properties.

TABLE 6.1 COST RECOVERY CHART

IRS Cost Recovery Percentages

27.5 Years Straight-Line Residential

Year	
1	3.485%
2–9	3.636
10	3.637
11–27	Alternates between 3.636 and 3.637
28	1.970

39 Years Straight-Line Nonresidential

Year	
1	1.282%
2	2.564
3–32	2.564
33	2.565
34	2.564
35	2.565
36	2.564
37	2.565
38	2.564
39	2.565
40	1.282

Note: The percentages will vary slightly depending on the month in which the asset is placed into service.

2. Your local multiple-listing service decides to buy its own printing press so that it can produce its own MLS book. If the press costs $40,000 and the multiple-listing service plans to depreciate it over ten years, how much depreciation will the MLS have left (the book value) at the end of four years, when it plans to trade for a new laser press?

The following graph shows the relationship of dollars to time in problem 2.

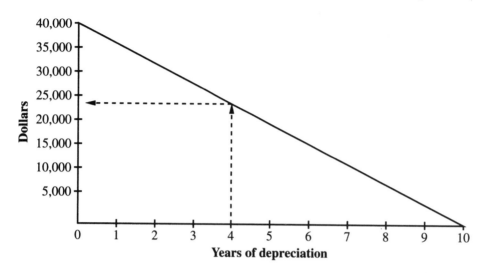

Years of depreciation

To determine the amount of depreciation left after four years, locate the number 4 on the time line, or horizontal axis, then move straight up until you intersect the diagonal line. At this point, move straight left to the dollar line, or vertical axis. The book value is $24,000.

3. Now you try it. From the graph illustrated, determine how much depreciation will be taken, or used up, at the end of seven years.

Accumulated Depreciation

The initial figure used in problem 3 was $40,000 and $28,000 was used up in seven years. The $28,000 is called *accumulated depreciation.*

$40,000 initial cost
− 12,000 depreciation still allowable
$28,000 accumulated depreciation

Application of Depreciation

4. Elaine bought a four-unit apartment house near the local community college. Her cost of the property was $120,000. The lot value was $22,500. She paid $16,000 cash and signed a note to the seller for the balance of $104,000 bearing 10% interest to be paid in monthly installments for 25 years. If Elaine's

first-year total operating costs, including taxes and insurance, were $2,000, the total rent income was $15,000 and the total payments on the mortgage loan were $11,340 (of which $985 was for principal), how much taxable income from this property did she have available if she used a 27.5-year depreciation schedule? (This assumes that the tax laws permitted her to use all of the depreciation.) How much depreciation per year is to be taken?

PROBLEMS FOR ADDITIONAL PRACTICE

When you have finished these problems, check your answers at the end of the chapter. If you miss any of the problems, review this chapter before going on to Chapter 7.

1. You want to buy a new $12,000 car for use in your real estate business. If you plan to use it 100% for business purposes and depreciate it over five years, how much depreciation can you take each year?

   a. $2,000
   b. $2,400

   c. $1,800
   d. $1,200

2. A house and lot are valued at $80,000. If the lot is worth $20,000 and the property is to be depreciated over 30 years, how much depreciation has been taken in three years?

   a. $2,000
   b. $6,000

   c. $2,667
   d. $8,000

3. You purchased a lot for $35,000 and built a house on it costing $80,000 seven years ago. If the house has depreciated at the rate of 3.636% per year straight-line, what is the current value of the house?

   a. $20,361.60
   b. $59,638.40

   c. $94,368.40
   d. $94,638.40

4. If the lot in the above problem appreciated at the rate of 2% per year straight-line, what is the current value of the lot?

   a. $35,700
   b. $4,900

   c. $39,900
   d. $30,100

5. What is the current value of the property (house and lot) introduced in problem 3, given the information in problems 3 and 4?

   a. $99,538.40
   b. $95,338.40

   c. $89,738.40
   d. $94,738.40

6. Using a depreciation factor of 2.56% per year, what is the depreciated value of an industrial building that has been in service for 17 years if the original cost of the building was $856,000?

   a. $372,360
   b. $482,099

   c. $600,564
   d. $483,469

7. What is the annual amount of depreciation on a $200,000 property if the building accounts for 80% of the total property value? The building is eight years old and is to be depreciated over 27.5 years.

   a. $46,545.46
   b. $5,818.18

   c. $7,272.73
   d. $58,181.82

8. A property was purchased four years ago for $220,000. 25% of the total value is attributed to the land. What is the current value of this property if the land depreciated at 2% per year straight-line and the building depreciated at 3.636% per year straight-line?

   a. $200,475.40
   b. $196,075.40

   c. $191,602.40
   d. $224,400.40

9. A property was acquired five years ago for $185,000, of which $45,000 was attributed to the land. If during the holding period the land appreciated at 6% per year straight-line and the building appreciated at $1\frac{1}{2}$% per year straight-line, what is the current value of the property?

   a. $182,000
   b. $198,500

   c. $209,000
   d. $201,200

10. What is the book value of a car three years old if you depreciate it over five years straight-line, you paid $23,500 for it and you used it for business purposes 80% of the time?

    a. $12,220
    b. $11,280

    c. $14,100
    d. $9,400

11. What is the total accumulated depreciation on a four-year-old, $3,200 computer system that is depreciating over seven years straight-line?

    a. $457.14
    b. $2,742.86

    c. $1,371.43
    d. $1,828.56

12. Using an annual depreciation rate of 2.778% straight-line, calculate the accumulated depreciation on a $450,000, ten-year-old commercial building.

    a. $125,010
    b. $324,990

    c. $405,000
    d. $437,496

13. What is the current book value of a $463,000, six-year-old building that is depreciating at the rate of 3.636% per annum straight-line?

    a. $101,017.34
    b. $361,991.92

    c. $141,844.68
    d. $321,155.32

14. If $20,000 cash is paid down on a $125,000 property having a land value of $25,000, how much can be depreciated?

    a. $105,000   c. $125,000

    b. $80,000   d. $100,000

15. Bob bought a new central air-conditioning system for his building. It cost $9,000 and is to be depreciated over nine years. How much depreciation has been taken after three years?

    a. $1,000   c. $3,000

    b. $9,000   d. $6,000

ANSWER KEY

SOLUTIONS: WARM-UP EXERCISES

1. (c): $75,000 − $15,000 = $60,000
   $60,000 ÷ 30 = $2,000

2. (a): $2,000 × 5 = $10,000

3. (b): $70,000 ÷ 12 = $5,833.33

4. (d): $70,000 − $15,000 = $55,000
   .025 × 6 = .15
   $55,000 × .15 = $8,250
   $55,000 − $8,250 = $46,750

5. (a): .04 × 6 = .24
   $15,000 × .24 = $3,600
   $15,000 + $3,600 = $18,600
   $18,600 + $46,750 = $65,350

SOLUTIONS: CHAPTER PROBLEMS

1. $4,000 ÷ 7 = $571.43

2. $40,000 ÷ 10 = $4,000
   $4,000 × 4 = $16,000
   $40,000 − $16,000 = $24,000

3. Starting at the 7 on the horizontal axis, go up to the depreciation line and over to the left. Only $12,000 remains, so $28,000 depreciation has been used.

4. $120,000 − $22,500 = $97,500
100% of building value ÷ 27.5 years = 3.636 or .03636
$97,500 × .03636 = $3,545.10

SOLUTIONS: PROBLEMS FOR ADDITIONAL PRACTICE

1. (b): $12,000 ÷ 5 = $2,400

2. (b): $80,000 − $20,000 = $60,000
$60,000 ÷ 30 = $2,000
$2,000 × 3 = $6,000

3. (b): .03636 × 7 = .25452
$80,000 × .25452 = $20,361.60
$80,000 − $20,361.60 = $59,638.40

4. (c): .02 × 7 = .14
$35,000 × .14 = $4,900
$35,000 + $4,900 = $39,900

5. (a): $39,900 + $59,638.40 = $99,538.40

6. (d): .0256 × 17 = .4352
$856,000 × .4352 = $372,531 (rounded)
$856,000 − $372,531 = $483,469

7. (b): $200,000 × .80 = $160,000
$160,000 ÷ 27.5 = $5,818.18

8. (c): $220,000 × .25 = $55,000
$220,000 × .75 = $165,000
.02 × 4 = .08
.08 × $55,000 = $4,400
$55,000 − $4,400 = $50,600
.03636 × 4 = .14544
.14544 × $165,000 = $23,997.60
$165,000 − $23,997.60 = $141,002.40
$50,600 + $141,002.40 = $191,602.40

9. (c): $185,000 − $45,000 = $140,000
.06 × 5 = .30
.30 × $45,000 = $13,500
$45,000 + $13,500 = $58,500
.015 × 5 = .075
.075 × $140,000 = $10,500
$140,000 + $10,500 = $150,500
$58,500 + $150,500 = $209,000

10. (a): $23,500 × .80 = $18,800
$18,800 ÷ 5 = $3,760
$3,760 × 3 = $11,280
$23,500 − $11,280 = $12,220

11. (d): $3,200 ÷ 7 = $457.14
$457.14 × 4 = $1,828.56

12. (a): .02778 × 10 = .2778
$450,000 × .2778 = $125,010

13. (b): .03636 × 6 = .21816
$463,000 × .21816 = $101,008.08
$463,000 − $101,008.08 = $361,991.92

14. (d): $125,000 − $25,000 = $100,000

15. (c): $9,000 ÷ 9 = $1,000
$1,000 × 3 = $3,000

Appraisal Methods

This chapter presents methods and formulas used in estimating property value. First you will be given a general description of the most commonly used methods of appraising property, including the

- sales comparison approach;
- cost approach; and
- income capitalization approach.

Then you will analyze each method in detail. Appraisal is *not* a science. An appraisal is an *estimate* of value, which depends on the experience and common sense of an appraiser, who must evaluate the data involved.

Appraisals are done by state-licensed or state-certified appraisers. In most states, salespeople and brokers are not legally permitted to do appraisals. However, they are frequently called upon to do broker price opinions and comparative market analyses (CMAs). The purpose of this chapter is to help you understand the appraisal process. An in-depth discussion of appraisals is beyond the scope of this text.

At the conclusion of your work in this chapter, you will be able to

- adjust comparables, applying the sales comparison approach;
- accurately calculate the replacement or reproduction cost and accrued depreciation for the application of the cost approach; and
- capitalize annual net operating income into an indication of value for an income-producing property.

WARM-UP EXERCISES

Because readers will have varying amounts of knowledge and experience, the problems that follow will allow you to determine your familiarity with the material to be covered. Try all of the problems before checking your answers against the answer key at the end of the chapter.

1. What is the estimated replacement cost of the following building if the cost is estimated to be $28.50 per square foot?

a. $63,000   c. $62,500

b. $61,275   d. $62,000

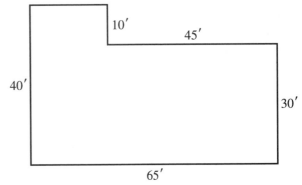

2. Using the replacement cost of the building in question 1, what is the value of the property if the building has $6,250 of accrued depreciation and is sitting on a $25,000 lot?

a. $61,275   c. $80,025

b. $31,250   d. $68,900

3. An apartment building earns an annual net operating income of $25,000. If the property sells for $175,000, what is the overall capitalization rate for this property?

a. 14%   c. 14.5%

b. 14.3%   d. 14.7%

4. If you were purchasing an apartment building for $265,000 and wished a 24% overall return on your investment, what annual net operating income would the property have to produce to meet your required return?

a. $63,600.00   c. $63,000.00

b. $110,416.67   d. $63,500.00

5. The subject property is a three-bedroom, two-and-a-half-bath house with no garage. Market research indicates that a two-car garage adds $7,500 value and a half-bath adds $1,800 value. A three-bedroom, two-bath house with a two-car garage on the next block sold for $115,600 two weeks ago. What is the indicated market value of the subject property by the sales comparison approach?

a. $124,900   c. $121,300

b. $106,300   d. $109,900

VALUE

Value is not a static number but rather a concept involving the *benefits* the item returns to its owner or prospective owner. If you agree with this statement, it is easier to understand the use of the term *value* not only in real estate practice but in other areas, as well. For example, how much would you pay for five gallons of gasoline if your car ran out of fuel as it rolled into the service station driveway? How much would you pay for that same five gallons of gasoline if your car ran out of fuel 50 miles from a service station at midnight on a cold February night? Did the "value" of the fuel change for the service station owner? Did it change for you?

Or how about the value of a 2,500-square-foot, four-bedroom house bought when energy was cheap and the children were all living at home compared to that same house today, when all of the children are married, both spouses are in poor health and retired and energy is expensive. Is the value still similar for the owners? Do the owners currently receive the same benefits of ownership that they once did?

Usually, exact property values are not possible to obtain. In the field of real estate, varying methods of estimating property value are used. Real estate is traditionally appraised by three methods: the *sales comparison approach* (also called the *market data approach*), the *cost approach* and the *income capitalization approach.*

The *sales comparison approach* is used to estimate the value of a parcel of real estate by

- comparing the given real estate to comparable (or similar) properties in the subject neighborhood and
- making plus or minus dollar adjustments to each comparable's sales price for significant differences between the comparable and the subject property.

A

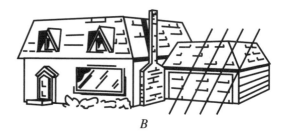

B

For example, if House *A* (pictured above) is being appraised via the sales comparison approach to value, the appraiser finds a comparable house—for example, House *B,* which sold for $56,000. In comparing the two, the only major difference between the houses may be that House *B* has a garage, valued at $4,000, whereas House *A* has no garage. Therefore, $4,000 must be subtracted from the sales price of House *B* to arrive at the sales comparison approach appraisal of House *A,* which is $52,000.

In estimating value by the *cost approach,* the appraiser will

- estimate the cost of replacing the buildings on the land at current prices;
- subtract the estimated amount of accumulated depreciation from the cost of the buildings;
- estimate the value of the land; and
- add the land value to the depreciated building value to arrive at the current property value.

The *income capitalization approach* is used to estimate the value of a property on the basis of the income it produces. It is calculated by

- subtracting the operating expenses from the gross income of the property to determine the net operating income and

- dividing the net operating income by an appropriate *capitalization rate*—a rate that is estimated to represent the proper relationship between the value of that property and the net operating income it produces.

Market Value

Market value is an estimate of the most probable price a property would bring if exposed for sale in the open market. Reasonable time is allowed in which to find a purchaser who buys with the knowledge of all of the uses and purposes for which the property is adapted and for which it is capable of being used.

SALES COMPARISON APPROACH

The sales comparison approach to value is the method most frequently used in estimating the value of residential properties. Many salespeople do not use the other two approaches to value because the salespeople typically provide broker price opinions or CMAs, not appraisals.

Belonging to a multiple-listing service (MLS) with reliable, up-to-date information greatly simplifies the use of the sales comparison approach to value. For instance, if a salesperson can find only *one* similar, or comparable, house, as shown in the example above, the estimate of the value of House *A* depends completely on the information obtained from the sale of House *B* and the similarities between the two. However, if a salesperson scans a list of similar properties and selects three or four of those most similar to the subject house, the salesperson's estimate of value will be much more accurate. The larger database provides better statistics.

In selecting similar or comparable houses, a salesperson must be careful to consider the following:

- Sales or financing concessions
- Date of sale/time
- Location
- Quality of construction
- Age
- Condition
- Amenities and features
- Room count and square footage
- Lot size
- Style or type of house
- Any unusual features, such as a converted garage now used as a bedroom or the large size of a particular model when compared to the rest of the neighborhood

Without printed data furnished by an appraisal file or an MLS, a sales comparison approach would be much more difficult and subjective rather than objective. Most real estate offices also have forms or computer programs used to accumulate data on current listings and similar houses that have sold. Similar houses currently on the market tend to establish the maximum value of the property being appraised. Furthermore, these comparisons allow owners to recognize their competition before they list or market their property.

The dates of sale of similar houses and information about how they were financed also greatly influence the adjusted values of houses. Because the market changes, it is more accurate to use the most recent sales.

For example, during a period of rapid economic expansion, house values may increase, or appreciate, by large amounts. Inflation certainly enters into this and prices sometimes increase dramatically. By considering the date of sale, a salesperson can determine a comparative sales price by using the current rate of appreciation within a particular market.

Older sales figures particularly must be adjusted to allow for the lapse of time since the sales. When an adjustment is made for the date of sale, a method similar to computing simple interest is used. For example, if you choose 6% per year as your appreciation adjustment factor (i.e., the amount you estimate real estate has gained in value due to inflation and other causes), you can reduce that to a monthly factor of 0.5% (.06 ÷ 12 = .005, or 0.5%). The monthly factor can then be multiplied by the number of months elapsed since the sale you are evaluating.

1. If housing prices appreciate at a rate of 8% per year, what would be the adjusted value of a house that sold for $53,000 three years ago? (Round to the nearest dollar.)

The type of financing used in each sale affects the net amount received by the seller and this has an indirect bearing on the probable sales price of the house. For example, some buyers may be able to pay cash for a house. This type of sale tends to be the most reliable because financing plays no part at all. Another seller with an assumable loan at a below-market interest rate might obtain a higher price for his or her house. Still another seller might have to pay very large loan costs in order to sell, which results in a much lower net price received by the seller. In this case, some of the high loan costs could be included in the sales price. Therefore, these costs must be subtracted from the sales price in order to remove this effect of financing from the sales price. Still another seller might have such a compelling reason to sell that he or she will carry a large second lien note at a below-market interest rate. If each of the foregoing sales involved similar models in the same subdivision within a short period of time, the sales prices could vary considerably depending on the type of financing. Appraisers obtain this data from various sources, including MLS membership and verification from the seller or buyer or from a broker involved in the sale.

Table 7.1 shows a useful format for gathering data concerning the sale of houses that are similar to and located near the subject house. It permits the user to adjust the sales prices for differences in extras, date of sale and method of financing. For this exercise, use an appreciation rate of 6% per year, or 0.5% per month. (**Note:** The use of a factor for appreciation or depreciation depends on a great many variables, such as prevailing economic conditions, geographic location of the property and so on. Therefore, *careful* use should be made of such a factor.) After you read the explanation of the chart, fill in the missing amounts, considering appreciation and financing.

In Table 7.1, the first adjustment is for "extras." For House 1, subtract $10,000 for the pool because the subject house does not have one. This gives an estimate of the sales price for a house that, like the subject house, has no pool.

$70,000 actual sales price for House 1
− 10,000 estimated value of pool
$60,000 price of House 1 adjusted for pool

Next adjust House 1's price for the sale date. Use an appreciation factor of 6% per year (or 0.5% per month) to account for elapsed time between sale dates.

TABLE 7.1

House	Age	Rooms	Extras	Sales Price	Sale Date	Adjusted Price	How Financed	Final Adjustment	Size	$ per Sq. Ft.
1	5 yrs.	3–2–2	Fireplace Pool <$10,000>	$70,000 <10,000> $60,000	1–1–96	$63,300	Cash	$63,300	1,500 sq. ft.	$42.20
2	4 yrs.	3–2–2	No fireplace + $1,000	$63,000 + 1,000 $64,000	12–1–96	$64,000	Equity <$1,000>	$63,000	1,480 sq. ft.	$42.57
3	5 yrs.	3–2–2	Fireplace	$62,000	6–1–96		FHA <$1,800>		1,460 sq. ft.	
4*	5 yrs.	3–2–2	Fireplace	$61,000	8–1–96		Equity + 2nd + $1,000		1,500 sq. ft.	
Subject	4 yrs.	3–2–2	Fireplace		Current Date 12–1–96				1,490 sq. ft.	

*This house involved a distress sale and the seller agreed to carry back a large second lien note.

$$\$60,000 \times .005 = \$300 \text{ monthly appreciation}$$

$$\$300 \times 11 \text{ months} = \$3,300 \text{ total appreciation}$$

$$\$60,000 + \$3,300 = \$63,300 \text{ adjusted price}$$

Because this was a cash sale, no adjustment is made for financing, so the final adjustment leaves the price at $63,300.

This house has 1,500 square feet of living area (excluding garages and open porches), so:

$$\$63,300 \div 1,500 \text{ square feet} = \$42.20 \text{ per square foot}$$

The procedure is the same for House 2. First add $1,000 for a fireplace because all of the similar houses, including the subject house, have one. This results in an adjusted sales price of $64,000. The sale date is current, so no adjustment for date of sale is necessary. However, the house may have sold for about $1,000 more because of the attractive low-interest assumable loan. Therefore, adjust downward by this $1,000 to $63,300. The house has 1,480 square feet of living area, which yields a rate of $42.57 per square foot:

$$\$63,000 \div 1,480 \text{ square feet} = \$42.57 \text{ per square foot}$$

2. Now fill in the missing data for Houses 3 and 4 in Table 7.1.

Check your answers against the completed table in the answer key. These numbers can help you estimate a value for the subject house. Many real estate licensees calculate a numerical average of the adjusted sales price per square foot for the comparables and use that average as the value per square foot of the subject property. The average value is multiplied by the square footage to estimate the value of the subject house. This method is acceptable because the final calculation represents an *estimate* of value, not an appraisal.

To compute an average, add the individual values together, then divide by the number of values you have added.

EXAMPLE: To compute the average of a set of numbers—such as 12, 17, 23 and 14.2—first add those numbers:

$$12 + 17 + 23 + 14.2 = 66.2$$

Four values are being averaged, so divide by 4:

$$66.2 \div 4 = 16.55$$

Thus, the average of the four values is 16.55.

The next step in estimating the value of the subject house would be to take the average value per square foot and multiply it by the number of square feet in the subject house, to arrive at the total estimated value or price. Please note that a professional appraiser would probably use a more sophisticated method of arriving at the value per square foot of the subject house. Multiplying this different value per square foot by the square footage of the subject house would give the appraiser a different estimate of the value of the subject house.

Forms

The simple form that you used for accumulating data illustrates how the date of sale and the financing affect the accuracy of the data. In times when appreciation or inflation is great, the sales price *must* be adjusted to reflect the date of sale of each comparable property.

Another form used nationwide is the appraisal form produced by the Federal National Mortgage Association (FNMA), illustrated on pages 113 and 114. Notice that this is an *appraisal* form and not one just for estimating value. Therefore, it provides for adjustments to account for date of each sale, differences in amenities, or desirabilities, and the effects of financing on each property. Because this form is so detailed and elicits data not customarily used in a simple estimate of value (as in the solicitation of a listing), most brokers have devised forms similar to the one used in the example.

Please note that this chapter describes estimation of market value by a salesperson rather than appraisal of a property by a professional. There is a distinct difference.

COST APPROACH

The *cost approach* can be expressed as a formula:

Building replacement cost − Depreciation + Land value = Estimated property value

Building replacement cost is the dollar amount that would be required to build a comparable building today Note that this would result in a new building. If the subject building is not new, depreciation must be considered.

Depreciation represents the difference (loss) in value between a new building of the same type as the subject (the replacement) and one in the present condition of the structure being appraised. This has *nothing* to do with IRS (Internal Revenue Service) depreciation cost recovery. When depreciation is used in calculating an appraisal, it involves the actual wearing out of an improvement based on its actual age and compared to its projected remaining economic life. There are three types of depreciation that apply here— physical deterioration, functional obsolescence and external obsolescence.

Uniform Residential Appraisal Report

UNIFORM RESIDENTIAL APPRAISAL REPORT   File No.

Property Description

Property Address	City State Zip Code
Legal Description	County
Assessor's Parcel No.	Tax Year R.E. Taxes $ Special Assessments $

SUBJECT

Borrower   Current Owner   Occupant [ ] Owner [ ] Tenant [ ] Vacant

Property rights appraised [ ] Fee Simple [ ] Leasehold   Project Type [ ] PUD [ ] Condominium (HUD/VA only)   HOA$ _____ /Mo.

Neighborhood or Project Name   Map Reference   Census Tract

Sales Price $ Date of Sale   Description and $ amount of loan charges/concessions to be paid by seller

Lender/Client   Address

Appraiser   Address

NEIGHBORHOOD

Location	[ ] Urban	[ ] Suburban	[ ] Rural	Predominant occupancy	Single family housing		Present land use %	Land use change
					PRICE $ (000)	AGE (yrs)		
Built up	[ ] Over 75%	[ ] 25-75%	[ ] Under 25%				One family ____	[ ] Not likely [ ] Likely
Growth rate	[ ] Rapid	[ ] Stable	[ ] Slow	[ ] Owner	Low		2-4 family ____	[ ] In process
Property values	[ ] Increasing	[ ] Stable	[ ] Declining	[ ] Tenant	High		Multi-family ____	To: _____
Demand/supply	[ ] Shortage	[ ] In balance	[ ] Over supply	[ ] Vacant (0-5%)	Predominant		Commercial ____	
Marketing time	[ ] Under 3 mos.	[ ] 3-6 mos.	[ ] Over 6 mos.	[ ] Vacant (over 5%)			( )	

Note: Race and the racial composition of the neighborhood are not appraisal factors.

Neighborhood boundaries and characteristics: _____

Factors that affect the marketability of the properties in the neighborhood (proximity to employment and amenities, employment stability, appeal to market, etc.): _____

Market conditions in the subject neighborhood (including support for the above conclusions related to the trend of property values, demand/supply, and marketing time -- such as data on competitive properties for sale in the neighborhood, description of the prevalence of sales and financing concessions, etc.): _____

PUD

Project Information for PUDs (If applicable) - - Is the developer/builder in control of the Home Owners' Association (HOA)? [ ] Yes [ ] No

Approximate total number of units in the subject project _____ . Approximate total number of units for sale in the subject project _____ .

Describe common elements and recreational facilities: _____

SITE

Dimensions _____		Topography _____
Site area _____	Corner Lot [ ] Yes [ ] No	Size _____
Specific zoning classification and description _____		Shape _____
Zoning compliance [ ] Legal [ ] Legal nonconforming (Grandfathered use) [ ] Illegal [ ] No zoning		Drainage _____
Highest & best use as improved [ ] Present use [ ] Other use (explain)		View _____

Utilities	Public	Other	Off-site Improvements	Type	Public	Private	
Electricity	[ ]	____	Street	____	[ ]	[ ]	Landscaping _____
Gas	[ ]	____	Curb/gutter	____	[ ]	[ ]	Driveway Surface _____
Water	[ ]	____	Sidewalk	____	[ ]	[ ]	Apparent easements _____
Sanitary sewer	[ ]	____	Street lights	____	[ ]	[ ]	FEMA Special Flood Hazard Area [ ] Yes [ ] No
Storm sewer	[ ]	____	Alley	____	[ ]	[ ]	FEMA Zone ____ Map Date ____
							FEMA Map No. ____

Comments (apparent adverse easements, encroachments, special assessments, slide areas, illegal or legal nonconforming zoning use, etc.): _____

DESCRIPTION OF IMPROVEMENTS

GENERAL DESCRIPTION	EXTERIOR DESCRIPTION	FOUNDATION	BASEMENT	INSULATION
No. of Units ____	Foundation ____	Slab ____	Area Sq. Ft. ____	Roof [ ]
No. of Stories ____	Exterior Walls ____	Crawl Space ____	% Finished ____	Ceiling [ ]
Type (Det./Att.) ____	Roof Surface ____	Basement ____	Ceiling ____	Walls [ ]
Design (Style) ____	Gutters & Dwnspts. ____	Sump Pump ____	Walls ____	Floor [ ]
Existing/Proposed ____	Window Type ____	Dampness ____	Floor ____	None [ ]
Age (Yrs.) ____	Storm/Screens ____	Settlement ____	Outside Entry ____	Unknown [ ]
Effective Age (Yrs.) ____	Manufactured House ____	Infestation ____		

ROOMS	Foyer	Living	Dining	Kitchen	Den	Family Rm.	Rec. Rm.	Bedrooms	# Baths	Laundry	Other	Area Sq. Ft.
Basement												
Level 1												
Level 2												

Finished area **above** grade contains: Rooms;   Bedroom(s);   Bath(s);   Square Feet of Gross Living Area

INTERIOR	Materials/Condition	HEATING		KITCHEN EQUIP.		ATTIC		AMENITIES		CAR STORAGE:	
Floors	____	Type	____	Refrigerator	[ ]	None	[ ]	Fireplace(s) # ____	[ ]	None	[ ]
Walls	____	Fuel	____	Range/Oven	[ ]	Stairs	[ ]	Patio ____	[ ]	Garage # of cars	
Trim/Finish	____	Condition	____	Disposal	[ ]	Drop Stair	[ ]	Deck ____	[ ]	Attached	
Bath Floor	____	COOLING		Dishwasher	[ ]	Scuttle	[ ]	Porch ____	[ ]	Detached	
Bath Wainscot	____	Central	____	Fan/Hood	[ ]	Floor	[ ]	Fence ____	[ ]	Built-In	
Doors	____	Other	____	Microwave	[ ]	Heated	[ ]	Pool ____	[ ]	Carport	
		Condition	____	Washer/Dryer	[ ]	Finished	[ ]			Driveway	

COMMENTS

Additional features (special energy efficient items, etc.): _____

Condition of the improvements, depreciation (physical, functional, and external), repairs needed, quality of construction, remodeling/additions, etc.: _____

Adverse environmental conditions (such as, but not limited to, hazardous wastes, toxic substances, etc.) present in the improvements, on the site, or in the immediate vicinity of the subject property: _____

Valuation Section   **UNIFORM RESIDENTIAL APPRAISAL REPORT**   File No.

COST APPROACH

ESTIMATED SITE VALUE . . . . = $ _____

ESTIMATED REPRODUCTION COST-NEW OF IMPROVEMENTS:

Dwelling _____ Sq. Ft @ $ _____ = $ _____

_____ Sq. Ft @ $ _____ = _____

= _____

Garage/Carport _____ Sq. Ft @ $ _____ = _____

Total Estimated Cost-New . . . . = $ _____

Less   Physical | Functional | External

Depreciation _____ = $ _____

Depreciated Value of Improvements . . . . = $ _____

"As-is" Value of Site Improvements . . . . = $ _____

INDICATED VALUE BY COST APPROACH . . . . = $ _____

Comments on Cost Approach (such as, source of cost estimate, site value, square foot calculation and, for HUD, VA and FmHA, the estimated remaining economic life of the property): _____

SALES COMPARISON ANALYSIS

ITEM	SUBJECT	COMPARABLE NO. 1		COMPARABLE NO. 2		COMPARABLE NO. 3	
Address							
Proximity to Subject							
Sales Price	$	$		$		$	
Price/Gross Liv. Area	$	$		$		$	
Data and/or							
Verification Sources							
VALUE ADJUSTMENTS	DESCRIPTION	DESCRIPTION	+ (−) $ Adjustment	DESCRIPTION	+ (−) $ Adjustment	DESCRIPTION	+ (−) $ Adjustment
Sales or Financing Concessions							
Date of Sale/Time							
Location							
Leasehold/Fee Simple							
Site							
View							
Design and Appeal							
Quality of Construction							
Age							
Condition							
Above Grade Room Count	Total Bdrms Baths	Total Bdrms Baths		Total Bdrms Baths		Total Bdrms Baths	
Gross Living Area	Sq. Ft.	Sq. Ft.		Sq. Ft.		Sq. Ft.	
Basement & Finished Rooms Below Grade							
Functional Utility							
Heating/Cooling							
Energy Efficient Items							
Garage/Carport							
Porch, Patio, Deck, Fireplace(s), etc.							
Fence, Pool, etc.							
Net Adj. (total)		+ − $		+ − $		+ − $	
Adjusted Sales Price of Comparable		$		$		$	

Comments on Sales Comparison (including the subject property's compatibility to the neighborhood, etc.): _____

ITEM	SUBJECT	COMPARABLE NO. 1	COMPARABLE NO. 2	COMPARABLE NO. 3
Date, Price and Data Source for prior sales within year of appraisal				

Analysis of any current agreement of sale, option, or listing of the subject property and analysis of any prior sales of subject and comparables within one year of the date of appraisal:

INDICATED VALUE BY SALES COMPARISON APPROACH . . . . $ _____

INDICATED VALUE BY INCOME APPROACH (If Applicable) Estimated Market Rent $_____ /Mo. x Gross Rent Multiplier _____ = $ _____

This appraisal is made ☐ "as is" ☐ subject to the repairs, alterations, inspections, or conditions listed below ☐ subject to completion per plans and specifications.

Conditions of Appraisal: _____

RECONCILIATION

Final Reconciliation: _____

The purpose of this appraisal is to estimate the market value of the real property that is the subject of this report, based on the above conditions and the certification, contingent and limiting conditions, and market value definition that are stated in the attached Freddie Mac Form 439/Fannie Mae Form 1004B (Revised _____).

I (WE) ESTIMATE THE MARKET VALUE, AS DEFINED, OF THE REAL PROPERTY THAT IS THE SUBJECT OF THIS REPORT, AS OF _____

(WHICH IS THE DATE OF INSPECTION AND THE EFFECTIVE DATE OF THIS REPORT) TO BE $ _____

APPRAISER:	SUPERVISORY APPRAISER (ONLY IF REQUIRED):	
Signature	Signature	☐ Did ☐ Did Not
Name	Name	Inspect Property
Date Report Signed	Date Report Signed	
State Certification # _____ State	State Certification # _____ State	
Or State License # _____ State	Or State License # _____ State	

Land value represents the present market value of the land alone. It does not include the value of improvements. Land value is arrived at through an analysis of current sales of comparable land in the general area. *It is computed separately because land is not depreciable.*

Physical deterioration may be defined as the physical wearing out of a structure.

EXAMPLES: A building that needs a new roof.

Peeling paint and broken windows.

A furnace with a cracked heat exchanger.

Functional obsolescence occurs as a result of an undesirable layout or an outdated design.

EXAMPLES: A two-story, five-bedroom house with only one bathroom that is located on the first floor.

A house with a coal furnace.

A house with multicolor shag carpeting and avocado green appliances.

A house with no dishwasher or garbage disposal in a neighborhood where all other homes have them.

External (economic and/or environmental) *obsolescence* involves a loss of value from causes outside the property itself.

EXAMPLES: Loss of value due to a new highway constructed adjacent to a property (dirt and noise).

A machine shop, an elementary school or a drive-through restaurant built across from an apartment hotel designed for retirees.

Excessive taxes, zoning changes, proximity of nuisances and changes in land use.

Now use the cost approach formula to arrive at an estimate of value for the real estate described in problems 3 through 7.

3. An appraiser estimates the value of a piece of land at $20,000 and the replacement cost of the building on that land at $90,000. The depreciation has been calculated to be $10,000. What is the estimated value of the real estate?

The estimated replacement cost of a building is often given as an amount per square foot or cubic foot.

4. A house has a total finished floor area of 1,450 square feet. Mr. Jorgenson has appraised the building and estimated its replacement cost at $36 per square foot.

    a. What is the estimated replacement cost of the building?

    b. If the value of the land is $18,500 and the depreciation is $5,200, what is the estimated value of the real estate?

5. Mr. Robinson's house is 24 feet by 37 feet, with a finished family room addition that measures 15 feet by 20 feet. An appraiser has estimated the replacement cost at $35.25 per square foot, the land value at $14,000 and the depreciation at $8,400. What is the estimated value of the real estate?

6. What is the estimated replacement cost of the building shown below if the cost estimate is $38.75 per square foot? What is the value of the real estate if the land is estimated at $11,000 and depreciation at $5,500? Round off your answer to the nearest hundred dollars.

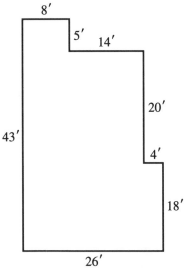

7. Compute the estimated value of the real estate pictured below. An appraiser has told you that the replacement cost is $2.25 per cubic foot, the depreciation is $10,800 and the land value is $15,500. Round off your answer to the nearest hundred dollars.

Calculating Depreciation

Depreciation is the loss of value suffered by a building. It is the difference between an existing building and a brand new building of like specifications.

Straight-Line Method   The *straight-line method* (also known as the economic age-life method) of depreciation spreads the total depreciation over the useful life of a building in equal annual amounts, using the formula below. Remember, this "useful life" has nothing at all to do with the life used for IRS depreciation or cost recovery.

$$\frac{\text{Replacement cost}}{\text{Years of useful life}} = \text{Annual depreciation charge}$$

A building most frequently becomes useless through external or functional obsolescence rather than physical deterioration. For this reason, appraisers often refer to the useful life of real estate as the "estimated economic life." Note that the "useful life," "economic life" and "actual life" of a building are rarely the same.

An appraiser estimates the remaining economic life of a property after considering the physical, functional and external factors.

EXAMPLE: An appraiser has estimated the replacement cost of a building at $100,000. The building is ten years old and has an estimated useful life of 50 years. What is the annual depreciation charge? What is the total depreciation for ten years? What is the current value of the building?

Step 1. Compute the annual depreciation charge.

$$\frac{\text{Replacement cost}}{\text{Years of useful life}} = \text{Annual depreciation charge}$$

$$\frac{\$100,000}{50} = \$2,000$$

Step 2. Find the amount of depreciation over ten years.

$$\frac{\text{Annual depreciation}}{\text{charge}} \times \frac{\text{Number of}}{\text{years}} = \text{Total depreciation}$$

$$\$2,000 \times 10 = \$20,000$$

Step 3. Find the current value of the buildings.

> Replacement cost − Depreciation = Current value of building

$$\$100,000 - \$20,000 = \$80,000$$

8. If the building in the preceding example was 30 years old, what would its current value be?

9. If the building in the example was located on a piece of land worth $25,000, what would be the estimated value of the property after 30 years of use (computed in problem 8)?

10. If the building in the example originally cost $75,000, what would be the current estimated value of the property?

Depreciation can also be expressed as a *percentage* or *rate*. To find the depreciation rate by the straight-line method, divide the total value (100%) by the building's estimated useful years of life.

$$\frac{100\%}{\text{Years of useful life}} = \text{Annual depreciation rate}$$

EXAMPLE: If a building has a useful life of 25 years, $\frac{1}{25}$ of the building's value is depreciated in one year. That is, the building depreciates at a rate of 4% per year.

$$\frac{100\%}{\text{Years of useful life}} = \text{Annual depreciation rate}$$

$$\frac{100\%}{25} = 4\%$$

11. a. If a building has an estimated useful life of 40 years, what is its annual rate of depreciation?

b. By what percentage will that building depreciate in 15 years?

c. If the building is 15 years old and has a current replacement cost of $180,000, what is the total amount that it has depreciated?

d. If the land on which the building is located is valued at $40,000, what is the estimated value of the total real estate?

12. The replacement cost of a building has been estimated at $115,000 and the building has an estimated useful life of 50 years. The building is nine years old.

a. What is the annual depreciation rate?

b. What is the total amount of depreciation that the appraiser will deduct?

INCOME CAPITALIZATION APPROACH

The *income capitalization approach* is a technique used in appraising income-producing real estate. It is a method of estimating the value of a property by dividing the annual net operating income (NOI—gross income minus expenses) produced by the property by the desired capitalization rate.

Net operating income is found by constructing an operating statement, using annual amounts for each line item.

Annual Operating Statement

Potential Gross Income
(Rental income at 100% occupancy)

Less: Allowance for vacancy and credit loss
(Reduction for unrented space and uncollectable rents)

Plus: Other income
(Laundry room coins, vending machine revenue, fees, parking charges, etc.)

equals

Effective Gross Income

Less: Annual operating expenses
(The costs ordinary and necessary to keep the property open and operating)
1. **Fixed expenses**—real estate taxes, insurance, etc.
   (Are not tied to occupancy)
2. **Variable expenses**—maintenance, utilities provided by owner, etc.
   (Items that increase or decrease with increased or decreased occupancy levels)
3. **Reserves for replacements**—appliances, carpet, etc.

equals

Net Operating Income
(The income available to the property after all operating expenses have been paid)

Notice that in the income capitalization approach, expenses do not include payments of principal and interest on any note. To do so would distort the data because some properties are debt free. Therefore, the net remaining after expenses are subtracted ought to be sufficient to service any debt (make the payments). If it is not, negative cash flow occurs. Finally, note that the terms *net annual income, cash flow, net spendable income* and *taxable income* are not synonymous. Detailed discussion of each, however, is beyond the scope of this text.

$$\frac{\text{Annual NOI}}{\text{Annual rate of return}} = \text{Value}$$

Does the formula look familiar? It's really the same formula you've used in previous chapters:

$$\frac{\text{Annual NOI (part)}}{\text{Over-all capitalization rate (rate)}} = \text{Value (total)}$$

EXAMPLE: What is the estimated value of an apartment building that is expected to produce an annual NOI of $14,000? An appraiser estimates that 10% is a suitable capitalization rate for comparable properties. This percentage is the rate of return demanded by an investor, but it is subject to limitations beyond the scope of this text. (For example, it ignores fluctuations in the projected income.)

By inserting the appropriate figures into the formula, you get:

NOI ÷ Rate = Value
$14,000 ÷ 10% = ?
$14,000 ÷ .10   = $140,000

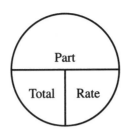 *or*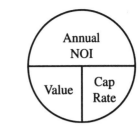

13. Fill in the following equations. Remember, *total* is the same as *value*, *part* is the same as *NOI* and *rate* stands for *overall capitalization rate*.

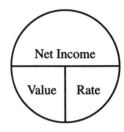

_____ × _____ = NOI

_____ ÷ _____ = Value

_____ ÷ _____ = Capitalization rate

14. If you had $120,000 to invest and you wanted a 10% return on your investment, what net income would a property have to produce to meet your required return?

a. First fill in the known parts of the equation.
value =   rate =   income =

b. Restate the problem.

c. What formula will you use?

d. Solve the problem.

15. Assume that a property produces an NOI of $26,250 per year. What capitalization rate is this if you purchased the property for $210,000?

a. Restate the problem.

b. What formula will you use?

c. Solve the problem.

16. An apartment building earns an NOI of $10,000 per year. What price would a buyer pay for the property if the capitalization rate is 10%?

a. Restate the problem.

b. What formula will you use?

c. Solve the problem.

17. A purchaser paid $175,000 for an apartment building that produced annual NOI of $16,850. Find the rate of return on the cost.

a. Restate the problem.

b. What formula will you use?

c. Solve the problem.

18. A purchaser bought a parcel of commercial real estate for $320,000 and wants a 12% capitalization rate. What annual NOI does she expect?

a. Restate the problem.

b. What formula will you use?

c. Solve the problem.

19. The effective gross income from an apartment building is $27,500 and annual expenses total $14,000. If the owner expects to get a 9% return on his investment, what is the indicated value of the property? Remember, effective gross income minus expenses equals NOI.

A small change in the rate of return, or capitalization rate, makes a big difference in the value. So, again, be aware of the importance of estimates in *all* of the methods used in the appraisal, or estimation of value, of real estate.

Gross Rent Multipliers (GRMs)

The income capitalization approach is used for income-producing properties. Residential properties are sometimes evaluated using a gross rent multiplier (GRM), which may be either a monthly multiplier or an annual multiplier.

To arrive at a multiplier, search the market to find houses that sold recently and that had tenants who occupied the properties at the time of sale.

Divide each sales price by the gross rent to find the GRM. Multiply the gross rent of the subject property by the GRM to find the indicated value of the subject property.

EXAMPLE: A house that rented for $500 per month recently sold for $60,000.
To find the monthly GRM:

$60,000 sales price ÷ $500 monthly gross rent = 120 monthly GRM

To find the annual GRM:

$500 monthly gross rent × 12 months = $6,000 annual GRM
$60,000 sales price ÷ $6,000 annual gross rent = 10 annual GRM

The subject home rents for $625 per month. Find its indicated value.

Using the monthly GRM:

$625 monthly gross rent × 120 monthly GRM = $75,000 indicated value

Using the annual GRM:

$625 monthly gross rent × 12 months = $7,500 annual gross rent
$7,500 annual gross rent × 10 annual GRM = $75,000 indicated value

---

Reconciliation of Data

After an appraiser has completed the tasks of gathering the data and calculating values based on the three methods (or approaches to value), a determination must be made as to which method is most valid for that specific appraisal. This involves the reconciliation of data and a comparison of the various values. It is quite important to note that the reconciliation of data is *not* the averaging of data. These reconciliation operations are beyond the scope of this text.

SUMMARY

In summary, each of the three approaches to value must be used on an appropriate type of property. Following is a general list of types of property lending themselves to the various approaches or methods:

- Sales comparison approach
  a. Single-family, owner-occupied homes, including condominiums
  b. Vacant lots
  c. Resort or recreation property

- Cost approach—All types of property with buildings and other improvements constructed thereon; especially well suited to newer buildings and special-use properties
- Income capitalization approach—Properties producing rent or income

There are, of course, many appraisals made by professionals who use two or all three of these methods. In the FNMA appraisal form shown in this chapter, all three approaches are used. In these appraisals, the appraiser must reconcile all of the data from all of the methods used and write a report supporting the appraisal presented.

PROBLEMS FOR ADDITIONAL PRACTICE

When you have finished these problems, check your answers at the end of the chapter. If you miss any of the problems, review this chapter before going on to Chapter 8.

1. A building, 100 feet by 250 feet by 20 feet, has a replacement cost of $1.50 per cubic foot. The land is valued at $150,000 and the building's depreciation has been estimated at $75,000. What is the value of this property via the cost approach to value?

   a. $907,500
   b. $825,000

   c. $900,000
   d. $675,000

2. The replacement cost of a building has been estimated at $150,000. The building was estimated to have a useful life of 50 years; it is now two years old. The land is valued at $50,000. What is the estimated value of this real estate via the cost approach to value?

   a. $192,000
   b. $200,000

   c. $194,000
   d. $198,000

3. A property valued at $100,000 produces a net operating income of $12,000 per year. What is the overall capitalization rate for this property?

   a. 12%
   b. 11.5%

   c. 13.6%
   d. 10%

4. If the owner is selling the above property and a prospective buyer wishes a 15% capitalization rate, what amount will the buyer pay for this property?

   a. $85,500
   b. $80,500

   c. $80,000
   d. $95,000

5. In computing value by the cost approach, the appraiser estimated the remaining economic life, or years of useful life, of a building to be 40 years. The replacement cost of the building is estimated at $170,000 and the age of the building is eight years. The current value of the building is

   a. $136,000.
   b. $164,687.

   c. $127,000.
   d. $170,000.

6. In the appraisal of a seven-story commercial building, the appraiser estimated the replacement cost per square foot to be $27. If the building is 92 feet wide and 117 feet deep, the replacement cost is estimated at

a. $1,729,483.

b. $1,979,845.

c. $2,034,396.

d. $290,628.

7. What capitalization rate is indicated by a property producing $10,000 annual net operating income and for which an investor paid $120,000?

a. 10%

b. 12%

c. 8.33%

d. 9.6%

8. An appraiser has estimated the annual net operating income from a commercial building to be $142,700. When capitalized at a rate of 10.5%, the estimated property value is

a. $1,498,350.

b. $1,427,000.

c. $1,392,195.

d. $1,359,048.

9. An apartment property has been appraised for $175,000, using a capitalization rate of 9.5%. The estimated annual net operating income is

a. $17,500.

b. $16,625.

c. $17,927.

d. $18,421.

10. If the effective gross annual income from a property is $112,000 and the total expenses for the year are $53,700, what capitalization rate was used to obtain a valuation of $542,325?

a. 10.75%

b. 10.50%

c. 10.25%

d. 9.75%

11. What is the current value of a house originally costing $35,000 if the house has appreciated 12%?

a. $66,250

b. $39,200

c. $78,400

d. $74,200

12. If the rate of straight line appreciation is 10%, what is the current value of a house that was appraised at $40,000 four years ago?

a. $56,000

b. $53,240

c. $66,667

d. $58,564

13. Charles Wilson bought a condominium for $60,000. Six months later, he was transferred and had to sell the property for $54,600. Which of the following calculations would you use to find his percentage of loss?

a. $5,400 ÷ $60,000

b. $5,400 ÷ $54,600

c. $54,600 ÷ $60,000

d. $60,000 ÷ $54,600

14. What is the indicated value via the sales comparison approach of a four-bedroom, two-bath, two-car-garage home with a pool? Market research indicates that a pool is worth $6,000, a bathroom is worth $2,800 and a two-car garage is worth $5,000 more than a one-car garage. A similar four-bedroom, three-bath home recently sold for $127,500. It had a one-car garage and no pool.

    a. $135,700   c. $124,700
    b. $121,100   d. $141,300

15. The subject property is similar to the comparable property in every way other than it has no fireplace. The comparable sold last week for $86,700. Your market study determines that a fireplace is worth $1,200. What is the indicated value of the subject property via the sales comparison approach?

    a. $86,700   c. $85,500
    b. $87,900   d. $87,000

ANSWER KEY

SOLUTIONS: WARM-UP EXERCISES

1. (b): $40' \times 65' = 2,600$ square feet
    $10' \times 45' = 450$ square feet
    2,600 square feet $-$ 450 square feet $= 2,150$ square feet
    2,150 square feet $\times$ $28.50 = $61,275

2. (c): $61,275 $-$ $6,250 + $25,000 = $80,025

3. (b): $25,000 $\div$ $175,000 = .14286$ or 14.3%

4. (a): $265,000 $\times$ .24 = $63,600

5. (d): $115,600 + $1,800 $-$ $7,500 = $109,900

SOLUTIONS: CHAPTER PROBLEMS

1. $8\% \times 3$ years $= 24\%$
    $24\% = .24$
    $53,000 $\times$ .24 = $12,720
    $53,000 + $12,720 = $65,720

2.

House	Age	Rooms	Extras	Sale Price	Sale Date	Adjusted Price	How Financed	Final Adjustment	Size	$ per Sq. Ft.
1	5 yrs.	3–2–2	Fireplace Pool <$10,000>	$70,000 <10,000> $60,000	1–1–96	$63,300	Cash	$63,300	1,500 sq. ft.	$42.20
2	4 yrs.	3–2–2	No fireplace + $1,000	$63,000 + 1,000 $64,000	12–1–96	$64,000	Equity <$1,000>	$63,000	1,480 sq. ft.	$42.57
3	5 yrs.	3–2–2	Fireplace	$62,000	6–1–96	$63,860	FHA <$1,800>	$62,060	1,460 sq. ft.	$42.51
4	5 yrs.	3–2–2	Fireplace	$61,000	8–1–96	$62,220	Equity + 2nd + $1,000	$63,220	1,500 sq. ft.	$42.15
Subject	4 yrs.	3–2–2	Fireplace		Current Date 12–1–96				1,490 sq. ft.	

House 3:

You need make no adjustment for extras because House 3 is similar to the subject house, but update the sales price at 0.5% per month, resulting in $63,860. Because this was a new FHA loan, estimate that the seller had to pay $1,800 in loan costs. Thus, after you subtract this amount to arrive at a cash equivalent price, the final adjusted price is $62,060. This house has 1,460 square feet of heated and cooled space (excluding the garage and covered porches), so its price per square foot is $42.51.

House 4:

Again, no adjustment need be made for extras because House 4 is similar to the subject house, but you must account for the lapse of time since it sold. At 0.5% per month, this adjusts the sales price to $62,220. This was a "distress sale" and the seller agreed to carry back a portion of the equity in the form of a second lien note. This might affect the sales price, so add $1,000, for a final adjusted price of $63,220. The house has 1,500 square feet of living area. This yields $42.15 as the price per square foot.

Please notice that several estimates were made in this problem. They must be based on experience and judgment. Remember, appraisal is not a science. These are some of the reasons that seem to make it more of an art.

3. $90,000 – $10,000 + $20,000 = $100,000

4. a. 1,450 square feet × $36 per square foot = $52,200
   b. $52,200 – $5,200 + 18,500 = $65,500

5. Compute the area.
$L \times W = A$
24' × 37' = 888 square feet
15' × 20' = 300 square feet
888 square feet + 300 square feet = 1,188 square feet

Compute the building replacement cost.
1,188 square feet × $35.25 = $41,877

Compute the estimated value.
$41,877 – $8,400 + $14,000 = $47,477

6. Compute the area.
   $43' \times 26' = 1{,}118$ square feet
   $4' \times 20' = 80$ square feet
   $5' \times 18' = 90$ square feet
   $1{,}118 - 80 - 90 = 948$ square feet

   Compute the building replacement cost.
   948 square feet $\times$ \$38.75 = \$36,735

   Compute the estimated value.
   \$36,735 − \$5,500 + \$11,000 = \$42,235 or \$42,200 (rounded)

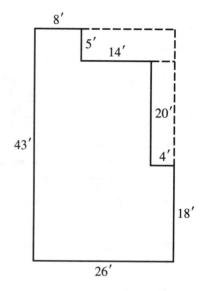

7. Compute the volume.
   $\text{Volume}_1 = L \times W \times H$
   $41' \times 23' \times 15' = 14{,}145$ cubic feet (first story)
   $\text{Volume}_2 = \dfrac{1}{2}(b \times h \times w)$
   $\dfrac{1}{2}(23' \times 7' \times 41') = 3{,}300.5$ cubic feet (second story)

   Total volume = 14,145 cubic feet + 3,300.5 cubic feet = 17,445.5 cubic feet

   Compute the building replacement cost.
   17,445.5 cubic feet $\times$ \$2.25 = \$39,252.38

   Compute the estimated value.
   \$39,252.38 − \$10,800 + \$15,500 = \$43,952.38 or \$44,000 (rounded)

8. $\$2{,}000 \times 30 = \$60{,}000$
   $\$100{,}000 - \$60{,}000 = \$40{,}000$

9. $\$100{,}000 - \$60{,}000 + \$25{,}000 = \$65{,}000$

10. The current value would remain the same—\$65,000. The original value of the building is not considered in this formula—only the appraiser's estimate of its current replacement cost.

11. a. Calculate the depreciation rate.
       $100\% \div 40 = .025$
    b. Calculate the depreciation rate for 15 years.
       $.025 \times 15 = .375$ or 37.5%
    c. Calculate the depreciation value for 15 years.
       $.375 \times \$180{,}000 = \$67{,}500$
    d. Calculate the estimated value.
       $\$180{,}000 - \$67{,}500 + \$40{,}000 = \$152{,}500$

12. a. $100\% \div 50 = .02$
    b. $.02 \times 9 = .18$
       $.18 \times \$115{,}000 = \$20{,}700$

13. Value $\times$ Capitalization rate = NOI
    NOI $\div$ Capitalization rate = Value
    NOI $\div$ Value = Capitalization rate

14. a. value = $120,000   rate = 10%   income = unknown (annual NOI needed)
   b. What is 10% of $120,000?
   c. Value × Rate = NOI
   d. $120,000 × .10 = $12,000

15. a. What percent of $210,000 is $26,250?
   b. NOI ÷ Total = Rate
   c. $26,250 ÷ $210,000 = .125 or 12.5%

16. a. $10,000 is 10% of what amount?
   b. NOI ÷ Rate = Value
   c. $10,000 ÷ .10 = $100,000

17. a. $16,850 is what percent of $175,000?
   b. NOI ÷ Total = Rate
   c. $16,850 ÷ $175,000 = .096 or 9.6%

18. a. What is 12% of $320,000?
   b. Value × Rate = NOI
   c. $320,000 × .12 = $38,400

19. a. First compute the net income.
   $27,500 − $14,000 = $13,500
   Then ask, $13,500 is 9% of what amount? (Use the formula NOI ÷ Rate = Value.)
   $13,500 ÷ .09 = $150,000

SOLUTIONS: PROBLEMS FOR ADDITIONAL PRACTICE

1. (b): 100′ × 250′ × 20′ = 500,000 cubic feet
   500,000 cubic feet × $1.50 = $750,000
   $750,000 − $75,000 + $150,000 = $825,000

2. (c): $150,000 ÷ 50 = $3,000
   $3,000 × 2 = $6,000
   $150,000 − $6,000 = $144,000
   $144,000 + $50,000 = $194,000

3. (a): $12,000 ÷ $100,000 = .12 or 12%

4. (c): $12,000 ÷ .15 = $80,000

5. (a): $170,000 ÷ 40 × 8 = $34,000
   $170,000 − $34,000 = $136,000

6. (c): 92′ × 117′ × 7 × $27 = $2,034,396

7. (c): $10,000 ÷ $120,000 = .0833 (rounded) or 8.33%

8. (d): $142,700 ÷ .105 = $1,359,048

9. (b): $175,000 × .095 = $16,625

10. (a): $112,000 − $53,700 = $58,300
$58,300 ÷ $542,325 = .1075 or 10.75%

11. (b): $35,000 × .12 = $4,200
$35,000 + $4,200 = $39,200

12. (a): .10 × 4 = .40
$40,000 × .40 = $16,000
$40,000 + $16,000 = $56,000

13. (a): $60,000 − $54,600 = $5,400
$5,400 ÷ $60,000 = .09 or 9%

14. (a): $127,500 + $5,000 + $6,000 − $2,800 = $135,700

15. (c): $86,700 − $1,200 = $85,500

CHAPTER

Interest

Interest is the cost (rent paid) of using someone else's money. That charge is typically expressed as a percentage (rate) of the loan amount (total) that is charged on an annual basis. In this chapter, you will learn to

- calculate the interest paid when given the time, rate and principal;
- calculate the principal loan amount when given the time, rate and interest paid; and
- determine the interest rate when given the time, principal and interest paid.

Mathematically, interest problems are another type of calculation using concepts learned in Chapter 2:

Total (loan amount) × Rate (*annual* interest rate) = Part (*annual* $ interest)
Part (*annual* $ interest) ÷ Total (loan amount) = Rate (*annual* interest rate)
Part (*annual* $ interest) ÷ Rate (*annual* interest rate) = Total (loan amount)

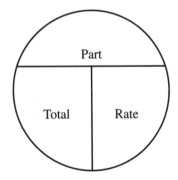
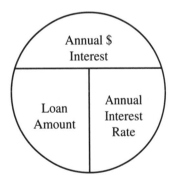

Because readers will have varying amounts of knowledge and experience, the problems that follow will allow you to determine your familiarity with the material to be covered. Try all of the problems before checking your answers against the answer key at the end of the chapter.

1. A bank issued a loan of $21,000 at 11% simple interest for two and a half years. If the loan was paid in full at the end of two and a half years, how much interest was paid to the bank?

    a. $5,775.00   c. $6,612.53
    b. $4,620.00   d. $6,006.43

2. If a bank wished to earn $6,300 on a loan of $50,000 over twelve months, what interest rate would the bank have to charge?

    a. 11%   c. 12%
    b. 12.5%   d. 12.6%

3. If a bank loans Maggie Smith $15,000 and charges her 8.5% simple interest, what will Maggie pay the bank at the end of seven months to pay off the loan?

    a. $743.75   c. $15,743.75
    b. $16,275.00   d. $1,275.00

4. What is the balance in Collin Miller's savings account at the end of four years if he deposits $18,000 and is paid 4% annual interest compounded semiannually? (No money is withdrawn.)

    a. $20,247.55   c. $19,468.80
    b. $18,720.00   d. $21,089.87

5. If Curt Shrum's money market account has a balance of $48,605.36 at the end of four years and interest was compounded yearly at an annual rate of 6%, what amount did he originally deposit in the account?

    a. $42,446   c. $38,500
    b. $40,425   d. $45,854

Interest, as stated earlier, is the cost of using someone else's money. A person who borrows money is required to repay the loan *plus* a charge for interest. This charge will depend on the amount borrowed (*principal*), the length of time the money is used (*time*) and the percentage of interest agreed on (*rate*). Repayment, then, involves the *return of* the principal *plus* a *return on* the principal, which is called *interest*.

A person who signs a 10% interest-bearing note for $500 that will mature in one year will be required to pay interest for one year (time) at 10% (rate) on the $500 (principal), as well as the face value of the note itself ($500).

Interest rates are expressed as annual rates, although interest may be paid monthly. A 10% interest rate means that the interest charged annually will be 10% of the principal.

There are two types of interest: simple interest and compound interest. The first part of this chapter will deal with simple interest and the latter section will cover compound interest. Most real estate loans involve simple interest paid *in arrears,* or *after* the use of the money has occurred.

SIMPLE INTEREST

The basic formula for computing simple interest is as follows:

Principal (total) × Annual interest rate (rate) = Annual $ interest (part)

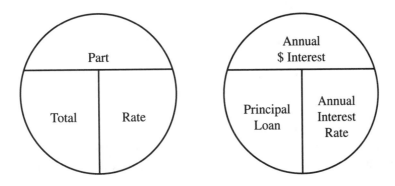

EXAMPLE: What is the annual interest earned by a bank on a $50,000 loan at 9% annual interest?

$50,000 (total) × .09 (rate) = $4,500 (part)

or

$50,000 (loan) × .09 (annual rate) = $4,500 (annual interest)

Often loans are paid back at intervals greater than one year. If a loan is paid back at the end of multiple years, multiply the dollars of annual interest by the number of years for which interest is owed.

EXAMPLE: What amount of simple interest would be due at the end of two years on a $25,000 loan at 11% annual interest?

$25,000 (total) × .11 (rate) = $2,750 (part)

or

$25,000 (loan) × .11 (annual rate) = $2,750 (annual interest)
$2,750 (annual interest) × 2 (years) = $5,500

Loans may also be paid back at the end of a time period less than one year. When this is the case, determine a monthly or daily amount of interest and multiply it by the number of months or days for which interest is owed.

EXAMPLE: What amount of simple interest would be due at the end of three months on a $6,000 loan at 10% annual interest?

$6,000 (total) × .10 (rate) = $600 (part)

or

$6,000 (loan) × .10 (annual rate) = $600 (annual interest)

$600 (annual interest) ÷ 12 (months) × 3 (months due) = $150

Using what you have just learned, solve the following interest problems.

1. Calculate the interest on a $1,000 loan at 10% for three years.

2. Find the amount of interest on a $6,000 loan at 11% for nine months.

3. Mrs. Johnson borrowed $4,000 to paint her house and the lender charged 9.5% interest. The loan was repaid in three months. What amount was repaid (the loan in full plus interest)?

When two elements in the interest formula are known, the third can be calculated.

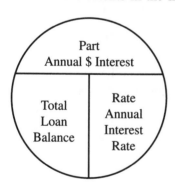

Loan amount × Rate = Annual $ interest

Annual $ interest ÷ Rate = Loan amount

Annual $ interest ÷ Loan amount = Rate

EXAMPLE: What amount of money was loaned if the borrower paid $450 in interest at the end of four months and was charged 9% annual interest?

$450 ÷ 4 (months) × 12 (months) = $1,350 (annual interest)

$1,350 (part) ÷ .09 (rate) = $15,000 (total)

EXAMPLE: What interest rate did the borrower pay if she borrowed
$23,000 and paid $2,070 in interest at the end of nine months?

$2,070 ÷ 9 (months) × 12 (months) = $2,760 (annual interest)
$2,760 (part) ÷ $23,000 (total) = .12, or 12% (rate)

Use what you have just learned to solve the following problems.

4. If the interest rate is 10% per year, how much money will you have to lend in order to get $75 interest
for six months?

5. A borrower paid $24 in interest charges at the end of three months. If the annual interest rate was 8%,
what was the amount of the loan?

6. How many months will it take for $800 to yield $95 in interest at a rate of 9.5%?

7. John Morse received $750 in interest on a loan of $12,000 for six months. What interest rate did he charge?

Interest payments may be made annually (once a year), semiannually (twice a year), quarterly (four times
a year) or monthly (twelve times a year). To calculate the interest payment amount, compute the annual
interest amount, then divide by the number of payments per year.

EXAMPLE: What will the quarterly payments be on a loan of
$5,000 at $10\frac{1}{2}$% per annum?

Step 1. Compute the annual interest.

$$\$5,000 \times .105 = \$525$$

Step 2. Divide by the number of payments per year.

$$\$525 \div 4 = \$131.25$$

The quarterly interest payments will be $131.25 each.

8. What will be the quarterly interest payments for a $600,000 loan with an interest rate of $8\frac{7}{8}\%$?

9. A loan for $15,000 with an interest rate of $9\frac{3}{4}\%$ requires monthly interest payments of how much?

10. If the appraised value of a house is $210,000, how much will semiannual interest payments be on a $168,000 loan at $8\frac{1}{4}\%$ interest?

11. A loan has an interest rate of 12% and requires quarterly interest payments of $750. What is the principal amount of the loan?

12. A loan has an interest rate of 8.5% and requires semiannual payments of $637.50. What is the principal amount of the loan?

13. A $10,000 loan requires quarterly interest payments of $250. What is the interest rate of the loan?

14. A $42,000 loan requires semiannual interest payments of $2,152.50. What annual interest rate is being charged?

15. The interest on a $90,000 loan is to be paid every two months. At $8\frac{7}{8}\%$ annual interest, what will be the amount of the bimonthly interest payment?

COMPOUND INTEREST

The term *compound interest* means that the interest is periodically added to the principal, with the result that the new balance (principal plus interest) draws interest. The annual interest rate may be calculated at different intervals, such as annually, semiannually, quarterly, monthly or daily. When the interest comes due during the compounding period (for instance, at the end of the month), the interest is calculated and accrues, or is added to the principal. Compound interest is generally paid on deposits in savings banks.

EXAMPLE: Consider a savings account with a starting balance of $10,000, earning compound interest at 10% per year, compounded annually. To determine how much money will be in the account at the end of two years, use the following steps:

Step 1. Calculate the interest for the first earning period.

$$\$10,000 \times .10 = \$1,000$$

Step 2. Add the first period's interest to the principal balance of the loan.

$$\$10,000 + \$1,000 = \$11,000$$

Step 3. Calculate the interest for the next earning period on the new principal balance.

$$\$11,000 \times .10 = \$1,100$$

If you want to compound for additional periods, simply repeat steps 2 and 3 as many times as necessary.

The example problem asks for the balance at the end of two years.

$10,000 beginning balance
$ 1,000 first year's interest
$11,000 balance at end of first year
$ 1,100 second year's interest
$12,100 balance at end of second year

The balance at the end of the second year includes the original principal amount of $10,000 plus the accrued compound interest calculated annually at the rate of 10%.

If this account were earning only *simple* interest, the interest would be calculated as follows:

$10,000 (principal) × .10 (rate) = $1,000 (annual interest)
$1,000 × 2 (years) = $2,000

Compound interest made a difference of:

$2,100 (compound interest) − $2,000 (simple interest) = $100

16. If you have a $20,000 certificate of deposit earning interest at the rate of 4.5% annually, but the interest is compounded monthly, what will be your account balance at the end of three months?

Remember, the compounding period and the interest rate per year (called the *nominal* rate) do not have to be the same. When they are not, you must first compute the interest rate *per compounding period.* In our problem, this is:

$$\frac{\text{Rate:}}{\text{Compounding Period:}} \quad \frac{4.5\% \text{ or } .045 \text{ annual rate}}{12 \text{ months}} = .00375 \text{ monthly rate}$$

Now, the calculation proceeds as in the previous example.

The following table compares $10,000 earning simple interest and the same amount earning compound interest. The term is five years. The annual interest rate is 7%.

	Simple		Compound	
	Interest Earned	Balance	Interest Earned	Balance
Beginning		$10,000		$10,000
Year 1	$ 700.00	10,700	$ 700.00	10,700
Year 2	700.00	11,400	749.00	11,449
Year 3	700.00	12,100	801.43	12,250.43
Year 4	700.00	12,800	857.53	13,107.96
Year 5	700.00	13,500	917.56	14,025.52
Total	$3,500.00		$4,025.52	

Simple interest is computed only on the principal. *Compound interest* is computed on the principal plus accrued interest.

PROBLEMS FOR ADDITIONAL PRACTICE

When you have finished these problems, check your answers at the end of the chapter. If you miss any of the problems, review this chapter before going on to Chapter 9.

1. Carl Bach has borrowed $2,000 at 10.5% interest. The loan will be repaid in nine months. What amount will be repaid when the nine months have elapsed?

a. $210.00   c. $157.70

b. $2,157.50   d. $2,210.00

2. The interest on a 10% loan was $72 for six months. What was the principal amount of the loan?

a. $720.00   c. $2,480.00

b. $4,320.00   d. $1,440.00

3. How many months will it take for $15,000 to yield $1,125 at 10% interest?

a. 12

b. 15

c. 9

d. 8

4. Mrs. Ranty was charged $1,295 on a $14,000 loan for one year. What was the rate of interest?

a. $9\frac{1}{4}\%$

b. 9%

c. $9\frac{3}{4}\%$

d. $9\frac{7}{8}\%$

5. What will quarterly interest payments be on a $16,500 loan at 11.5% interest for one year?

a. $632.50

b. $474.38

c. $790.63

d. $453.75

6. Mary Donaldson has invested $12,000 at 6% annual interest compounded monthly. What is the balance in her account at the end of eight months?

a. $12,180.00

b. $12,480.00

c. $12,488.49

d. $12,364.53

7. Jerry Cain had $6,945.75 at the end of three years in a money market account at his credit union, which compounded interest annually. If he was paid 5% per annum, what was the original amount deposited in the account?

a. $6,305.00

b. $6,000.00

c. $6,630.50

d. $6,450.00

8. A homeowner borrows $1,500 from a lender at 11% interest. When this loan is paid off at the end of seven months, the total paid will be

a. $1,500.00.

b. $83.13.

c. $1,596.25.

d. $1,642.50.

9. A couple spent $1,200 on furnishings at a department store, charging it on their credit card. They were out of town and did not pay their bill when due. The following month's bill showed a finance charge of $18 added to the $1,200. What was the rate of interest used to compute the finance charge?

a. 6%

b. 12%

c. 18%

d. 24%

10. Andrea Cavanaugh took her $5,000 certificate of deposit to the bank as collateral for a loan of $2,300, which she wanted in order to buy furniture and equipment for her new office. The bank gave her the loan and had her sign a six-month note at 13% interest. The amount of interest Andrea will owe when the note matures is

a. $207.00.

b. $225.00.

c. $149.50.

d. $127.00.

11. A bank issued a loan of $20,000 at 11% simple interest for four and a half years. If the loan was paid in full at the end of four and a half years, how much money did the bank receive?

    a. $8,550   c. $21,900

    b. $29,900   d. $11,450

12. If a bank wished to earn $9,000 on a loan of $20,000 over four and a half years, what simple interest rate would it have to charge?

    a. 9%   c. 10%

    b. 45%   d. 12.2%

13. Which of the following short-term loans will yield the greatest amount of interest?

    a. $2,000 at 20% for $2\frac{1}{2}$ years

    b. $10,000 at 5% for 2 years

    c. $60,000 at 10% for 2 months

    d. All of the above yield the same interest.

14. If an interest payment of $150 is made every three months on a $5,000 loan, what is the interest rate?

    a. 6%   c. 3%

    b. 12%   d. 9%

15. A loan is given for 80% of the appraised value of a house. If the interest on the loan is $12,500 semi-annually at an annual rate of 10%, what is the appraised value of the house?

    a. $500,000   c. $400,000

    b. $625,000   d. $312,500

ANSWER KEY

SOLUTIONS: WARM-UP EXERCISES

1. (a): $21,000 × .11 = $2,310

        $2,310 × 2.5 = $5,775

2. (d): $6,300 ÷ $50,000 = .126 or 12.6%

3. (a): $15,000 × .085 = $1,275

        $1,275 ÷ 12 × 7 = $743.75

4. (d): .04 ÷ 2 periods per year = .02 per period

        4 years = 8 compounding periods

        Multiply the principal by 100% + 2% (or 1.02) eight times.

        $18,000 × 1.02 × 1.02 × 1.02 × 1.02 × 1.02 × 1.02 × 1.02 × 1.02 = $21,089.87 (rounded)

5. (c): $48,605.36 ÷ 1.06 ÷ 1.06 ÷ 1.06 ÷ 1.06 = $38,500 (rounded)

SOLUTIONS: CHAPTER PROBLEMS

1. $1,000 × .10 = $100
$100 × 3 = $300

2. $6,000 × .11 = $660
$660 ÷ 12 × 9 = $495

3. $4,000 × .095 = $380
$380 ÷ 12 × 3 = $95 (rounded)
$4,000 + $95 = $4,095

4. $75 ÷ 6 × 12 = $150
$150 (part) ÷ .10 (rate) = $1,500 (total)

5. $24 ÷ 3 × 12 = $96
$96 (part) ÷ .08 (rate) = $1,200 (total)

6. $800 × .095 = $76
$95 ÷ $76 = 1.25
1.25 × 12 = 15

7. $750 ÷ 6 × 12 = $1,500
$1,500 (part) ÷ $12,000 (total) = .125 or 12.5% (rate)

8. $600,000 (total) × .08875 (rate) = $53,250 (part)
$53,250.00 ÷ 12 × 3 = $13,312.50
or
$53,250.00 ÷ 4 = $13,312.50

9. $15,000 (total) × .0975 (rate) = $1,462.50 (part)
$1,462.50 ÷ 12 = $121.88 (rounded)

10. $168,000 (total) × .0825 (rate) = $13,860 (part)
$13,860 ÷ 12 × 6 = $6,930

11. $750 ÷ 3 × 12 = $3,000
$3,000 (part) ÷ .12 (rate) = $25,000 (total)

12. $637.50 ÷ 6 × 12 = $1,275
$1,275 (part) ÷ .085 (rate) = $15,000 (total)

13. $250 ÷ 3 × 12 = $1,000 (rounded)
$1,000 (part) ÷ $10,000 (total) = .10 or 10% (rate)

14. $2,152.50 ÷ 6 × 12 = $4,305
$4,305 (part) ÷ $42,000 (total) = .1025 or 10.25% (rate)

15. $90,000 (total) × .08875 (rate) = $7,987.50 (part)
$7,987.50 ÷ 12 × 2 = $1,331.25

16. .045 ÷ 12 = .00375

$20,000 × 1.00375 × 1.00375 × 1.00375 = $20,225.85 (rounded)

SOLUTIONS: PROBLEMS FOR ADDITIONAL PRACTICE

1. (b): $2,000 × .105 = $210

$210 ÷ 12 × 9 = $157.50

$2,000 + $157.50 = $2,157.50

2. (d): $72 ÷ 6 × 12 = $144

$144 ÷ .10 = $1,440

3. (c): $15,000 × .10 = $1,500

$1,125 ÷ $1,500 = .75

.75 × 12 = 9

4. (a): $1,295 ÷ $14,000 = .0925 or 9.25%

5. (b): $16,500 × .115 = $1,897.50

$1,897.50 ÷ 12 × 3 = $474.38 (rounded)

6. (c): .06 ÷ 12 = .005

$12,000 × 1.005 × 1.005 × 1.005 × 1.005 × 1.005 × 1.005 × 1.005 × 1.005 = $12,488.49

7. (b): $6,945.75 ÷ 1.05 ÷ 1.05 ÷ 1.05 = $6,000

8. (c): $1,500 × .11 = $165

$165 ÷ 12 × 7 = $96.25

$96.25 + $1,500 = $1,596.25

9. (c): $18 × 12 = $216

$216 ÷ $1,200 = .18 or 18%

10. (c): $2,300 × .13 = $299

$299 ÷ 12 × 6 = $149.50 (rounded)

11. (b): $20,000 × .11 = $2,200

$2,200 × 4.5 = $9,900

$9,900 + $20,000 = $29,900

12. (c): $9,000 ÷ 4.5 = $2,000

$2,000 ÷ $20,000 = .10 or 10%

13. (d)

14. (b): $150 ÷ 3 × 12 = $600

$600 ÷ $5,000 = .12 or 12%

15. (d): $12,500 ÷ 6 × 12 = $25,000 (rounded)

$25,000 ÷ .10 = $250,000

$250,000 ÷ .80 = $312,500

The Mathematics of Real Estate Finance

Real estate finance is such a critical area of the real estate business that entire courses and textbooks are devoted to it. The purpose of this chapter is to introduce the student to some of the most common and elementary calculations involved in the area of finance.

In this chapter, you will be introduced to the calculation of loan qualification ratios, loan-to-value ratios, down payments, mortgage amounts, loan discount points, mortgage insurance premiums, amortization, funding fees and commitment fees. At the conclusion of your work in this chapter, you will be able to

■ calculate a loan amount;
■ calculate a down payment;
■ calculate a monthly payment for an amortized loan payment;
■ calculate points;
■ compute an amortized loan payment; and
■ use the lender's qualifying ratios to determine how much verifiable gross monthly income a purchaser must show to qualify for a particular loan amount.

WARM-UP EXERCISES

Because readers will have varying amounts of knowledge and experience, the problems that follow will allow you to determine your familiarity with the material to be covered. Try all of the problems before checking your answers against the answer key at the end of the chapter.

1. Ms. Wilson can obtain a 90% loan on a home selling for $385,000. Her required cash down payment will be

   a. $346,500.
   b. $77,000.

   c. $38,500.
   d. $308,000.

2. If Ms. Wilson is required to pay 1.5 discount points, a 1-point loan origination fee and a private mortgage insurance premium of .873 points, how much cash will she need to deliver to the closing table, including her down payment calculated in problem 1?

   a. $11,687.45   c. $47,162.50
   b. $50,187.45   d. $12,986.05

3. Shirley and Jerry Cain want to purchase a home for $135,000 with a 95% conventional loan. The lender uses a qualifying ratio of 25% of gross monthly income for the principal and interest payment. How much verifiable gross monthly income must the Cains show in order to qualify for a 15-year loan at 9% that requires monthly payments of $10.14 per $1,000 of the loan amount?

   a. $5,201.84   c. $6,502.38
   b. $1,300.46   d. $5,475.60

4. Mr. Murray can obtain a 30-year, 90% nonconforming conventional loan at 8.75%. The loan requires monthly principal and interest payments of $7.87 per $1,000. If the annual insurance premium is $1,800 and the annual ad valorem tax bill is calculated at $3.80 per $100 of value—using an assessment ratio of 53% of market value—what will be his monthly PITI payment if he purchases a home for $456,000?

   a. $10,983.84   c. $9,183.84
   b. $3,229.85   d. $4,145.17

5. Arnie Jones has decided to offer $135,000 for Bob and Mary Smith's home. The bank will loan him 80% of the purchase price for 30 years at 9% interest. What will be the amount of his principal and interest payment if the requirement is $8.05 monthly for each $1,000 borrowed?

   a. $1,086.75   c. $2,173.50
   b. $869.40   d. $1,869.40

LOAN-TO-VALUE RATIO

In the financing of real estate, the lender will typically loan a certain percentage of the sales price or the appraised value, *whichever is less*. The relationship between the value (sales price) and the loan amount is known as the *loan-to-value ratio* (LTV). The interest, then, is charged only on the amount of the loan, not on the sales price.

EXAMPLE:

> $80,000 sales price (value)
> $72,000 loan

describes a 90% loan-to-value ratio. Here is how it works:

$$\frac{\$72,000 \text{ loan}}{\$80,000 \text{ value}} = .90, \text{ or } 90\% \text{ LTV}$$

1. If a buyer obtains an 80% loan on a $90,000 sale, what is the loan amount?

2. If the loan in problem 1 has a 12% interest rate, what is the amount of interest due for the first month? (See Chapter 8 if you need help.)

The amount of interest charged and the total amount of money to be repaid relate *only* to the loan amount (the loan principal) and not to the sales price or value. (A VA loan, however, can have a 100% loan-to-value ratio.)

AMORTIZED LOANS

In Chapter 8, you learned to calculate simple interest. Loans earn a return, or profit, on the principal loan amount. Before the 1930s, the typical real estate loan was a *term loan,* which required the borrower to pay interest only (monthly, quarterly or annually) until the maturity date, when the entire principal balance became due and payable in full.

Following the Great Depression, lenders decided that it was better to have the borrower make regular periodic payments, which would, over the term of the loan, liquidate the indebtedness as well as pay all of the interest. This is what is known as an *amortized loan.* An amortized loan can call for a fixed monthly payment of principal, plus accrued interest. In this approach, the payment amount is less each month as the amount of the outstanding principal is reduced with each monthly payment. Known as a *direct reduction loan,* it is not commonly used by lenders.

EXAMPLE: A $90,000 loan is granted for 15 years at 10% annual interest, with monthly payments of $500 principal plus accrued interest. The first three payments would look like this:

	Total Payment	Principal	Interest	Ending Balance
Payment 1	$1,250.00	$500.00	$750.00	$89,500
Payment 2	$1,245.83	$500.00	$745.83	$89,000
Payment 3	$1,241.67	$500.00	$741.67	$88,500

A more common approach to amortized loans is to have a *fixed* monthly payment, which includes principal and interest, but with a changing amount being credited to each.

EXAMPLE: Using the same loan as in the previous example, but with a fixed payment amount, the first three payments would be:

	Total Payment	Principal	Interest	Ending Balance
Payment 1	$967.15	$217.15	$750.00	$89,782.86
Payment 2	$967.15	$218.96	$748.19	$89,563.90
Payment 3	$967.15	$220.78	$746.37	$89,343.12

Lenders prefer the second approach to amortized loans because it enables the borrower to qualify for a larger loan due to the smaller initial payments and because there is a reduced amount of risk connected with level-payment loans.

To calculate the monthly payment for a level-payment amortized loan:

- Use a financial calculator.

  number of payments = $\boxed{\text{N}}$

  annual interest rate ÷ 12 = $\boxed{\text{\%i}}$

  loan amount = $\boxed{\text{PV}}$

  compute for $\boxed{\text{PMT}}$
- Refer to a loan amortization book.
- Use a loan constant chart.
- Use a loan payment factor from a chart such as Table 9.1.

Calculating payments for these loans will be discussed more fully later in this chapter.

LOAN PAYMENT FACTORS

Table 9.1 shows a family of numbers known as *loan payment factors*. These factors are based on a $1,000 loan. Therefore, it is necessary to divide the loan amount by 1,000. To use these factors, just locate the appropriate interest rate in the left-hand column and relate this to the appropriate loan term or length of repayment period. For simplicity, we show only 30-, 25-, 20- and 15-year terms. After choosing the correct factor, multiply it by the amount of the loan, divided by 1,000, as discussed above.

To illustrate, suppose that we wish to know the payment required to amortize a $100,000 loan at 11% interest over a 30-year term. First divide the $100,000 loan amount by 1,000 ($100,000 ÷ $1,000 = 100). Then locate 11.000% in the left-hand column and find the factor that corresponds to the 30-year repayment term. This factor is $9.52. Now multiply this factor by 100, the number of thousands in the loan amount. This calculation yields a $952 monthly payment.

TABLE 9.1
LOAN PAYMENT FACTORS
Principal and Interest Factors per $1,000 of Loan Amount
Based on Monthly Payments

RATE	30 Yrs.	25 Yrs.	20 Yrs.	15 Yrs.	RATE	30 Yrs.	25 Yrs.	20 Yrs.	15 Yrs.
7.000%	6.65	7.07	7.75	8.99	12.125%	10.38	10.62	11.10	12.08
7.125	6.74	7.15	7.83	9.06	12.250	10.48	10.72	11.19	12.16
7.250	6.82	7.23	7.90	9.13	12.375	10.58	10.81	11.27	12.24
7.375	6.91	7.31	7.98	9.20	12.500	10.67	10.90	11.36	12.33
7.500	6.99	7.39	8.06	9.27	12.625	10.77	11.00	11.45	12.41
7.625	7.08	7.47	8.13	9.34	12.750	10.87	11.09	11.54	12.49
7.750	7.16	7.55	8.21	9.41	12.875	10.96	11.18	11.63	12.57
7.875	7.25	7.64	8.29	9.48	13.000	11.06	11.28	11.72	12.65
8.000	7.34	7.72	8.36	9.56	13.125	11.16	11.37	11.80	12.73
8.125	7.42	7.80	8.44	9.63	13.250	11.26	11.47	11.89	12.82
8.250	7.51	7.83	8.52	9.70	13.375	11.36	11.56	11.98	12.90
8.375	7.60	7.97	8.60	9.77	13.500	11.45	11.66	12.07	12.98
8.500	7.69	8.05	8.68	9.85	13.625	11.55	11.75	12.16	13.07
8.625	7.78	8.14	8.76	9.92	13.750	11.65	11.85	12.25	13.15
8.750	7.87	8.22	8.84	9.99	13.875	11.75	11.94	12.34	13.23
8.875	7.96	8.31	8.92	10.07	14.000	11.85	12.04	12.44	13.32
9.000	8.05	8.39	9.00	10.14	14.125	11.95	12.13	12.53	13.40
9.125	8.14	8.48	9.08	10.22	14.250	12.05	12.23	12.62	13.49
9.250	8.23	8.56	9.16	10.29	14.375	12.15	12.33	12.71	13.57
9.375	8.32	8.65	9.24	10.37	14.500	12.25	12.42	12.80	13.66
9.500	8.41	8.74	9.32	10.44	14.625	12.35	12.52	12.89	13.74
9.625	8.50	8.82	9.40	10.52	14.750	12.44	12.61	12.98	13.83
9.750	8.59	8.91	9.49	10.59	14.875	12.54	12.71	13.08	13.91
9.875	8.68	9.00	9.57	10.67	15.000	12.64	12.81	13.17	14.00
10.000	8.78	9.09	9.65	10.75	15.125	12.74	12.91	13.26	14.08
10.125	8.87	9.18	9.73	10.82	15.250	12.84	13.00	13.35	14.17
10.250	8.96	9.26	9.81	10.90	15.375	12.94	13.10	13.45	14.25
10.375	9.05	9.35	9.90	10.98	15.500	13.05	13.20	13.54	14.34
10.500	9.15	9.44	9.98	11.05	15.625	13.15	13.30	13.63	14.43
10.625	9.24	9.53	10.07	11.13	15.750	13.25	13.39	13.73	14.51
10.750	9.33	9.62	10.15	11.18	15.875	13.35	13.49	13.82	14.60
10.875	9.43	9.71	10.24	11.29	16.000	13.45	13.59	13.91	14.69
11.000	9.52	9.80	10.32	11.37	16.125	13.55	13.69	14.01	14.77
11.125	9.62	9.89	10.41	11.44	16.250	13.65	13.79	14.10	14.86
11.250	9.71	9.98	10.49	11.52	16.375	13.75	13.88	14.19	14.95
11.375	9.81	10.07	10.58	11.60	16.500	13.85	13.98	14.29	15.04
11.500	9.90	10.16	10.66	11.68	16.625	13.95	14.08	14.38	15.13
11.625	10.00	10.26	10.75	11.76	16.750	14.05	14.18	14.48	15.21
11.750	10.09	10.35	10.84	11.84	16.875	14.16	14.28	14.57	15.30
11.875	10.19	10.44	10.92	11.92	17.000	14.26	14.38	14.67	15.39
12.000	10.29	10.53	11.01	12.00					

We can simplify this process by combining the steps this way:

$$\frac{\$100,000}{\$1,000} \times \$9.52 = \$952$$

Calculate the loan payment if the term is shortened to 25 years.

Use the calculation below to check your answer:

$$\frac{\$100,000}{\$1,000} \times \$9.80 = \$980$$

MORTGAGE INSURANCE PREMIUMS

Because of the increased risk to lenders that results from making a loan with a high loan-to-value ratio, lenders demand additional protection. This has come to be known as *mortgage insurance*. Do not confuse this with credit life insurance, which is designed to pay off a loan if the borrower dies. Mortgage insurance protects the lender if the buyer defaults or if the property does not sell for a sufficient amount at a foreclosure sale to pay off the defaulted loan.

FHA MORTGAGE INSURANCE PREMIUMS (MIPs)

The Federal Housing Administration (FHA) originated this concept. As of 1995, an up-front premium of 2.25 points and an annual premium of .5 points are charged for the life of a loan unless the borrower makes a down payment in excess of 10% of the purchase price or the appraised value, whichever is less. The up-front premium can be paid in cash at the closing or financed as part of the loan. The annual premium is divided by 12 and collected monthly. The FHA insurance premium is identified as MIP. The FHA insures more than 50 types of loans. Check with your lender or local FHA field office for current premiums for a particular loan program.

The following example shows how to calculate the MIPs required for an FHA-insured loan.

EXAMPLE: Assume the loan amount totals $90,000:

Up-front monthly premium: $90,000 × .0225 = $2,025
Annual premium: $90,000 × .005 = $450
$450 ÷ 12 months = $37.50 monthly premium

Therefore, $37.50 is added to the monthly payment.

VA FUNDING FEES

VA-guaranteed loans are underwritten by the Department of Veterans Affairs and require the borrower or seller, as agreed by the parties, to pay a funding fee. This fee is always subject to change; however, as of 1995, it is influenced by the amount of down payment made by the veteran.

No down payment requires 2 points.
A down payment of 5% or more requires 1.5 points.
A down payment of 10% or more requires 1.25 points.

EXAMPLE: Assume a home has a purchase price of $125,000:

> No down payment:
> $125,000 × .02 = $2,500 funding fee

> 5% down payment:
> $125,000 × .05 = $6,250 down payment
> $125,000 − $6,250 = $118,750 loan
> $118,750 × .015 = $1,781.25 funding fee

> 10% down payment:
> $125,000 × .10 = $12,500 down payment
> $125,000 − $12,500 = $112,500 loan
> $112,500 × .0125 = $1,406.25 funding fee

PRIVATE MORTGAGE INSURANCE (PMI) PREMIUMS

Loans that are neither insured nor guaranteed by the government are known as *conventional loans*. When a lender grants a conventional loan for an amount greater than 80% of the sales price or the appraised value, whichever is less, the borrower will be required to obtain private mortgage insurance (PMI).

The premiums for PMI are expressed and calculated in points. The premium cost will depend on several factors, such as the amount of coverage required, the loan-to-value ratio, the repayment term of the loan, the geographic location of the property and other factors related to the lender's risk associated with a particular loan.

The premium amount will also be influenced by how and when premiums are paid. A variety of options is available to purchasers of PMI. The insurance premium may be paid

- up front, in a one-time amount;
- by financing it in the loan;
- in an upfront payment, followed by annual renewal premiums; or
- only in annual premiums.

PMI may be required for the entire term of the loan or, at the discretion of the lender, until the loan balance is reduced to an amount less than 80% of the market value of the property.

When you know the required current charges for a particular loan, use the following formula to compute the dollar amount of the up-front or annual premium:

$$\text{Loan amount} \times \text{Required points} = \text{PMI premium}$$

EXAMPLE: A lender requires an upfront premium of 1 point on a conventional loan of $95,000 and an annual premium of .32 points.

Upfront premium: $95,000 × .01 = $950
Annual renewal premium: $95,000 × .0032 = $304 ÷ 12 = 25.33 per month

The annual renewal premium is collected each month with the monthly payment.

For a further discussion of PMI, the authors recommend that you consult a *current* real estate finance text, such as *Essentials of Real Estate Finance,* by David Sirota, which is published by Real Estate Education Company of Chicago.

LOAN COMMITMENT FEES

If a builder desires to finance the construction of a new house, a short-term construction loan (also called an *interim* loan) is required. However, before the short-term lender funds the loan, it will require a loan commitment from a long-term lender to pay off its short-term loan and take it out of that property—hence, the term *take-out,* or *stand-by,* commitment. The long-term lender charges a *commitment fee* for this service of committing funds for a permanent loan. A typical commitment fee is 1% of the amount of the new long-term loan. This fee is generally nonrefundable. However, in some cases, it is credited against the total loan discount charged to the seller. If such is the case, it is greatly to the builder's benefit to require the buyer to obtain the loan from the same lender that provided the builder's commitment.

EXAMPLE: If a proposed long-term or permanent loan is $150,000 and the commitment fee is 1%, how much must the builder pay to the lender?

$150,000 × .01 = $1,500

Loan commitment fees are not restricted to new construction loans. They frequently are charged on non-residential loans and may be charged on certain residential loans, particularly the larger ones.

LOAN ORIGINATION FEES

Lenders charge a service fee to originate a new loan. This fee is usually expressed in points, although some lenders charge a flat fee. The most typical loan requires a 1-point origination fee.

EXAMPLE: The Smith family is getting a $325,000 loan to purchase their new home. The lender will charge a $\frac{1}{2}$-point loan commitment fee and a 1-point loan origination fee. The commitment fee will be paid at loan approval and the origination fee will be paid at closing. How much will each be?

Commitment fee: $325,000 × .005 = $1,625
Origination Fee: $325,000 × .01 = $3,250

LOAN DISCOUNT POINTS

A point always equals 1% of the loan amount. As discussed earlier in this chapter, FHA mortgage insurance premiums, VA funding fees, private mortgage insurance premiums, loan commitment fees and loan origination fees are stated in points.

Lenders may also charge discount points to adjust the yield or profit on a loan. Sometimes these points are called *buydowns* because they enable the lender to offer a lower face rate. The discount points are also referred to as *loan equalization factors*. The use of discount points began after World War II, when the government limited the amount of interest that could be charged on an FHA-insured or a VA-guaranteed loan. Conventional rates were set by the market place and were often higher than those permitted by the government for government-backed loans. The money for these government-backed loans came from the private sector. To be attractive to investors and to make funds available for these loans, the government permitted lenders to charge discount points to equalize the yield or profit of the government-backed loans to those originated as conventionally backed loans.

The government no longer dictates interest rates or who may pay points for government-backed loans. Interest rates for all loans are determined by the marketplace. Discount points are still used by lenders to offer a variety of loan options to their customers.

To calculate a point, simply multiply the loan amount by 1%, or .01.

EXAMPLE: A lender requires $1\frac{3}{4}$ discount points on a $125,000 loan.

$1\frac{3}{4}$ points = .0175 points

$125,000 × .0175 = $2,187.50 for discount points

BUYER'S LOAN QUALIFICATION RATIOS

Prior to approving a prospective buyer's loan application, the lender wants to be sure that the applicant has the financial ability to repay the loan and that the applicant has a history of paying off other debts satisfactorily. Likewise, before a real estate licensee invests a great deal of time and expense in working with a buyer, the licensee should perform a "prequalification" of the buyer. Of course, this is not directly related to the actual loan qualification to be done by the lender.

Lenders verify a buyer applicant's income and relate this to (1) the amount of the payments on the requested loan and (2) the total amount of all other payments now owed by the buyer. To accomplish this, lenders use arbitrary ratios. In the case of FHA and VA loans, the U.S. government sets these ratios. In the case of secondary market lenders such as FNMA and FHLMC, these agencies set the ratios. Or if a lender plans to retain the loan in its own portfolio, the ratios are set individually. It is important to remember that each agency or lender is free to change the numbers in each ratio, as well as which items are included in that ratio. These ratios also may vary depending on the loan-to-value ratio and whether the interest is fixed or is subject to adjustment. Therefore, our discussion is intended to be general in nature.

Qualification ratios are usually described as *PITI* and *LTD* ratios. The "PITI" ratio is a percentage of the buyer's income to be applied to the principal, interest, tax and insurance payment and the LTD ratio is a percentage of the buyer's income to be applied to all of the buyer's present monthly payments plus the PITI payment, as described above. Buyers must satisfy both ratios in order to obtain loan approval.

Qualification Ratios

Let us now explore the calculation of these loan qualification ratios. Suppose that the PITI and LTD ratios for a 90% loan are 28% and 36% (expressed as 28/36), respectively. This means that the buyer's PITI payment should not exceed 28% of his or her gross monthly income and that the mortgage loan payment plus all other debts should not exceed 36% of gross monthly income. (If the buyer is able to obtain a 95% loan, the lender may require ratios of 25/33 due to the fact that the loan has more risk because of the buyer's smaller cash investment.)

$$\text{Total} \times \text{Rate} = \text{Part}$$
$$\text{Income} \times \text{Ratio} = \text{Allowable Payment Amount}$$

EXAMPLES: Mr. and Mrs. Rudy Ramirez have a combined gross monthly income of $3,600. They have selected a $100,000 house and plan to obtain a $90,000 loan at 10.5% for 30 years. The monthly principal and interest payment on this house is $823.27, the hazard insurance premium is $41, the taxes are $95 and the financed private mortgage insurance premium is $26.25. Their only long-term debt is a $300 car payment. Can they qualify for the loan?

$823.27 principal and interest + $41 insurance + $95 taxes + $26.25 PMI = $985.52 total house payment

$985.52 total house payment ÷ $3,600 income = 27.4% (rounded—must not exceed 28%)

$985.52 total house payment + $300 car payment = $1,285.52 total debt payment

$1,285.52 total debt payment ÷ $3,600 income = 35.7% (rounded—must not exceed 36%)

Mr. and Mrs. Ramirez qualify for the loan because their ratios are less than those required. They could not qualify if they had a $100 monthly boat payment, for example, because their second ratio would be too high even though their first ratio is satisfactory. However, if they could pay off the boat with funds currently on hand (not borrowed), the loan could be approved.

Now you try a few simple loan qualification problems.

3. Roy and Rita wish to obtain a new loan. Their combined monthly income is $4,200. What amount of monthly payment can they qualify for if the lender uses the 28/36 ratios and if they have no other debts?

4. John and Debbie Keating have been told that the monthly payment for PITI on the house they have selected is $1,234.56. If area conventional lenders are qualifying prospective buyers at 28/36, what is the required monthly income for the Keatings?

5. Kit and Charlotte's combined monthly income is $5,000. What monthly PITI can they qualify for if area conventional lenders are qualifying at 28/36?

6. What is the maximum monthly debt the Keatings (see problem 5) can have and still qualify for the loan?

CALCULATION OF LOAN AMOUNTS AND DOWN PAYMENTS

The amount of money that a lender requires a buyer to pay toward the purchase price is called the *down payment*. The difference between the sales price and this down payment is the amount of the loan that the lender is willing to make on the subject property. This loan amount must be substantiated by an appraisal. The amount of the down payment and the loan amount (the loan-to-value ratio) are determined by the type of loan to be obtained.

VA Loans

A VA-guaranteed loan requires no down payment up to the maximum allowable loan amount, which is based on the amount of the veteran's entitlement. Of course, the buyer may make a down payment in order to keep the payments lower, and to reduce the funding fees discussed earlier.

FHA Loans

FHA-insured loans require a variety of down payments and loan amounts. We will not attempt to address any but one common FHA loan type because this is not a finance textbook. Most FHA buyers prefer to make a minimum down payment and therefore obtain the maximum loan amount. In order for a buyer to obtain the maximum loan for FHA mortgage insurance purposes, the FHA permits the buyer to add the amount of the buyer's closing costs (not including the prepaid items) to the sales price. This amount is called the FHA *acquisition cost*. It is the basis upon which the loan amount is calculated.

Let's say that the sales price is $70,000. The FHA provides a table of allowable buyer's closing costs, which varies by geographic area. Suppose that these amount to $1,350. Acquisition cost is then $70,000 plus $1,350, which equals $71,350. If the acquisition cost is more than $50,000, the FHA uses a two-tiered loan-to-value ratio. It will insure 97% of the first $25,000 and 95% of the excess, up to the maximum loan amount, which varies from one part of the United States to another.

In order to calculate the maximum loan amount for this property:

$$\$71,350 \text{ acquisition cost} - \$25,000 = \$46,350$$
$$\$46,350 \times .95 = \$44,032.50$$
$$\$25,000 \times .97 = \$24,250$$
$$\$44,032.50 + \$24,250 = \$68,282.50$$

The FHA would round down this amount to the next $50, which is $68,250. Therefore, $68,250 is the maximum loan for FHA mortgage insurance purposes. We must now subtract this amount from the lesser of the sales price or the appraised value (not the acquisition cost).

$$\$70,000 \text{ sales price} - \$68,250 = \$1,750 \text{ cash down payment required}$$

Note: In addition to this amount, the buyer would be required to pay $1,350 at closing as the FHA allowable closing costs plus the amount of the prepaid items. The total cash required to close would be $1,750 plus $1,350 which equals $3,100 plus prepaid items and tax and insurance reserve impounds.

7. If an FHA buyer's allowable closing costs are $1,450 on a house priced at $80,000, calculate the maximum loan for FHA mortgage insurance purposes.

8. What is the amount of down payment on the transaction shown in problem 7?

Conventional Loans

The maximum conventional loan available is 100%; however, 97%, 95%, 90% and 80% are more common. There are stringent underwriting requirements for high loan-to-value ratio loans. Private mortgage insurance is required by the lender on any loan greater than 80% of the market value (or the sales price, whichever is less). The amount of the premium for this PMI varies among insurers and also among types of loans. For example, a fixed-rate loan will have a smaller PMI premium than an adjustable-rate loan.

EXAMPLE: If the sales price is $100,000 and the buyer requests a 90% loan, how much cash down payment must the buyer make if the property appraises for $97,000?

Remember, the loan amount is based on the *lesser* of the sales price *or* the appraised value. In this case, the seller may not be willing to reduce the sales price to an amount equal to the appraised value. Thus, the buyer may either terminate the contract (which is a typical contract provision) or pay a larger down payment. Let's look at the figures:

$97,000 appraised value × .90 = $87,300 maximum loan amount

$100,000 sales price − $87,300 maximum loan amount = $12,700 required down payment

If the seller reduces the sales price to the appraised value of $97,000, the down payment will be $9,700.

MORTGAGE LOANS—OVERVIEW

Mortgage loans are usually made with a repayment period of 15 or 30 years. Payments of both principal (face value of the mortgage) and interest are required during the term of the loan. A mortgage debt divided into equal, regular payments (usually monthly) over a period of time is called an *amortized mortgage.*

Under the terms of an amortized loan, the borrower makes a fixed monthly payment that includes one month's interest on the unpaid principal, plus a payment of part of the principal. The beginning monthly installments pay primarily interest and only a small portion of each payment is applied to the reduction of the principal. As the principal is gradually repaid and the balance reduced, also reducing the interest to be paid, an increasing percentage of the monthly payment can be applied to repayment of the principal, until the loan is repaid entirely.

A chart of typical amortized loan payments is shown in Figure 9.1. Notice how the amount of principal paid in each installment *increases,* while the amount of interest paid *decreases.* The reason for this is that interest is charged only on the outstanding balance of the loan. The last payment—in this example, number 300—is not shown. Note that the percentages in each payment total 100%. This is because each payment on such a loan involves only principal reduction and interest on the balance, although the percentage changes with each payment.

Many mortgage lenders require the borrower to pay a monthly amount, in addition to the monthly amortization payment, to establish a reserve to pay real estate taxes and insurance premiums when they become due. The amount of this reserve will be indicated when it is to be included in a problem in this text. It is not a part of the *loan* payment, however.

AMORTIZATION CALCULATIONS

You should be able to handle all the problems in this chapter by applying what you have learned about percentages, principal and interest. Work all dollar amounts out to three decimal places and round off to two places only in the last step of a problem. Work carefully. If your answer does not agree with the one given, review until you understand the correct solution. Then adjust your work before going on to the next problem.

FIGURE 9.1
Amortized Mortgage for $80,000 at 13.5% Interest for 25 Years

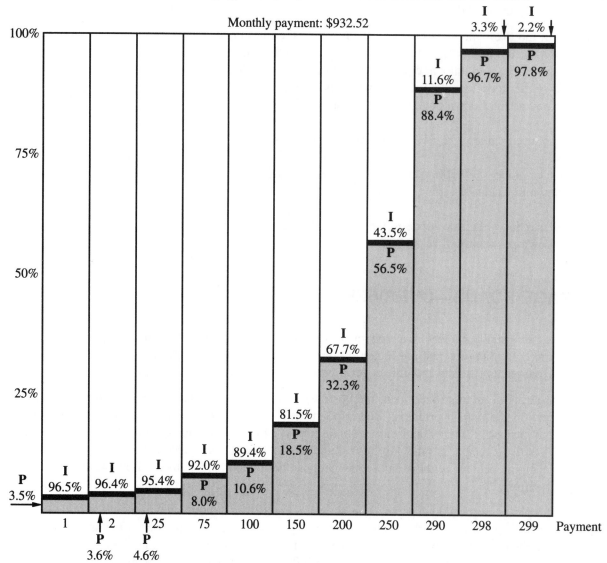

Monthly payment: $932.52

9. Mrs. Walsh owns a residence valued at $77,000 and has been granted a 30-year mortgage loan equal to 75% of the value of the property. If the interest rate is 9%, compute the amount of interest charged for the first month of the loan. (Remember the loan-to-value ratio; in this example, it is 75%.)

10. Using Table 9.1, what will Mrs. Walsh's monthly principal and interest payment be (see problem 9)?

EXAMPLE: Using the information in problem 9, if Mrs. Walsh's monthly payment is $464.89, what will be the balance of the principal of her loan next month?

Step 1. Compute the monthly interest on the full principal. This was calculated in the last problem). The answer is $433.13.

Step 2. Find the amount of payment that will be applied to reducing the principal.

$464.89 total payment
− 433.13 monthly interest
$ 31.76 amount applied to principal

Step 3. Compute the new principal balance.

$57,750.00 old principal balance
−   31.76 reduction
$57,718.24 new principal balance

Please note again that there will be a few cents difference in the answer if you leave the numbers in the calculator and perform the chain functions, as opposed to writing down each answer, clearing the calculator, then reentering the numbers for the next step in the problem. Greater accuracy with a calculator is obtained if the numbers are left in the calculator and the next calculation is then performed.

11. Now calculate the balance of the principal of Mrs. Walsh's loan when the interest for the third payment is computed.

Accrued Interest and Loan Reduction

Typically, interest on a real estate loan is paid *after* it has been earned, or accrued, by the lender. For this reason, interest is paid in arrears, which means that the June payment on a loan includes both the interest earned during May and a remainder, which reduces the June principal.

Occasionally, interest may be paid in advance, but changes in the tax laws no longer invite this method of payment. A limited exception to this is found in nearly every new loan, however. Because a loan may be finalized, or closed, on any day of the month, the buyer at closing usually pays interest from that day of closing through the end of the month. This is called *prepaid* interest. Then the first regular monthly payment will be on the first day of the *following* month. That payment will include the interest for the intervening first full month of the loan. The buyer is not getting a free ride, as some think. Examine the diagram below for a better understanding of this.

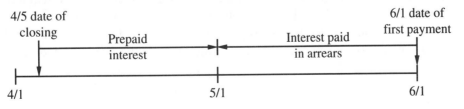

12. On May 1, Thomas Carter borrowed $45,000 at 11% interest. The loan was amortized over a 20-year period at $464.48 per month. How much of the June 1 payment was applied to interest and how much was applied to principal?

13. Using the information given in the problem 12, divide the July 1 payment between interest and principal.

14. W. C. Olcott has obtained a $31,500 loan at $10\frac{1}{2}$% interest. Mr. Olcott's monthly payment has been figured at $474.74, which includes interest and principal *plus* tax and insurance premiums. If tax and insurance premiums total $1,920 per year, what will be the principal balance of the loan after the first payment is made?

15. Nikki Holloway, who has a house valued at $60,000, obtained a $10,000 home improvement loan to build a room addition. The loan is payable at the rate of $100 per month, plus 14% interest on the decreasing principal balance. The loan was made on March 1 and principal and interest payments are due on the first day of each month. What amount will be due on April 1? On May 1?

PROBLEMS FOR ADDITIONAL PRACTICE

1. Two discount points cost a seller $1,650. What is the amount of his loan?

a. $168,367

b. $82,500

c. $165,000

d. $3,300

2. For how much monthly PITI payment can Ryan qualify if he earns $3,300 monthly and the lender applies 28/36 qualifying ratios?

a. $1,188

b. $825

c. $1,150

d. $924

3. Mark and Jennifer Freeman can get a 90% conventional loan for 20 years at 9%. It will require a monthly principal and interest payment of $10.14 per $1,000 of the loan amount. For how much financing can they qualify if Mark's annual salary is $60,000 and Jennifer earns $1,800 monthly? (The lender will permit them to devote up to 25% of their gross monthly income to a principal and interest payment.)

a. $1,687.50

b. $81,000.00

c. $167,653

d. $184,911.24

4. Using the information in problem 3, calculate the price of the house Mark and Jennifer can purchase? Divide loan amount by loan-to-value ratio to get purchase price.

   a. $186,281

   b. $81,000.00

   c. $166,420.12

   d. $184,911.24

5. If a lender agrees to make an 80% loan on a house that sells for $116,900 and that appraises for $114,500, what is the amount of the loan?

   a. $93,200

   b. $23,300

   c. $91,600

   d. $22,900

6. To obtain an FHA-insured loan, the Johnsons will have to pay a MIP of 2.25 points, which will be financed into the loan. What will be the amount of their loan if FHA insures 97% of the first $25,000 and 95% of the balance of the cost of their new home, which appraises for $110,000? (The maximum loan the FHA will insure in their area is $125,000.)

   a. $80,750

   b. $105,000

   c. $104,500

   d. $107,362.50

7. Kim and Rodger Donaldson earn a combined annual income of $96,400. They can get a 20-year, 90% conventional loan at 8.75% interest that will require monthly payments of $8.84 per $1,000 borrowed. A house they really like has annual taxes of $3,200 and can be insured for $1,500 per year. If the lender uses 28/36 qualifying ratios and they have no other debts, how much financing can Kim and Rodger qualify for?

   a. $210,142.53

   b. $282,272.12

   c. $233,492.12

   d. $254,449.10

8. Using the information in problem 7, calculate the maximum sales price Kim and Rodger can afford.

   a. $210,142.91

   b. $233,491.70

   c. $254,449.10

   d. $282,272.12

9. If Kim and Rodger (see problems 7 and 8) are required to pay a 1.5-point origination fee, a .75-point PMI premium and 1 discount point plus $2,860 in other closing costs, how much cash will they need to bring to the closing if they have already deposited $10,000 earnest money with the escrow officer?

   a. $33,038.80

   b. $23,038.80

   c. $30,178.80

   d. $20,178.80

10. If Carl Snyder has an annual gross income of $48,000, for how much monthly PITI payment can he qualify if the lender uses 29/41 qualifying ratios?

    a. $1,160

    b. $1,640

    c. $1,120

    d. $1,140

11. What is the 2.25-point MIP on an $80,000 FHA-insured loan?

    a. $800

    b. $1,800

    c. $2,000

    d. $2,600

12. What is the maximum amount of money Lee Harris would have available for a car note if he earns $65,400 per year, wants to obtain the maximum amount of home loan possible and can get a 95% conventional loan for 30 years at 9.25%? (The lender will require 25/33 qualifying ratios and a monthly payment of $8.23 per $1,000 borrowed.)

a. $1,798.50
b. $1,362.50

c. $5,450.00
d. $436.00

13. Mrs. York can obtain an 80% conventional loan to purchase a home selling for $428,000. If the property appraises for $425,000, what will be the required down payment?

a. $42,500
b. $85,000

c. $85,600
d. $42,800

14. How much verifiable gross monthly income will Sarah and Mark Williamson need in order to purchase a new home for $186,000 if they can obtain an 80% conventional loan for 15 years at 10% annual interest? (The annual insurance premium will be 2% of the value of the home and the ad valorem taxes will be charged at $3.85 per $100 of market value. The loan will require a monthly principal and interest payment of $10.75 for each $1,000 of the loan amount and the lender will use 28/36 qualifying ratios. The property appraises for $186,000 and the Williamsons have no other debts.)

a. $2,976.00
b. $8,951.25

c. $7,161.00
d. $10,599.60

15. If the Williamsons (see problem 14) pay 2 discount points to obtain the loan, what amount will be charged on the closing statement?

a. $7,161.00
b. $2,976.00

c. $8,951.25
d. $1,599.60

ANSWER KEY

SOLUTIONS: WARM-UP EXERCISES

1. (c): $385,000 × .90 = $346,500
$385,000 − $346,500 = $38,500

2. (b): 1.5 + 1 + .873 = 3.373
3.373 = 3.373% or .03373
$346,500 × .03373 = $11,687.45 (rounded)
$11,687.45 + $38,500 = $50,187.45

3. (a): $135,000 × .95 = $128,250
$128,250 ÷ $1,000 = 128.25
128.25 × $10.14 = $1,300.46 (rounded)
$1,300.46 ÷ .25 = $5,201.84

4. (d): $456,000 × .90 = $410,400
$410,400 ÷ $1,000 × $7.87 = $3,229.85
(rounded)
$456,000 × .53 ÷ 100 × $3.80 = $9,183.84
$9,183.84 + $1,800 ÷ 12 = $915.32
$3,229.85 + $915.32 = $4,145.17

5. (b): $135,000 × .80 = $108,000
$108,000 ÷ $1,000 = 108
108 × $8.05 = $869.40

SOLUTIONS: CHAPTER PROBLEMS

1. $90,000 \times .80 = $72,000

2. $72,000 \times .12 \div 12 = $720

3. $4,200 \times .28 = $1,176

4. $1,234.56 \div .28 = $4,409.14 (rounded)

5. $5,000 \times .28 = $1,400

6. $5,000 \times .36 = $1,800
$1,800 - $1,400 = $400

7. $80,000 + $1,450 = $81,450
$81,450 - $25,000 = $56,450
$56,450 \times .95 = $53,627.50
$25,000 \times .97 = $24,250
$24,250 + $53,627.50 = $77,877.50 or $77,850 (rounded)

8. $80,000 - $77,850 = $2,150

9. $77,000 \times .75 = $57,750
$57,750 \times .09 \div 12 = $433.13

10. $57,750 \div $1,000 \times $8.05 = $464.89 (rounded)

11. Pmt 2: $57,718.24 \times .09 \div 12 = $432.89
　　　　$464.89 - 432.89 = $32.00
　　　　$57,718.24 - $32.00 = $57,686.24
　　Pmt 3: $57,686.24 \times .09 \div 12 = $432.65
　　　　$464.89 - 432.65 = $32.24
　　　　$57,686.24 - $32.24 = $57,654.00

12. $45,000 \times .11 \div 12 = $412.50
$464.48 - $412.50 = $51.98

13. $45,000 - $51.98 = $44,948.02
$44,948.02 \times .11 \div 12 = $412.02 (rounded)
$464.48 - $412.02 = $52.46

14. $1,920 \div 12 = $160
$474.74 - $160 = $314.74
$31,500 \times .105 \div 12 = $275.63 (rounded)
$314.74 - $275.63 = $39.11
$31,500 - $39.11 = $31,460.89

15. April 1: $10,000 \times .14 \div 12 = $116.67 (rounded)
$116.67 + $100 = $216.67
May 1: $10,000 - $100 = $9,900
$9,900 \times .14 \div 12 = $115.50
$115.50 + $100 = $215.50

SOLUTIONS: PROBLEMS FOR ADDITIONAL PRACTICE

1. (b): $1,650 ÷ .02 = $82,500

2. (d): $3,300 × .28 = $924

3. (c): $60,000 ÷ 12 + $1,800 = $6,800
$6,800 × .25 = $1,700
$1,700 ÷ $10.14 × $1,000 = $167,653 (rounded)

4. (a): $167,653 ÷ .90 = $186,281 (rounded)

5. (c): $114,500 × .80 = $91,600

6. (d): $110,000
$\underline{-25,000} × .97 = $24,250
$\underline{85,000 × .95 = $80,750}$
$105,000 × .0225 = $2,362.50
$105,000 + $2,362.50 = $107,362.50

7. (a): $96,400 ÷ 12 × .28 = $2,249.33 (rounded)
$3,200 + $1,500 = $4,700
$4,700 ÷ 12 = $391.67 (rounded)
$2,249.33 − $391.67 = $1,857.66
$1,857.66 ÷ $8.84 × $1,000 = $210,142.53

8. (b): $210,142.53 ÷ .90 = $233,491.70

9. (b): $233,491.70 × .10 = $23,349.17
1.5 + .75 + 1 = 3.25
$210,142.53 × .0325 = $6,829.63 (rounded)
$6,829.63 + $2,860 + $23,349.17 − $10,000 = $23,038.80

10. (a): $48,000 ÷ 12 = $4,000
$4,000 × .29 = $1,160

11. (b): $80,000 × .0225 = $1,800

12. (d): 33% − 25% = 8%
$65,400 ÷ 12 = $5,450
$5,450 × .08 = $436

13. (b): $425,000 × .20 = $85,000

14. (b): $186,000 × .80 = $148,800
$148,800 ÷ $1,000 × $10.75 = $1,599.60
$186,000 × .02 = $3,720
$7,161 + $3,720 ÷ 12 = $906.75
$1,599.60 + $906.75 = $2,506.35
$2,506.35 ÷ .28 = $8,951.25

15. (b): $148,800 × .02 = $2,976

Ad Valorem Taxes

It often will be necessary for you as a real estate salesperson or broker to calculate real estate taxes, in addition to having a basic understanding of how taxes are levied.

At the conclusion of your work in this chapter, you will be able to compute annual ad valorem taxes

■ based on the market value of property and an assessment ratio;
■ based on assessed value, using a tax rate per $100 value;
■ given in mills; and
■ using an equalization factor.

You also will be able to calculate penalties for delinquent ad valorem taxes.

Much of the material presented in this chapter may not apply to your state because each state has its own way of calculating ad valorem taxes.

WARM-UP EXERCISES

Because readers will have varying amounts of knowledge and experience, the problems that follow will allow you to determine your familiarity with the material to be covered. Try all of the problems before checking your answers against the answer key at the end of the chapter.

1. A property has a market value of $67,000. The assessment ratio used in the area is 82% of market value. The tax rate is $2.50 per $100 of assessed value. What are the annual taxes for this property?

   a. $1,675.00   c. $1,373.50
   b. $2,042.68   d. $1,375.00

2. A property is assessed at $55,600. What is the annual tax bill, with taxes assessed at 23 mills?

   a. $127,880.00   c. $1,278.80
   b. $12,788.00   d. $12.78

3. How much annual tax will be paid on a parcel of real estate assessed at $182,500, using an equalization factor of 1.30 and a tax rate of $4.18 per $100 of equalized value?

   a. $9,917.05

   b. $5,868.08

   c. $7,628.50

   d. $3,084.25

4. What is the assessed value of a property with a market value of $4,860,300, using an equalization factor of .53?

   a. $91,703.77

   b. $2,575,959

   c. $257,595.90

   d. $25,759,590

5. Real estate taxes in the amount of $1,460 are due and payable on December 31. A late penalty of .75% per month or any part thereof is levied for taxes paid after the due date. What amount will be due if the taxes are paid on April 4 of the following year?

   a. $1,470.95

   b. $1,492.85

   c. $1,518.40

   d. $1,503.80

TAXES BASED ON ASSESSED VALUE

Taxes levied against real estate so that each taxpayer will share the cost of various government activities in proportion to the value of his or her property are known as *ad valorem* taxes. *Ad valorem* means according to value, so an ad valorem tax is a real estate tax based on the value of property.

Valuing and assessing real estate for tax purposes is usually the responsibility of the tax assessor or, in some states, the tax appraisal district, but you will find it helpful to have a basic understanding of how the amount of tax is derived. To figure the amount of tax that will be imposed on a parcel of real estate, you must know two things: the percentage or ratio of assessment to market value used in your area and the tax rate, usually expressed as dollars or cents per hundred or per thousand dollars of assessment.

Suppose, for example, that the assessed value of a particular property is 70% of market value, which is estimated at $50,000, and the official tax rate in the city or town is $4 per $100 of assessment. The amount of city tax on the property is computed as follows:

Step 1. Compute the assessed value. In some jurisdictions, this step is not necessary because assessed value and market value are the same. Property may be assessed at 100% of market value.

$$\text{Market value} \times \text{Assessment ratio} = \text{Assessed value}$$

$$\$50,000 \times .70 = \$35,000$$

Step 2. Compute the tax (tax rate expressed in dollars per hundred).

> Assessed value ÷ 100 × Tax rate = Annual tax

$35,000 ÷ 100 × $4 = Annual tax

Annual tax = $1,400

EXAMPLE: Assessed value at 100% of market value.

A property is assessed at $143,500 and was recently purchased for $144,000. What are the annual school taxes if the tax rate is $2.20 per $100 valuation?

Assessed value ÷ 100 × Tax rate = Annual tax
$143,500   ÷ 100 × $2.20 = $3,157

EXAMPLE: Assessed value as a percentage or ratio of assessment to market value.

A property has a market value of $125,600 in a jurisdiction that assesses property at 53% of market value. What is the current year's tax bill to the city if the tax rate is $.92 per $100 of assessed value?

Market value × Assessment ratio = Assessed value
$125,600   ×   .53   = $66,568

Assessed value ÷ 100 × Tax rate =   Annual tax
$66,568   ÷ 100 × $.92   = $612.43 (rounded)

When taxes are based on an assessment equal to 100% of market value, eliminate step 1 of this example.

Caution: Taxes on real estate are determined by state and local laws. The material presented here is in general form. Be sure to inquire about tax procedures in your own locality.

1. A house has a market value of $80,000. The assessment ratio is 70%. What is the assessed value?

2. If property is assessed at 40% of its market value, what would be the assessed value of a parcel worth $47,500?

3. If property is valued at $65,000 and assessed for 60% of its value, what is the tax if the rate is $5.30 per $100 of assessed value?

4. If the annual tax on a property comes to $1,467, what is the assessed value of that property, given a tax rate of $1.63 per $100 of assessed value and assuming that this property is assessed at 100% of its market value?

5. A house has a market value of $44,200. The assessment ratio is 50% of market value and the tax rate is $35 per $1,000 of assessed value. What is the annual tax on the property?

Notice that tax rates may be expressed in any of 4 ways. The following rates are equivalent:

$3.50 per $100
$35 per $1,000
3.5% (.035)
35 mills

TAXES GIVEN IN MILLS

The tax rate can be expressed as so many *mills* on each dollar of assessed value. A mill is $\frac{1}{10}$ of one cent. In decimal form, 1 mill is written as .001. To convert mills to decimal form, divide the number of mills by 1,000.

6. Complete the table below:

$$1 \text{ mill} = \frac{1}{10}\cent = \$.001$$
$$10 \text{ mills} = 1\cent = \$.01$$
$$100 \text{ mills} = 10\cent = \underline{\quad\quad}$$

7. Write 54 mills in decimal form.

EXAMPLE: A property is assessed at $75,500. The tax rate is 23 mills. Compute the amount of tax on the property.

$$23 \text{ mills} \div 1,000 = .023$$

Assessed value × Tax rate decimal = Annual tax
$75,500   ×   .023   = $1,736.50

8. A property is assessed at $125,600. The tax rate is 48 mills. Compute the annual tax.

9. Taxes are based on an assessment ratio of 53% of market value. This year, the school system collects 33 mills per $1 of assessed value. Compute the annual school tax for a property valued at $225,000.

10. Property taxes on a parcel of real estate were $1,641.60. The property was assessed at 45% of market value and the tax rate was 57 mills per $1 of assessed value. What was the market value of the real estate?

TAXES USING AN EQUALIZATION FACTOR

In some taxing districts, assessed values are adjusted in order to make them comparable to those of surrounding areas. The assessed value of a property is multiplied by an *equalization factor* determined by the assessor's office.

Assessed value × Equalization factor = Equalized assessment

The equalized assessment value is then multiplied by the tax rate to compute the amount of the tax bill.

Equalized assessment × Tax rate = Tax

11. If real estate is assessed at $82,500, to be adjusted by an equalization factor of 1.30, and the tax rate is $4.35 per $100 of assessed equalized value, how much tax will have to be paid?

PENALTIES FOR DELINQUENT TAXES

Unpaid taxes are subject to penalty charges—for example, 1% per month during the delinquency period.

EXAMPLE: Assume that an owner's annual real estate tax of $780 is payable in two equal installments. The due dates are May 1 and September 1. What is the amount of the penalty that will accrue if no tax payments are made until October 30, at which time the full tax is paid? (Assume that delinquent taxes are subject to a penalty of 1% a month.)

Step 1. Calculate the installment payments.

$$\$780 \div 2 = \$390 \text{ per installment}$$

Step 2. Determine the first penalty charge.

$$\$390 \times .06 \text{ penalty May 1 to October 30} = \$23.40$$

Step 3. Determine the second penalty charge.

$$\$390 \times .02 \text{ penalty September 1 to October 30} = \$7.80$$

Step 4. Add both penalties to arrive at the total.

$$\$23.40 + 7.80 = \$31.20$$

Delinquent real estate taxes are normally collected when the property is sold at a tax sale or at a private sale. If the delinquent owner is allowed a redemption period by local law, extra penalties are usually added until the time the property is redeemed or a tax deed is issued to the purchaser at the tax or private sale.

12. Real estate taxes in the amount of $927 were not paid by a July 1 due date. The property was sold at a tax sale on October 1. The penalty *before* the tax sale was 1% interest per month. The penalty *after* the tax sale was 12% for each six-month period after the sale, without proration. The redemption fee was $5. Find the cost to redeem the property on November 1.

EXEMPTIONS

Some states permit certain exemptions on property taxes and, in some cases, this option to grant exemptions extends to lesser taxing entities, such as counties, cities and school districts. The taxing authority subtracts, or exempts, a prescribed amount of value from the assessed value before applying the other factors.

For example, a state might exempt $10,000 for homestead purposes. If the property composing the homestead is assessed at $60,000, the $10,000 exemption is subtracted and usual factors are applied to the $50,000 valuation.

Or an exemption might be granted to senior citizens and, again, the amount of the exemption would be subtracted from the assessed value. In some cases, exemptions on land used for agricultural purposes are allowed and the assessed value is based on the productivity value, not the market value of the land. Generally, property owners must make a written application for any type of property tax exemption.

PROBLEMS FOR ADDITIONAL PRACTICE

When you have finished these problems, check your answers at the end of the chapter. If you miss any of the problems, review this chapter before going on to Chapter 11.

1. A property has a market value of $76,000. The taxes in the area are levied on 66% of market value at a rate of $2.50 per $100 of assessed value. How much tax will be charged in one year?

   a. $836.00
   b. $1,900.00

   c. $1,254.00
   d. $501.60

2. Mr. and Mrs. Billings own a house that is valued at $45,000. The assessed value is 55% of market value and the equalization factor is 1.3. The tax rate is 53.5 mills. What will be the tax bill for one year?

   a. $1,324.13
   b. $920.93

   c. $1,705.28
   d. $1,721.36

3. A property is valued at $46,000. The taxes are levied on 45% of market value and an equalization factor of 1.4 is used. The tax rate is $30 per $1,000 of assessed value. The owners of this property were delinquent in paying the second installment of their tax bill this year, by two months plus two days. What will be the total amount of their second installment if the penalty is 1% per month? (Consider the installments to be equal. Remember, tax penalties are the seller's responsibility; they are not prorated.)

   a. $447.74
   b. $434.70

   c. $869.40
   d. $882.44

4. A residential property sold for $75,000. The assessed value for tax purposes is 22% of market value. What will be the amount of the tax bill if the tax rate is $6.25 per $100 of assessed value?

   a. $937.50
   b. $975.00

   c. $1,031.25
   d. $1,072.50

5. Julio Martinez, a property owner, received his tax bill for $1,232.50. The published tax rate is $2.25 per $100 of assessed value. What is the assessed value of this property?

   a. $8,936.63
   b. $17,000.00

   c. $54,777.00
   d. $18,390.00

6. Your current real estate tax bill is $1,944. The tax rate is $4.50 per $100 of the equalized assessed value. When the equalization factor is .80 what is the assessed valuation?

   a. $50,000
   b. $52,000

   c. $54,000
   d. $56,000

7. What is the market value of property on which the real estate tax is $1,595.54, when the assessment is 45% of market value, all assessments are equalized by a factor of .67 and the tax rate is 63 mills per dollar?

   a. $30,306
   b. $56,417
   c. $70,467
   d. $84,000

8. Find the tax rate per $100 of assessed value when the tax bill is $901.31 and the assessed value is 33% of the market value of $47,500.

   a. $5.75
   b. $6.00
   c. $57.50
   d. $.575

9. The Clarks received a tax bill for $870.54, half of which is payable on June 1 and the other half, on October 1. A penalty of 1% per month is provided for delinquent taxes. If the Clarks make payment in full on October 15, how much will they pay?

   a. $892.30
   b. $896.64
   c. $887.95
   d. $883.60

10. A house was assessed for taxes at 50% of market value. The tax rate was $3.75 per $100 of assessed value. Five years later, taxes had increased by $300. How much did the market value of the house increase?

    a. $8,000
    b. $16,000
    c. $2,250
    d. $60,000

11. A house is valued at $75,000 and assessed for 60% of its value. If the tax bill is $1,350, what is the rate per $100?

    a. $1.80
    b. $13.50
    c. $4.00
    d. $3.00

12. The tax rate can be expressed as a certain number of mills for each dollar of assessed value. Indicate which of the following decimal equivalents is correct.

    a. 19 mills = .19
    b. 23 mills = .023
    c. $2\frac{1}{4}$ mills = .225
    d. $2\frac{1}{2}$ mills = .025

13. The Johnson home has an assessed value of $68,900. The Johnsons are permitted a $10,000 exemption and will owe current annual tax based on $2.28 per $100 of valuation. Their tax bill will be

    a. $1,798.92.
    b. $1,570.92.
    c. $1,342.92.
    d. None of the above

14. What is the annual tax amount due on a property with a market value of $385,600, where an assessment ratio of 48% is used and the tax rate is $3.43 per $100 of valuation?

    a. $6,533.61
    b. $13,226.08
    c. $7,009.82
    d. $6,348.52

15. A city levies $.83 per $100 of assessed value. What is the annual tax bill for a property that the appraisal district has assessed at $83,750?

a. $695.13

b. $69.51

c. $6,951.25

d. $688.90

ANSWER KEY

SOLUTIONS: WARM-UP EXERCISES

1. (c): $67,000 × .82 ÷ 100 × $2.50 = $1,373.50

2. (c): 23 mills ÷ 1,000 = .023
$55,600 × .023 = $1,278.80

3. (a): $182,500 × 1.3 ÷ 100 × $4.18 = $9,917.05

4. (b): $4,860,300 × .53 = $2,575,959

5. (d): .0075 × 4 = .03
$1,460 × .03 = $43.80
$43.80 + $1,460 = $1,503.80

SOLUTIONS: CHAPTER PROBLEMS

1. $80,000 × .70 = $56,000

2. $47,500 × .40 = $19,000

3. $65,000 × .60 = $39,000
$39,000 ÷ $100 = 390
390 × $5.30 = $2,067

4. $1,467 ÷ $1.63 = 900
900 × $100 = $90,000

5. $44,200 × .50 = $22,100
$22,100 ÷ $1,000 = 22.10
22.10 × $35 = $773.50

6. $.10

7. $.054

8. $48 \div 1,000 = .048$
$125,600 \times .048 = \$6,028.80$

9. $33 \div 1,000 = .033$
$225,000 \times .53 = \$119,250$
$119,250 \times .033 = \$3,935.25$

10. $57 \div 1,000 = .057$
$1,641.60 \div .057 = \$28,800$
$28,800 \div .45 = \$64,000$

11. $82,500 \times 1.30 = \$107,250$
$107,250 \div \$100 = 1,072.50$
$1,072.50 \times \$4.35 = \$4,665.38$ (rounded)

12. $927 \times .03 = \$27.81$
$927 \times .12 = \$111.24$
$927 + \$27.81 + \$111.24 + \$5 = \$1,071.05$

SOLUTIONS: PROBLEMS FOR ADDITIONAL PRACTICE

1. (c): $76,000 \times .66 = \$50,160$
$50,160 \div \$100 = 501.60$
$501.60 \times \$2.50 = \$1,254$

2. (d): $45,000 \times .55 = \$24,750$
$24,750 \times 1.3 = \$32,175$
$32,175 \times .0535 = \$1,721.36$ (rounded)

3. (a): $46,000 \times .45 = \$20,700$
$20,700 \times 1.4 = \$28,980$
$28,980 \div \$1,000 = 28.98$
$28.98 \times \$30 = \$869.40$
$869.40 \div 2 = \$434.70$
$434.70 \times .03 = \$13.04$ (rounded)
$434.70 + \$13.04 = \$447.74$

4. (c): $75,000 \times .22 = \$16,500$
$16,500 \div \$100 = 165$
$165 \times \$6.25 = \$1,031.25$

5. (c): $1,232.50 \div \$2.25 = \$547.77$ (rounded)
$547.77 \times \$100 = \$54,777$

6. (c): $1,944 \div \$4.50 = 432$
$432 \times \$100 = \$43,200$
$43,200 \div .80 = \$54,000$

7. (d): $1,595.54 \div .063 = \$25,326.03$ (rounded)
$25,326.03 \div .67 = \$37,800.04$ (rounded)
$37,800.04 \div .45 = \$84,000$ (rounded)

8. (a): $47,500 × .33 = $15,675
$15,675 ÷ $100 = 156.75
$901.31 ÷ 156.75 = $5.75 (rounded)

9. (b): $870.54 ÷ 2 = $435.27
$435.27 × .01 = $4.35 (rounded)
$4.35 × 5 = $21.75
$435.27 + $21.75 = $457.02
$435.27 + $4.35 = $439.62
$457.02 + $439.62 = $896.64

10. (b): $300 ÷ $3.75 = 80
80 × $100 = $8,000
$8,000 ÷ .50 = $16,000

11. (d): $75,000 × .60 = $45,000
$45,000 ÷ $100 = 450
$1,350 ÷ 450 = $3

12. (b): 23 ÷ 1,000 = .023

13. (c): $68,900 − $10,000 = $58,900
$58,900 ÷ $100 × $2.28 = $1,342.92

14. (d): $385,600 × .48 = $185,088
$185,088 ÷ $100 × $3.43 = $6,348.52 (rounded)

15. (a): $83,750 ÷ $100 × $.83 = $695.13 (rounded)

Property Transfer Taxes

The transfer of real estate is taxed in many states. The amount of tax and the considerations that are exempt from this tax differ from state to state. You should be familiar with the amount of transfer tax charged in your state and the current exemptions from the tax. Some states exempt a transfer in which the total consideration is less than some statutory amount, or an existing mortgage is assumed by the purchaser. This does not refer to the amount stated in the deed, but to the actual sales price. Many states require a written declaration to be made and signed by one or both parties to a sale in which the selling price is disclosed, together with other facts. Some states have no transfer tax.

At the conclusion of your work in this brief chapter, you will be able to compute the transfer tax, using the approaches applied by some states. Remember to check the rates for your state if applicable.

WARM-UP EXERCISES

Because readers will have varying amounts of knowledge and experience, the problems that follow will allow you to determine your familiarity with the material to be covered. Try all of the problems before checking your answers against the answer key at the end of the chapter.

1. A parcel of real estate sold for $64,000 and the buyer assumed a mortgage balance of $23,600. The state in which the transaction took place levies a transfer tax of $.65 for each $500 or fraction thereof paid in cash at the time of transfer. What is the amount of transfer tax due?

   a. $20.21
   b. $52.00

   c. $52.65
   d. $31.20

2. A property is sold for $85,500 in cash. The state levies a transfer tax of $.43 for each $300 of the sales price. What amount of transfer tax is due?

   a. $125.00
   b. $122.55

   c. $73.53
   d. $173.53

TRANSFER TAX RATES

Many states require that a transfer tax be paid when an interest in real estate is sold and conveyed by a deed. Payment of the tax is usually made by purchasing stamps from a state or local official, affixing them to the deed and having them canceled. Many state transfer taxes were adopted on January 1, 1968, when the federal revenue stamp tax was repealed.

Details of the transfer tax differ among states. For example, many states exempt sales in which the consideration is less than $100. Other states tax only the net consideration if the buyer assumes the seller's existing mortgage.

A tax rate of $.50 or $.55 for each $500 or fractional part of $500 of the net taxable consideration is common. A percentage of the taxable consideration is another method used.

EXAMPLE: What value in state transfer stamps must be affixed to a deed when property is sold for $10,600 and the tax rate is $.50 per $500 or fraction thereof of the selling price? ("Fraction thereof" means that $501 is treated the same way as $599.)

$$\$10,600 \div \$500 = 21.2, \text{ or } 22 \text{ taxable parts}$$
$$22 \times \$.50 = \$11 \text{ tax}$$

Because the tax is $.50 per $500 or fraction thereof, any fractional part will incur $.50 tax. Therefore, 21 and a fractional part (.2) are, for this tax, the same as 22 parts.

1. A piece of property was sold in a state in which the stamp tax rate is $.55 for each $500 paid in cash at the time of the transfer. A mortgage balance, if assumed by the buyer, is not a taxable consideration. If the total price of the property was $54,000 and the buyer assumed a $24,000 mortgage, compute the amount of transfer tax paid. (The assumed mortgage is exempt.)

2. Real estate that sold for $57,750 was subject to a transfer tax of $.50 for each $500 or fraction thereof of the selling price. What amount of tax stamps must be purchased, affixed to the deed and canceled?

3. Real estate was sold for $64,750 and a state transfer tax was required at the rate of $.26 per $100 or fraction thereof of consideration. How much tax was paid?

4. Real estate was sold for $40,500, with the buyer assuming the seller's mortgage balance of $20,394. The tax rate was .005 of the consideration paid in cash at the sale closing. What was the amount of tax if the assumed mortgage was exempt?

Approximate Sales Price

EXAMPLE: In certain states, tax stamps are based on the amount of cash paid at the time of transfer. Calculate the *approximate sales price* of the real estate involved in a transaction in which the tax rate was $.50 for each $500 or fraction thereof, a total of $20.50 in stamps was affixed to the deed and the buyer assumed the seller's mortgage of $19,812.

Step 1. Calculate the parts.

$$\$20.50 \div \$.50 = 41$$

Step 2. Determine the cash paid.

$$41 \times \$500 = \$20,500$$

Step 3. Total the cash paid and the mortgage amount.

$$\$20,500 + \$19,812 = \$40,312 \text{ sales price}$$

In most states, only assumed loans are exempt when computing transfer taxes. New purchase-money loans are not deducted from the amount subject to the transfer tax whether the note is to the seller or to a third-party lender.

5. Mr. Toper sold his house to Ms. Reilly for $12,000 cash, a $40,000 first mortgage assumed by the buyer and a purchase-money mortgage note signed by Ms. Reilly for $13,000. The transaction took place in a state that has a tax rate of $1.75 per $100 or fraction thereof and exempts assumed mortgages. What was the amount of transfer tax on the sale?

6. Mark Blair is buying a $40,000 house. He assumed the mortgage, which was for 25% of the sales price, and negotiated a second mortgage for 50% of the balance, paying the rest in cash. If the transfer tax rate is $.55 per $500 or fraction thereof and assumed mortgages are exempt, what amount of transfer tax stamps must be affixed to the deed?

7. Tony and Georgina Finnelli have listed their house with Wagner Realty for $60,000. The best offer that they've received is from Paul and Stephanie Jackson, who are willing to assume the present mortgage of $20,000, pay $25,000 in cash and sign a purchase-money mortgage note for $10,000. The transfer tax rate is $.75 per $500 or fraction thereof and assumed mortgages are exempt. What amount of transfer tax will be charged if the Finnellis accept this offer?

8. Mr. and Mrs. Hanes are purchasing Mr. and Mrs. Ebert's house for $74,000, less the mortgage they will assume, which has a principal balance of $30,000 after the October 1 payment. The interest rate on this amortized mortgage is 8% and payments of $250 are due on the first day of each month, to be applied first against the interest for the previous month, with the balance to be applied to the principal. The last mortgage payment was made November 1. The closing of the transaction has been set for November 13. What amount of transfer tax stamps will have to be affixed to the deed if the state requires $.50 per $500 or fraction thereof and exempts assumed mortgages?

PROBLEMS FOR ADDITIONAL PRACTICE

When you have finished these problems, check your answers at the end of the chapter. If you miss any of the problems, review this chapter before going on to Chapter 12.

1. Real estate was sold for $84,000, with the buyer assuming a mortgage of $52,000. What amount of transfer tax is due if the tax is based on the cash exchanged at closing at the rate of $.45 per $500 or fraction thereof?

a. $75.60
b. $46.80

c. $57.60
d. $28.80

2. The Doyles are selling their house to the George family. The total sales price of the house is $54,000. The Georges will assume the present mortgage of $14,000 and the Doyles will take back a purchase-money mortgage note of $20,000. What will be the amount of transfer tax if the state requires $.50 per $500 or fraction thereof and exempts transactions of less than $100 and assumed mortgages?

a. $60
b. $40

c. $52
d. $80

3. Real estate is being sold for $85,000, with the purchaser assuming the $56,500 unpaid balance of the sellers' existing mortgage. What is the state transfer tax when the rate of tax is $.50 for each $500 or fraction thereof of the actual consideration less the amount of any assumed mortgage?

a. $28.50

b. $85.00

c. $56.50

d. $29.00

4. The sales price of a house is $112,000. The buyer is assuming the seller's $61,000 mortgage balance and is giving the seller a purchase-money mortgage note for $25,000. What amount of state transfer tax stamps is required if the state transfer tax is 2% of the value of the property?

a. $520

b. $1,020

c. $1,720

d. $2,240

5. The state transfer tax is $.30 for each $100 or fraction thereof of the full sales price. The county tax is $.50 for each $500 or fraction thereof of the sales price less the amount of any assumed mortgage. Compute the total transfer tax required for a sale at $95,000 with a $68,000 assumed mortgage.

a. $81.00

b. $108.00

c. $123.50

d. $312.00

6. The state transfer tax is $.50 for each $500 or fraction thereof of the sales price less the amount of any assumed mortgage. A report of properties sold lists the addresses and names of grantors and grantees and the amount of transfer tax paid. When an item on the report lists $89.50 as the transfer tax, the sales price of the property is probably

a. $89,500.

b. less than $89,000.

c. greater than $89,500 if the buyer assumed the seller's mortgage.

d. None of the above

7. The state transfer tax on deeds is $.12 for each $100 of sales price; the county tax is $.30 for each $100 of sales price. The sales price of a residence is $84,000 and is financed by a mortgage loan for 80% of the sales price. What amount of transfer tax is due? (There are no exemptions for assumed loans.)

a. $100.80

b. $352.80

c. $252.00

d. $325.00

ANSWER KEY

SOLUTIONS: WARM-UP EXERCISES

1. (c): $64,000 − $23,600 = $40,400
   $40,400 ÷ $500 = 80.8 or 81 (rounded)
   81 × $.65 = $52.65

2. (b): $85,500 ÷ $300 = 285
   285 × $.43 = $122.55

SOLUTIONS: CHAPTER PROBLEMS

1. $54,000 − $24,000 = $30,000
$30,000 ÷ $500 = 60
60 × $.55 = $33

2. $57,750 ÷ $500 = 115.5 or 116
116 × $.50 = $58

3. $64,750 ÷ $100 = 647.5 or 648
648 × $.26 = $168.48

4. $40,500 − $20,394 = $20,106
$20,106 × .005 = $100.53

5. $12,000 + $13,000 + $40,000 = $65,000
$65,000 − $40,000 = $25,000
or
$12,000 + $13,000 = $25,000
$25,000 ÷ $100 = 250
250 × $1.75 = $437.50

6. $40,000 × .25 = $10,000
$40,000 − $10,000 = $30,000
$30,000 ÷ $500 = 60
60 × $.55 = $33

7. $20,000 + $25,000 + $10,000 = $55,000
$55,000 − $20,000 = $35,000
$35,000 ÷ $500 = 70
70 × $.75 = $52.50

8. $30,000 × .08 = $2,400
$2,400 ÷ 12 = $200
$250 − $200 = $50
$30,000 − $50 = $29,950
$74,000 − $29,950 = $44,050
$44,050 ÷ $500 = 88.1 or 89
89 × $.50 = $44.50

SOLUTIONS: PROBLEMS FOR ADDITIONAL PRACTICE

1. (d): $84,000 − $52,000 = $32,000
$32,000 ÷ $500 = 64
64 × $.45 = $28.80

2. (b): $54,000 − $14,000 = $40,000
$40,000 ÷ $500 = 80
80 × $.50 = $40

3. (a): $85,000 − $56,500 = $28,500
$28,500 ÷ $500 = 57
57 × $.50 = $28.50

4. (d): $112,000 × .02 = $2,240

5. (d): $95,000 ÷ $100 = 950
950 × $.30 = $285
$95,000 − $68,000 = $27,000
$27,000 ÷ $500 = 54
54 × $.50 = $27
$285 + $27 = $312

6. (a): $89.50 ÷ .50 = $179
$179 × $500 = $89,500

7. (b): $84,000 ÷ $100 = 840
840 × $.12 = $100.80
840 × $.30 = $252
$100.80 + $252 = $352.80

Legal Descriptions

Property must be legally described and identified before a correct transfer can be made. Legal descriptions in many states are based on the rectangular survey system. In this chapter, we will cover the mathematical computations involved in property descriptions using the rectangular survey system. Subdivisions of larger tracts of undeveloped land generally have lot and block property descriptions, such as "Lot 12, Block 34, Green Garden Subdivision to the city of Able, County of Baker, State of Charlie." This form of legal description will not be discussed because no mathematical computations are involved. Occasionally, you may encounter a metes-and-bounds description. This chapter will introduce this method because it is important that you be able to convert such a description into a sketch (which may be drawn exactly to scale) of the shape of the subject property.

At the conclusion of your work in this chapter, you will be able to

■ accurately determine the number of acres in a tract of land described using the rectangular survey system and
■ sketch a tract of land described by the metes-and-bounds system.

Because readers will have varying amounts of knowledge and experience, the problems that follow will allow you to determine your familiarity with the material to be covered. Try all of the problems before checking your answers against the answer key at the end of the chapter.

1. Henry Williams owned the SW $\frac{1}{4}$ of a section of land. He sold the W $\frac{1}{2}$ of the NW $\frac{1}{4}$ of the SW $\frac{1}{4}$ at $275 an acre and he sold the SW $\frac{1}{4}$ of the SW $\frac{1}{4}$ at $250 an acre. How much money did Mr. Williams receive for the land?

   a. $5,500
   b. $10,000

   c. $15,500
   d. $12,500

2. How many acres did Mr. Williams sell in problem 1?

   a. 100   c. 80

   b. 60   d. 160

3. How many acres does Mr. Williams still own (see problems 1 and 2)?

   a. 100   c. 50

   b. 80   d. 40

4. How many acres are contained in the following tract of land?

". . . . to a point of beginning; thence South 45° 0′ 0″ West 300 feet; thence North 45° 0′ 0″ West 350 feet; thence North 45° 0′ 0″ East 300 feet; thence South 45° 0′ 0″ East 350 feet to the point of beginning."

   a. 2.41   c. 2.07

   b. 3.60   d. 2.81

5. How many acres are in the W $\frac{1}{2}$ of the NE $\frac{1}{4}$ of the SW $\frac{1}{4}$ of the NW $\frac{1}{4}$ of Section 34?

   a. 5   c. 2.5

   b. 50   d. 40

RECTANGULAR SURVEY SYSTEM

The basic unit of measurement in the *rectangular survey system method* is the *township*—an area 6 miles square (36 square miles).

A township is divided into 36 *sections,* each 1 mile square (1 square mile), and identified by numbers, always in the sequence shown at the right. Section 1 is always at the northeast corner of the township.

Each section, in turn, can be divided into halves, quarters and smaller subdivisions.

6 mi.					
6	5	4	3	2	1
7	8	9	10	11	12
18	17	16	15	14	13
19	20	21	22	23	24
30	29	28	27	26	25
31	32	33	34	35	36

6 mi.

1 mi.

1 mi.

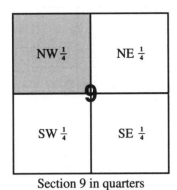

Section 9 in quarters

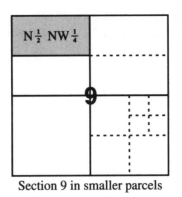

Section 9 in smaller parcels

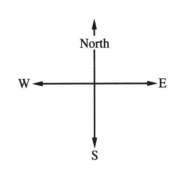

A section of land contains 640 acres and is 1 mile square, or 5,280 feet by 5,280 feet. The diagram at the left, above, shows a section divided into quarters. The shaded part is described as the NW $\frac{1}{4}$ (*northwest quarter*) of section 9. To find the number of acres in the shaded quarter, convert the fractions to decimals and multiply 640 by the decimals.

$$\frac{1}{4} = .25$$

$$640 \times .25 = 160 \text{ acres}$$

The shaded area in the middle diagram, above, is described as the N $\frac{1}{2}$ of the NW $\frac{1}{4}$ of section 9. (The location described is found by reading the parts of the description backwards. In this case, the NW $\frac{1}{4}$ of section 9 is found, then the N $\frac{1}{2}$ of that NW $\frac{1}{4}$.) The acres can be computed by either of two methods.

You can find the acreage of any part of a section by multiplying 640 (acres) by the fraction(s) *converted to decimals* in the description.

$$\frac{1}{2} = .50 \qquad \frac{1}{4} = .25$$

$$640 \times .50 \times .25 = 80 \text{ acres}$$

Pay careful attention to the words *of* and *and*. Each time you read *of* (such as, SW $\frac{1}{4}$ *of* section 3), multiply by the decimal shown. However, each time you read *and*, start a new calculation and add the result to prior results.

Another way to calculate the number of acres is to divide 640 by the denominators in the legal description.

EXAMPLE:

N $\frac{1}{2}$ of the SW $\frac{1}{4}$ of the NE $\frac{1}{4}$ of section 17

$\downarrow$ $\downarrow$ $\downarrow$

640 ÷ 2   ÷   4   ÷   4 = 20 acres

1. Determine the number of acres contained in the shaded area of the diagram at the right. The description of the parcel is as follows: SE $\frac{1}{4}$ of the SE $\frac{1}{4}$ of section 10.

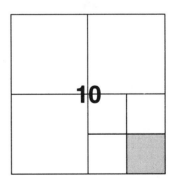

2. Find the number of acres contained in the shaded area of the diagram at the right. The property is described as follows: NW $\frac{1}{4}$ of the SW $\frac{1}{4}$ of the NE $\frac{1}{4}$ of section 12.

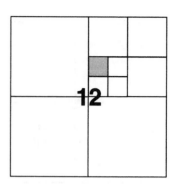

3. The diagram at the right shows a section of land. Determine the number of acres in each of the lettered areas.

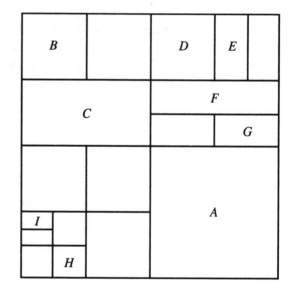

A. SE $\frac{1}{4}$

B. W $\frac{1}{2}$ of the N $\frac{1}{2}$ of the NW $\frac{1}{4}$ (or, NW $\frac{1}{4}$ of the NW $\frac{1}{4}$)

C. S $\frac{1}{2}$ of the NW $\frac{1}{4}$

D. NW $\frac{1}{4}$ of the NE $\frac{1}{4}$

E. W $\frac{1}{2}$ of the NE $\frac{1}{4}$ of the NE $\frac{1}{4}$

F. N $\frac{1}{2}$ of the S $\frac{1}{2}$ of the NE $\frac{1}{4}$

G. E $\frac{1}{2}$ of the S $\frac{1}{2}$ of the S $\frac{1}{2}$ of the NE $\frac{1}{4}$ (or, S $\frac{1}{2}$ of the SE $\frac{1}{4}$ of the NE $\frac{1}{4}$)

H. SE $\frac{1}{4}$ of the SW $\frac{1}{4}$ of the SW $\frac{1}{4}$

I. N $\frac{1}{2}$ of the NW $\frac{1}{4}$ of the SW $\frac{1}{4}$ of the SW $\frac{1}{4}$

4. How many acres does the shaded area in the diagram at the right contain?

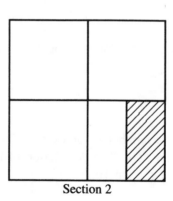

Section 2

5. Locate and shade in the NE $\frac{1}{4}$ of the NW $\frac{1}{4}$ of section 3, shown at the right. How many acres does the parcel contain?

Section 3

6. Locate and shade in the S $\frac{1}{2}$ of the S $\frac{1}{2}$ of the S $\frac{1}{2}$ of section 4, shown at the right. How many acres does the parcel contain?

Section 4

7. Dale Martin owns the SW $\frac{1}{4}$ of the SW $\frac{1}{4}$ of a section of unimproved land. If similar land in the area is selling for $1,240 per acre, how much is Mr. Martin's property worth?

8. The Valley Development Corporation bought a piece of land described as the W $\frac{1}{2}$ of the S $\frac{1}{2}$ of the S $\frac{1}{2}$ of the NE $\frac{1}{4}$ of section 24. If a total of $120,000 was paid for the land, how much did it cost per acre?

9. John Cordova owned the NE $\frac{1}{4}$ of a section. He sold the S $\frac{1}{2}$ of the NE $\frac{1}{4}$. How many acres does he still own?

10. Mr. Cordova sold the NW $\frac{1}{4}$ of the NE $\frac{1}{4}$ for $144,000. Based on this price per acre, how much would you pay for the E $\frac{1}{2}$ of the NE $\frac{1}{4}$ of the NE $\frac{1}{4}$?

11. Horace Tucker and William Lawson formed a corporation. Each conveyed real estate in return for shares of stock in the company, as indicated below:

Tucker: N $\frac{1}{2}$ of the NW $\frac{1}{4}$ of the SW $\frac{1}{4}$ of the SW $\frac{1}{4}$ *and* the SE $\frac{1}{4}$ of the SW $\frac{1}{4}$ of the SW $\frac{1}{4}$ of section 2

Lawson: SW $\frac{1}{4}$ of the NW $\frac{1}{4}$ of the SE $\frac{1}{4}$ of the NW $\frac{1}{4}$ of section 3 *and* the W $\frac{1}{2}$ of the SW $\frac{1}{4}$ of section 4

The corporation issued 500 shares of stock for each acre received.

a. How many shares did Tucker receive?
b. How many shares did Lawson receive?

METES-AND-BOUNDS DESCRIPTIONS

Another system of describing real estate is known as *metes and bounds.* This system relies on the metes (measures of distances) and bounds (directions or courses) as described by the surveyor in his or her field notes. Surveying is an exacting profession requiring licensure by most states. Real estate licensees should never attempt to prepare a metes-and-bounds legal description. For example, if the survey does not "close" (the point of ending is not the same as the point of beginning), the survey is defective. If the legal description is defective, the sales contract cannot be enforced, or the deed can be set aside.

Most real estate licensees will rarely need to construct a plat or scaled sketch from a set of field notes. However, if the need does arise, it is important to know how to do it.

First, we need to recognize that the directions stated in a metes-and-bounds description are the compass directions for all boundary lines. We might say that something lies *northwest* of a certain place or we might say that it lies *westnorth.* Although both words point us in the same direction, through accepted convention, we say *northwest, southeast* and so on. We recite the north or south direction *first,* followed by the direction of declination from north or south. So it is with metes-and-bounds descriptions. For example, the surveyor's call "N30°E" means that the direction of the subject line is 30 degrees east of due north. In other words, we look due north and then we pivot 30 degrees to the right and look again. If we now look due east and then we pivot 60 degrees to the left, we are looking in the same direction as before. This is because the compass is divided into 360 degrees, then further subdivided into minutes and seconds. Each degree is divided into 60 minutes (denoted by the symbol ′) and each minute is divided into 60 seconds (″).

In Figure 12.1, we see that, by convention, due north is toward the top of the page, east is to the right, south is toward the bottom and west is to the left. The compass circle is divided into four quadrants, as shown, so that our example of the call "N30°E" lies in the northeast or upper right quadrant. In like manner, the call "S45°W" lies in the southwest or lower left quadrant. Due north and due south are each 0 degrees; due east and due west are each 90 degrees.

In preparing a metes-and-bounds description, we must now add the *distances* to our call, which so far contains only directions. In surveyor's "shorthand," this is done by adding the distance or length of the line after the direction, so that a boundary line 1,000 feet long running in a northeasterly direction might appear as "N30°E 1,000 ft."—or "N30°30′30″E 1,000 ft.," if the line is not exactly 30 degrees east of north. Such a line would lie in a direction 30 degrees, 30 minutes and 30 seconds east of north.

FIGURE 12.1

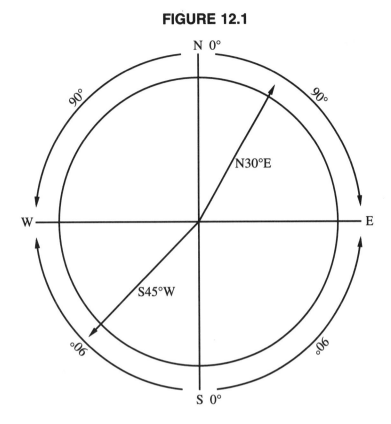

Let us examine a simple set of metes-and-bounds field notes. If the subject property is described as

Beginning at the southwest corner of the Robert B. Hart Survey, Tarrant County, Texas,

THENCE N0°E 2,640 feet;
THENCE N90°E 5,280 feet;
THENCE S0°W 2,640 feet;
THENCE S90°W 5,280 feet to the point of beginning,

we have a rectangular tract of land whose dimensions are 2,640 feet in the north-south direction and 5,280 feet in the east-west direction. This amounts to 320 acres, or one-half of a section (2,640 × 5,280 = 13,939,200; 13,939,200 ÷ 43,560 = 320).

To convert the metes-and-bounds description to a sketch or scaled drawing, we must use a protractor to measure the directions or angles and a scale or ruler to measure the distances. To used these tools, follow the steps below:

1. Place the center of the protractor (most protractors have a small hole at this point) directly over the point on the paper from which the indicated direction is to be measured.
2. Carefully align the protractor so that its straight bottom is exactly horizontal to the paper's edge. This will mean that the straight portion is lined up in the east-west direction on your paper.
3. Notice the direction from north of the metes-and-bounds call.
4. On the curved outer scale of the protractor, locate the number of degrees from north indicated by the call (in our example, it was 0 degrees).
5. Place a dot on the paper at 0 on the protractor.

6. Remove the protractor and, with a suitable scale, draw a line from the beginning point through the dot just made. The length of this line represents the distance shown in the call (in our example, it was 2,640 feet).

7. Move the protractor to the end of this line and position it so that its center (or the small hole) is directly over the end of the line just drawn.

8. Repeat the above steps until you arrive at the point of beginning. If you successfully arrive at this point, your survey is said to "close." If it does not close, either the field notes are defective or (more likely) you have erred in constructing the scaled sketch.

Draw your sketch of the above example here:

Your sketch should look like this:

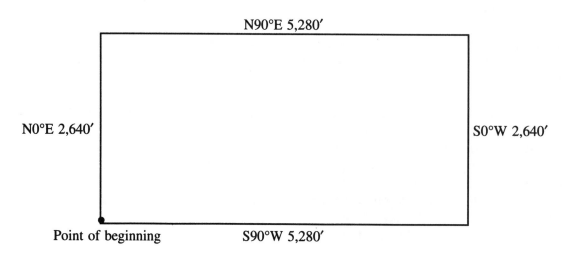

N90°E 5,280′

N0°E 2,640′   S0°W 2,640′

Point of beginning   S90°W 5,280′

Let's try another one:

Beginning at the northeast corner of the William H. Long Survey, Coleman County, Texas,

THENCE S45°W 1,000 feet;
THENCE S90°W 2,000 feet;
THENCE N45°E 1,000 feet;
THENCE N90°E 2,000 feet to the point of beginning

Your sketch should be in the shape of a parallelogram 2,000 feet in the east-west direction and 1,000 feet in the diagonal direction, which should be inclined below and to the left of the starting point. Draw your sketch here:

Your sketch should look like this:

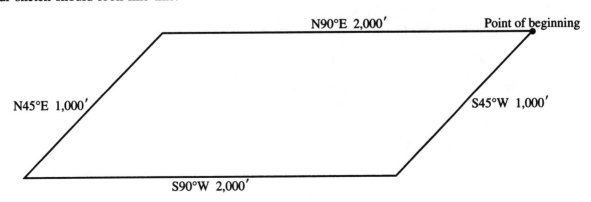

When you have finished these problems, check your answers at the end of the chapter. If you miss any of the problems, review this chapter before going on to Chapter 13.

1. The S $\frac{1}{2}$ of the SW $\frac{1}{4}$ of the NW $\frac{1}{4}$ of section 4 was sold for $1,150 per acre. How much did the parcel sell for?

   a. $29,000   c. $26,000
   b. $21,500   d. $23,000

2. If the S $\frac{1}{2}$ of the NW $\frac{1}{4}$ of the NE $\frac{1}{4}$ of the SW $\frac{1}{4}$ of section 24 sold for $1,325 per acre, what was the total price?

   a. $6,625   c. $53,000
   b. $13,250   d. $3,313

3. The Rand family owned the entire SW $\frac{1}{4}$ of section 5. They sold the S $\frac{1}{2}$ of the SW $\frac{1}{4}$ of the SW $\frac{1}{4}$ of section 5 at $2,000 per acre. They also sold the SW $\frac{1}{4}$ of the SE $\frac{1}{4}$ of the SW $\frac{1}{4}$ of section 5 at $2,500 per acre. How much money did the Rands receive?

   a. $25,000   c. $40,000
   b. $65,000   d. $45,000

4. Hannah Schwartz owned acreage described as the NW $\frac{1}{4}$ of section 7. She sold half of her property for $5,000 per acre and a quarter of the balance for $4,500 per acre. What was the total sales price?

   a. $400,000   c. $450,000
   b. $490,000   d. $500,000

5. Emil and Emett Emory owned section 17. They sold the following three tracts of land: W $\frac{1}{2}$ of the SW $\frac{1}{4}$; NE $\frac{1}{4}$ of the SW $\frac{1}{4}$; and N $\frac{1}{2}$ of the SE $\frac{1}{4}$. Their remaining acreage totals

   a. 400.   c. 440.
   b. 320.   d. 460.

6. Which of the following tracts is the largest?

   a. NW $\frac{1}{4}$ of the NW $\frac{1}{4}$ of the SE $\frac{1}{4}$ of section 1
   b. S $\frac{1}{2}$ of the SE $\frac{1}{4}$ of the SE $\frac{1}{4}$ of the NW $\frac{1}{4}$ of section 3
   c. SE $\frac{1}{4}$ of the SE $\frac{1}{4}$ of the NW $\frac{1}{4}$ *and* the SW $\frac{1}{4}$ of the NE $\frac{1}{4}$ of section 7
   d. All three tracts are of equal size.

7. Which of the following tracts totals 20 acres?

   a. N $\frac{1}{2}$ of the SW $\frac{1}{4}$ of the NE $\frac{1}{4}$ of the SW $\frac{1}{4}$ of section 6
   b. NW $\frac{1}{4}$ of the SE $\frac{1}{4}$ of the NW $\frac{1}{4}$ of section 9
   c. S $\frac{1}{2}$ of the NE $\frac{1}{4}$ of the SW $\frac{1}{4}$ of section 8
   d. S $\frac{1}{2}$ of the S $\frac{1}{2}$ of the S $\frac{1}{2}$ of section 10

8. What price per acre was paid for the W $\frac{1}{2}$ of the NE $\frac{1}{4}$ of the NE $\frac{1}{4}$ of section 1 and the SE $\frac{1}{4}$ of the NE $\frac{1}{4}$ of the NE $\frac{1}{4}$ of section 1 if the total parcel sold for $180,000?

a. $600

b. $3,000

c. $6,000

d. $4,500

9. How many square feet are in the following tract of land?

". . . . to a point of beginning; thence, due South for 400 feet; thence North 45° West 562.5 feet; thence due East 400 feet to the point of beginning."

a. 112,500

b. 160,000

c. 80,000

d. 225,000

10. How many acres are in the tract of land described in problem 9?

a. 1.84

b. 3.67

c. 2.58

d. 5.17

ANSWER KEY

SOLUTIONS: WARM-UP EXERCISES

1. (c): $640 \times .50 \times .25 \times .25 = 20$
$20 \times \$275 = \$5,500$
$640 \times .25 \times .25 = 40$
$40 \times \$250 = \$10,000$
$\$10,000 + \$5,500 = \$15,500$

2. (b): $20 + 40 = 60$

3. (a): $160 - 60 = 100$

4. (a): $300' \times 350' = 105,000$ square feet
$105,000$ square feet $\div 43,560 = 2.41$ acres (rounded)

5. (a): $640 \times .50 \times .25 \times .25 \times .25 = 5$

SOLUTIONS: CHAPTER PROBLEMS

1. $640 \times .25 \times .25 = 40$

2. $640 \times .25 \times .25 \times .25 = 10$

3. *A.* $640 \times .25 = 160$
 B. $640 \times .50 \times .50 \times .25 = 40$
 C. $640 \times .50 \times .25 = 80$
 D. $640 \times .25 \times .25 = 40$
 E. $640 \times .50 \times .25 \times .25 = 20$
 F. $640 \times .50 \times .50 \times .25 = 40$
 G. $640 \times .50 \times .50 \times .50 \times .25 = 20$
 H. $640 \times .25 \times .25 \times .25 = 10$
 I. $640 \times .50 \times .25 \times .25 \times .25 = 5$

4. $640 \times .50 \times .25 = 80$

5. $640 \times .25 \times .25 = 40$

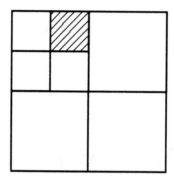

6. $640 \times .50 \times .50 \times .50 = 80$

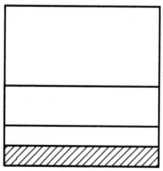

7. $640 \times .25 \times .25 = 40$
 $\$1,240 \times 40 = \$49,600$

8. $640 \times .50 \times .50 \times .50 \times .25 = 20$
 $\$120,000 \div 20 = \$6,000$

9. $640 \times .25 = 160$
 $160 \times .50 = 80$
 $160 - 80 = 80$

10. $640 \times .25 \times .25 = 40$
 $\$144,000 \div 40 = \$3,600$
 $640 \times .50 \times .25 \times .25 = 20$
 $20 \times \$3,600 = \$72,000$

11. a. $640 \times .50 \times .25 \times .25 \times .25 = 5$ b. $640 \times .25 \times .25 \times .25 \times .25 = 2.5$
 $640 \times .25 \times .25 \times .25 = 10$ $640 \times .50 \times .25 = 80$
 $10 + 5 = 15$ $80 + 2.5 = 82.5$
 $15 \times 500 = 7,500$ $82.5 \times 500 = 41,250$

SOLUTIONS: PROBLEMS FOR ADDITIONAL PRACTICE

1. (d): $640 \times .50 \times .25 \times .25 = 20$
$20 \times \$1,150 = \$23,000$

2. (a): $640 \times .50 \times .25 \times .25 \times .25 = 5$
$5 \times \$1,325 = \$6,625$

3. (b): $640 \times .50 \times .25 \times .25 = 20$
$20 \times \$2,000 = \$40,000$
$640 \times .25 \times .25 \times .25 = 10$
$10 \times \$2,500 = \$25,000$
$25,000 + \$40,000 = \$65,000$

4. (b): $640 \times .25 = 160$
$160 \times .50 = 80$
$80 \times .25 = 20$
$80 \times \$5,000 = \$400,000$
$20 \times \$4,500 = \$90,000$
$\$90,000 + \$400,000 = \$490,000$

5. (c): $640 \times .50 \times .25 = 80$
$640 \times .25 \times .25 = 40$
$640 \times .50 \times .25 = 80$
$80 + 40 + 80 = 200$
$640 - 200 = 440$

6. (c): a. $640 \times .25 \times .25 \times .25 = 10$
b. $640 \times .50 \times .25 \times .25 \times .25 = 5$
c. $640 \times .25 \times .25 \times .25 = 10$
$640 \times .25 \times .25 = 40$
$40 + 10 = 50$

7. (c): a. $640 \times .50 \times .25 \times .25 \times .25 = 5$
b. $640 \times .25 \times .25 \times .25 = 10$
c. $640 \times .50 \times .25 \times .25 = 20$
d. $640 \times .50 \times .50 \times .50 = 80$

8. (c): $640 \times .50 \times .25 \times .25 = 20$
$640 \times .25 \times .25 \times .25 = 10$
$10 + 20 = 30$
$\$180,000 \div 30 = \$6,000$

9. (c):

$400' \times 400' \div 2 = 80,000$ square feet

10. (a): 80,000 square feet $\div$ 43,560 square feet $= 1.84$ acres (rounded)

Prorations

To *prorate* certain expenses of a real estate transaction is to divide the items *proportionally* between the seller and the buyer. We prorate to equitably divide the on-going expenses of a property between the buyer and the seller. The seller gives money to the buyer for items that have not yet become due, such as interest. The buyer gives money to the seller for items that the seller paid in advance, but that have not been fully used, such as insurance premiums on a hazard insurance policy being assumed. Items that are typically prorated at the closing of a real estate transaction are

- ad valorem taxes;
- loan interest, when there is an assumption of an existing loan;
- insurance premiums;
- rents;
- maintenance fees; and
- propane, fuel oil, coal and so on.

Delinquent monthly payments, late charges and security deposits are not prorated, but simply transferred from the seller to the buyer at closing or paid to the third parties to whom they are owed from the seller's proceeds. Prorated items appear on a closing statement as debits or charges to one of the parties and as credits to the other party. Any prorated charge or prorated debit to one party is always a credit to the other party. For example, a charge to the seller for the ad valorem taxes from January 1 through closing will show as a credit to the buyer.

Some of the items that get prorated are paid *in advance,* such as insurance premiums and maintenance fees, and some are paid *in arrears,* such as taxes and interest. Items paid in advance are paid before a party receives the benefit or incurs the expense. Items paid in arrears will be paid in full by the buyer at a later date.

It should also be noted that prorations may be done *to* or *through* the day of closing. The purchase agreement (earnest money contract) between the buyer and the seller should specify which party will pay for the actual day of closing. When an item is prorated *to* closing, the buyer pays for the day of closing. When an item is prorated *through* closing, the seller pays for the day of closing.

When calculating prorations, some areas of the country typically use a *banker's* or a *statutory* year.

$$1 \text{ year} = 12 \text{ months of } 30 \text{ days}$$
$$1 \text{ year} = 360 \text{ days}$$

Other areas use a *calendar* year in the calculation of prorations.

1 year = 12 months of 28 to 31 days
1 year = 365 days in a *regular* calendar year
366 days in a *leap* year

On the real estate exam, salesperson and broker candidates may be asked to prorate *to* or *through* the day of closing using either the banker's (statutory) or calendar year. Read the problems carefully for these details.

At the conclusion of your work in this chapter, you will be able to accurately calculate prorations for taxes, interest, insurance and rents using both the 360-day and the 365-day years.

WARM-UP EXERCISES

Because readers will have varying amounts of experience and knowledge, the problems that follow will allow you to determine your familiarity with the material to be covered. Try all of the problems before checking your answers against the answer key at the end of the chapter.

1. Mr. Donaldson is selling his home. He made a monthly mortgage payment on July 1 that paid interest through June 30. His principal balance is now $22,450.40; the interest rate is 11%. The closing is set for July 21 and the buyer will assume the loan. What amount of accrued interest will be credited to the buyer? (Prorate through the date of closing using a regular calendar year.)

   a. $141.70
   b. $144.06

   c. $142.08
   d. $146.04

2. Patsy Miller has a one-year insurance policy that expires on December 14. The policy was purchased at a cost of $959. Figure the premium proration that the buyer will owe the seller at the closing on June 18. (Prorate through the date of closing using a banker's year.)

   a. $468.16
   b. $677.13

   c. $463.52
   d. $466.18

3. Taxes on Fredda York's home are $2.28 per $100 of assessed valuation. What amount would Ms. York be charged for an August 15 closing on her home, assessed at $187,650, using a calendar leap year and charging the seller to the day of closing?

   a. $2,653.56
   b. $2,660.83

   c. $2,665.25
   d. $2,687.78

4. Nancy Hendricks is selling her home, which has a garage apartment that rents for $465 per month. If the rent was paid on September 1, what amount will Ms. Hendricks be charged through the day of closing for the rent proration? (The closing is on September 18.)

a. $279

b. $186

c. $270

d. $180

5. Carl Willet is purchasing the home of Alan Smith. Taxes will be due on December 31. The sales agreement calls for the seller to pay expenses for the day of closing. If the annual taxes are $3,212, what credit will Mr. Willet receive at closing on August 8 using a statutory year?

a. $1,918.40

b. $1,945.04

c. $1,266.96

d. $1,246.19

For all proration problems, you must determine

- the annual cost (monthly cost for rent);
- the number of days to be charged;
- the amount to be credited or debited;
- the party to receive the credit; and
- the party to receive the debit.

The following charts create time-lines to show the period of time to be prorated for taxes, interest, insurance, rent and maintenance fees. Figure 13.1 prorates *through* the day of closing, which means the seller pays the expense for closing day. Figure 13.2 prorates *to* the day of closing, which means the buyer pays the expense for closing day.

FIGURE 13.1
PRORATIONS THROUGH THE DAY OF CLOSING

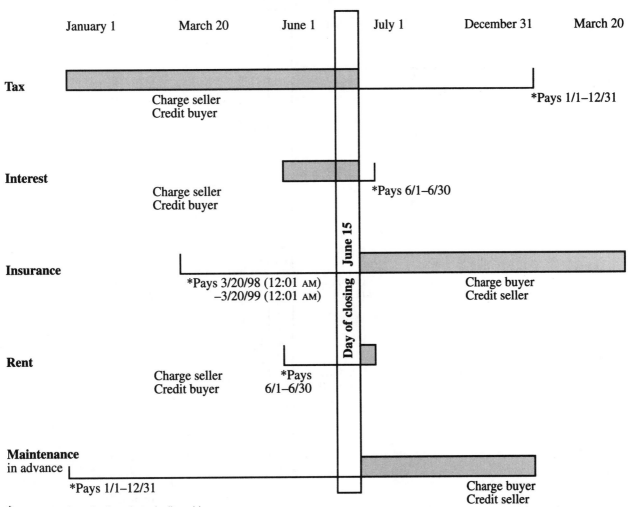

* Indicates when the item is typically paid.

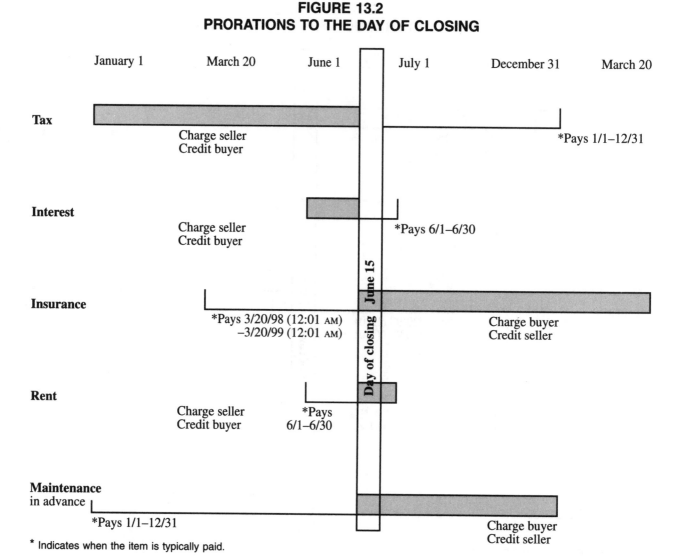

FIGURE 13.2
PRORATIONS TO THE DAY OF CLOSING

* Indicates when the item is typically paid.

PRORATING TAXES

When prorating ad valorem taxes, calculate the amount of money the seller will pay to the buyer for that portion of the year the seller owns the house. Taxes are usually paid in *arrears* and represent a *charge* to the seller and a *credit* to the buyer. Follow the three steps below:

Step 1. Determine the number of days to be charged to or through the closing date.

Step 2. Calculate the dollar amount per day.

Annual tax ÷ Days in year = $ per day

Step 3. Calculate the proration by multiplying the total from step 2 by the total from step 1.

$ per day × Days due = Proration

You may duplicate the following to help you calculate the ad valorem tax proration:

Step 1. Calculate the days due.

J   F   M   A   M   J   J   A   S   O   N   D = Days due

__ + __ + __ + __ + __ + __ + __ + __ + __ + __ + __ + __ = _____

Step 2. Calculate the $ per day.

Annual tax ÷ Days in year = $ per day
(Do not clear your calculator; do not round; move on to step 3.)

Step 3. Calculate the proration.

Step 2   × Step 1   = Step 3
$ per day × Days due = Proration
$_____ × _____ = $_____

EXAMPLE: Using a banker's or statutory year, prorate the taxes for a June 18 closing if the annual tax bill is $1,440 and is prorated through the day of closing.

Step 1.   J   F   M   A   M   J
          30 + 30 + 30 + 30 + 30 + 18 = 168 days due

Step 2.   Annual tax ÷ Days in year = $ per day
          $1,440 ÷ 360 = $4 per day

Step 3. $ per day × Days due = Proration
          $4 × 168 = $672 debit seller/credit buyer

Using a regular calendar year, it would look like this:

Step 1.   J   F   M   A   M   J
          31 + 28 + 31 + 30 + 31 + 18 = 169 days due

Step 2.   Annual tax ÷ Days in year = $ per day
          $1,440 ÷ 365 = $3.94521 per day

Step 3. $ per day × Days due = Proration
          $3.94521 × 169 = $666.74 debit seller/credit buyer (rounded)

In a leap year, it would look like this:

Step 1.   J   F   M   A   M   J
          31 + 29 + 31 + 30 + 31 + 18 = 170 days due

Step 2.   Annual tax ÷ Days in year = $ per day
          $1,440 ÷ 366 = $3.93443 per day

Step 3. $ per day × Days due = Proration
          $3.93443 × 170 = $668.85 debit seller/credit buyer (rounded)

Now you try one.

For a closing on August 28, what would you charge the seller if the annual tax bill is $1,680 and the proration is calculated through the day of closing?

Banker's year:

Step 1. J   F   M   A   M   J   J   A
    __ + __ + __ + __ + __ + __ + __ + __ = _____ days due

Step 2. Annual tax ÷ Days in year = $ per day
    $_____ ÷ _____ = $_____

Step 3. $ per day × Days due = Proration
    $_____ × _____ = $_____ debit seller/credit buyer

Calendar year (regular):

Step 1. J   F   M   A   M   J   J   A
    __ + __ + __ + __ + __ + __ + __ + __ = _____ days due

Step 2. Annual tax ÷ Days in year = $ per day
    $_____ ÷ _____ = $_____

Step 3. $ per day × Days due = Proration
    $_____ × _____ = $_____ debit seller/credit buyer

Calendar year (leap year):

Step 1. J   F   M   A   M   J   J   A
    __ + __ + __ + __ + __ + __ + __ + __ = _____ days due

Step 2. Annual tax ÷ Days in year = $ per day
    $_____ ÷ _____ = $_____

Step 3. $ per day × Days due = Proration
    $_____ × _____ = $_____ debit seller/credit buyer

Check your answers:

Banker's year:

Step 1. J   F   M   A   M   J   J   A
    30 + 30 + 30 + 30 + 30 + 30 + 30 + 28 = _238_ days due

Step 2. Annual tax ÷ Days in year = $ per day
    $1,680 ÷ 360 = $4.66667

Step 3. $ per day × Days due = Proration
    $4.66667 × _238_ = $1,110.67 debit seller/credit buyer

Calendar year (regular):

Step 1. J   F   M   A   M   J   J   A
    31 + 28 + 31 + 30 + 31 + 30 + 31 + 28 = _240_ days due

Step 2. Annual tax ÷ Days in year = $ per day
$1,680   ÷   365   = $4.60274

Step 3. $ per day × Days due = Proration
$4.60274 ×   240   = $1,104.66 debit seller/credit buyer

Calendar year (leap year):

Step 1. J   F   M   A   M   J   J   A
31 + 29 + 31 + 30 + 31 + 30 + 31 + 28 = 241   days due

Step 2. Annual tax ÷ Days in year = $ per day
$1,680   ÷   366   = $4.59016

Step 3. $ per day × Days due = Proration
$4.59016 ×   241   = $1,106.23 debit seller/credit buyer

If the purchase agreement called for the taxes to be prorated *to* the day of closing, each of the above examples would cost the seller one day less.

The above examples and the problems that follow assume that taxes are paid in arrears. When taxes are paid before the closing date, count the days from closing (prorated to) or from the day after closing (prorated through) through the end of the period for which the taxes have been paid in advance. Divide the tax bill by the number of days in the year and multiply by the number of days to be charged. When taxes have been paid in advance, you will debit the buyer and credit the seller.

1. Using a regular calendar year, prorate the taxes for a closing on November 30 on Mr. Langley's home, which has an annual tax bill of $2,840. The purchase agreement calls for Mr. Langley to pay through the day of closing.

2. Carl Davidson is selling his home to Erica Miller, who has agreed that all prorations will be calculated to the day of closing. If Mr. Davidson's home is assessed at $189,400 and the combined tax rate is $3.34 per $100 valuation, what will Mr. Davidson be charged at a May 23 closing? (Use a banker's year.)

PRORATING INTEREST ON LOANS BEING ASSUMED

Interest on loans is paid in *arrears*. Usually, the seller's loan payment is due on the first day of the month and includes the interest charge for the preceding month. For example, if you have a closing scheduled for March 23, you will charge the seller for 23 days of interest and credit it to the buyer. This is because the April 1 payment, which will be paid by the buyer when the loan is assumed, will include the interest charge for the entire month of March.

As with the proration of taxes, it is important to read the purchase agreement to see whether prorations are to be *to* or *through* the day of closing. In the examples that follow, the seller pays for the day of closing (through). If you were calculating *to* the day of closing, you would charge the seller for one day less.

You will again need to use three steps to prorate interest on loans being assumed:

Step 1. Determine the number of days to be charged to or through the closing date.

Step 2. Calculate the dollar amount per day.
Loan balance × Annual interest rate ÷ Days in year = $ per day

Step 3. Calculate the proration by multiplying the total from step 2 by the total from step 1.
$ per day × Days due = Proration, debit seller/credit buyer

You may duplicate the following to help you calculate the interest proration:

Step 1. Calculate the days due.

Count the days from the last payment to or through closing.

Step 2. Calculate the $ per day.

Loan balance × Annual interest rate ÷ Days in year = $ per day
(Do not clear your calculator; do not round; move on to step 3.)

Step 3. Calculate the proration.

Step 2   × Step 1   = Proration
$ per day × Days due = Proration
$_____ × _____ = $_____

EXAMPLE: Using a banker's year, calculate the proration of interest for an outstanding loan with a balance of $103,680 and an 8% annual interest rate. (Closing is scheduled for April 4 and the April 1 payment has been made.)

Step 1. April 4 = 4 days due

Step 2. Loan balance × Annual interest rate ÷ Days in year = $ per day
$103,680 × .08 ÷ 360 = $23.04

Step 3. $ per day × Days due = Proration
$23.04 × 4 = $92.16 debit seller/credit buyer

Using a regular calendar year, the above would look like this:

Step 1. April 4 = 4 days due

Step 2. Loan balance × Annual interest rate ÷ Day in year = $ per day
$103,680 × .08 ÷ 365 = $22.72438

Step 3. $ per day × Days due = Proration
$22.72438 × 4 = $90.90 debit seller/credit buyer

Now you try one.

For a closing on November 21, what credit would the buyer receive for interest on a loan being assumed if the loan balance is $68,374 and it carries an annual interest rate of 6.25%? (The purchase agreement calls for prorations to be calculated *to* the day of closing. Use a calendar year.)

Step 1. November 21 = _____ days due

Step 2. Loan balance × Annual interest rate ÷ Days in year = $ per day
$\qquad$ $\underline{\hspace{2cm}}$ × $\underline{\hspace{2.5cm}}$ ÷ $\underline{\hspace{2cm}}$ = $\underline{\hspace{1.5cm}}$

Step 3. $ per day × Days due = Proration
$\underline{\hspace{1.5cm}}$ × $\underline{\hspace{1.5cm}}$ = $\underline{\hspace{1.5cm}}$ debit seller/credit buyer

Check your answers:

Step 1. November 21 = 21 − 1 day = 20 days due
The buyer pays for the day of closing.

Step 2. Loan balance × Annual interest rate ÷ Days in year = $ per day
$68,374 × .0625 ÷ 365 = $11.70788

Step 3. $ per day × Days due = Proration
$11.70788 × 20 = $234.16 debit seller/credit buyer

3. Marion Murphy will assume a loan with an outstanding balance of $92,355 at an October 16 closing. The purchase agreement calls for the seller to pay through the day of closing. The annual interest rate on the loan is $6\frac{7}{8}\%$. What amount will the seller be charged at closing using a regular calendar year?

4. Prorate the interest using a banker's year for a March 17 closing if the loan balance is $43,560, the interest rate is 8.5% and the purchase agreement calls for all prorations to be to the day of closing.

PRORATING INSURANCE

Insurance premiums are paid in *advance* of the period covered by the policy. When an insurance policy is assumed by a buyer at closing, you will need to calculate the unused number of days and charge the buyer to reimburse the seller for the unused part of the premium.

Again, we shall use a three-step process to determine the insurance proration. In our examples, the seller pays *through* the day of closing. If a purchase agreement called for prorations to be *to* the day of closing, you would add a day when you calculate the days due.

The three steps are as follows:

Step 1. Calculate the number of days from the closing to the day of expiration of the policy.

Step 2. Calculate the dollar amount per day.
Annual premium ÷ Days in year = $ per day

Step 3. Calculate the proration by multiplying the total from step 2 by the total from step 1.
$ per day × Days due = Proration

You may duplicate the following to help you calculate insurance prorations:

Step 1. Calculate the days due.

Days in month of closing – Closing date = Days due in month of closing

Days due in month of closing + Days in full months between closing and expiration + Date of expiration (prorating to) or date before expiration (prorating through) = Total days due

_____ + _____ + _____ = _____
Days in month of closing   Full months   Days in month of expiration   Total days

Step 2. Calculate the $ per day.

Annual premium ÷ Days in year = $ per day
(Do not clear your calculator; do not round; move on to step 3.)

Step 3. Calculate the proration.

Step 2   × Step 1   = Proration
$ per day   Days due   Proration
$_____ × _____ = $_____

EXAMPLE: A buyer is assuming a one-year homeowner's policy that was taken out on May 27, 1994, for an annual premium of $456.25. What amount of money will the seller receive from the buyer at closing to reimburse him for the unused portion of the policy? (The closing will take place on October 5, 1994, and the sales agreement calls for prorations to be calculated through the day of closing.)

Calendar year (regular):

Step 1.   Days in month of closing
           – Closing date
           _____
           Days due in month of closing
           Oct. 31   N   D   J   F   M   A   M
           –   5
           _____
                    26 + 30 + 31 + 31 + 28 + 31 + 30 + 26 = 233 days due

Had the sales agreement called for proration *to* the day of closing, you would add one additional day, for a total of 234 days.

Step 2. Annual premium ÷ Days in year = $ per day
        $456.25   ÷   365   = $1.25

Step 3. $ per day × Days due = Proration
        $1.25   ×   233   = $291.25 debit buyer/credit seller

Banker's year:

Step 1. Oct. 30

$$\begin{array}{cccccccccc} & 5 & N & D & J & F & M & A & M \\ \hline & 25 & + 30 & + 30 & + 30 & + 30 & + 30 & + 30 & + 26 = 231 \text{ days due} \end{array}$$

Step 2. Annual premium ÷ Days in year = $ per day
$456.25 ÷ 360 = $1.26736

Step 3. $ per day × Days due = Proration
$1.26736 × 231 = $292.76 debit buyer/credit seller

Now you try two problems.

Using a banker's year, prorate a one-year insurance policy being assumed by the buyer that will expire on December 23, 1996. (The transaction will close on February 21, 1996. The annual premium paid by the seller was $874. Prorate through the day of closing.)

Step 1. Feb 30

$$\begin{array}{ccccccccccc} - & 21 & M & A & M & J & J & A & S & O & N & D \\ \hline & \_\_ & + \_\_ & + \_\_ & + \_\_ & + \_\_ & + \_\_ & + \_\_ & + \_\_ & + \_\_ & + \_\_ & = _____ \text{ days due} \end{array}$$

Step 2. Annual premium ÷ Days in year = $ per day
$_____ ÷ _____ = $_____

Step 3. $ per day × Days due = Proration
$_____ × _____ = $_____ debit buyer/credit seller

Check your answers:

Step 1. Feb 30

$$\begin{array}{ccccccccccc} - & 21 & M & A & M & J & J & A & S & O & N & D \\ \hline & 9 & + 30 & + 30 & + 30 & + 30 & + 30 & + 30 & + 30 & + 30 & + 30 & + 22 = 301 \text{ days due} \end{array}$$

Step 2. Annual premium ÷ Days in year = $ per day
$874 ÷ 360 = $2.42778

Step 3. $ per day × Days due = Proration
$2.42778 × 301 = $730.76 debit buyer/credit seller

Using a calendar year, prorate an insurance policy that will be assumed at an August 28, 1995, closing. The policy was taken out on October 4, 1994, and will expire at 12:01 AM on October 4, 1995. The earnest money contract calls for all items to be prorated through the day of closing. The premium paid was $456.25.

Step 1. August 31

$$\begin{array}{cccc} - & 28 & S & O \\ \hline & \_\_ & + \_\_ & + \_\_ = _____ \text{ days due} \end{array}$$

Step 2. Annual premium ÷ Days in year = $ per day
$_____ ÷ _____ = $_____

Step 3. $ per day × Days due = Proration
$_____ × _____ = $_____ debit buyer/credit seller

Check your answers:

Step 1. August 31
   −   28   S   O
         _3_ + _30_ + _3_ = 36 days due

Step 2. Annual premium ÷ Days in year = $ per day
   $456.25   ÷   365   = $1.25

Step 3. $ per day × Days due = Proration
   $1.25   ×   36   = $45   debit buyer/credit seller

5. Mary Hughes paid $684 for a policy taken out on April 5. The buyer will assume the policy. Calculate the proration through the day of closing on December 19, preceding a leap year.

6. What is the charge to the buyer for an assumed insurance policy at an April 15 closing? The one-year policy was purchased by June Daubenspeck on May 15 of the previous year and the purchase agreement calls for all prorations to be to the day of closing using a banker's year. Mrs. Daubenspeck paid $650 for the annual premium.

PRORATING RENT

When a transaction involving rental units closes, only rents that have been paid before the closing day will be prorated. Usually, rents will be prorated through the day of closing. The seller will give the rent to the buyer for the days after closing through the end of the month. Any security deposit being held by the seller is not prorated and should be transferred to the buyer at closing. The buyer will be expected to refund it to the tenant at the end of the lease.

There are three steps in prorating rent:

Step 1. The number of days owed by the seller to the buyer.
   Total days in month − Closing date = Days due

Step 2. Calculate the dollar amount per day.
   Monthly rent ÷ Days in month = $ per day

Step 3. Calculate the proration by multiplying the total from step 2 by the total from step 1.
   $ per day × Days due = Proration

EXAMPLE: A duplex with a garage apartment is being sold and will close on September 16. All rents have been paid for September. Each side of the duplex rents for $500 per month and the garage apartment rents for $350 per month. Each tenant has paid the equivalent of one month's rent as a security deposit. How much will the buyer be credited at closing using a banker's year?

Step 1. September = 30 days
    Closing – <u>16</u>
        14 days due

Step 2. $500 + 500 + 350 = $1,350 total monthly rent
    Monthly rent ÷ Days in month = $ per day
    $1,350   ÷   30   = $45

Step 3. $ per day × Days due = Proration
    $45   ×   14   = $630 debit seller/credit buyer

The seller owes the buyer a total of $1,980 ($630 prorated rent + $1,350 security deposit).

Now you try one.

   Prorate the rent for a four-plex that will close on May 23. Three units are occupied, with the seller holding a security deposit of $200 for each unit. The rent of $400 per month per unit has been paid for May.

Step 1. May   = _____ days
    Closing – _____
      _____ days due

Step 2. Monthly rent ÷ Days in month = $ per day
    $_____ ÷ _____ = $_____

Step 3. $ per day × Days due = Proration
    $_____ × _____ = $_____
          + $_____ security deposit
          $_____ debit seller/credit buyer

Check your answers:

Step 1. May   = _____<u>31</u> days
    Closing – _____<u>23</u>
       ·8 days due

Step 2. Monthly rent ÷ Days in month = $ per day
    <u>$1,200</u>   ÷ <u>31</u> = <u>$38.70968</u>

Step 3. $ per day × Days due = Proration
    <u>$38.70968</u> × <u>8</u> = <u>$309.68</u>
        + <u>$600.00</u> security deposit
        <u>$909.68</u> debit seller/credit buyer

7. Philip Duram is purchasing Ute Cezeaux's duplex. The closing date is August 11. What credit will he receive if both tenants have paid their rent on August 1? (The upper unit rents for $1,250 and the lower unit rents for $1,650.)

8. Prorate the rent on a garage apartment for a February 16 closing in a leap year if the unit rents for $500 per month and the February rent has been paid.

PRORATING MAINTENANCE FEES

Homeowners' association dues and maintenance fees are typically paid in *advance* in January for the entire year. However, these charges may be assessed and collected monthly, quarterly or annually. The problems in this section will illustrate annual fees. To prorate, use the following three steps:

Step 1. Calculate the number of days from closing through the last day of December.

Step 2. Calculate the dollar amount per day.
Annual fee ÷ Days in year = $ per day

Step 3. Calculate the proration by multiplying the total from step 2 by the total from step 1.
$ per day × Days due = Proration

EXAMPLE: The annual maintenance fee of $250 was paid on January 1. What would you credit the seller for a September 15 closing using a banker's year, with the seller paying through the day of closing?

Step 1. September = 30 days
$$\underline{-15} \quad O \quad N \quad D$$
$$15 + 30 + 30 + 30 = 105 \text{ days due}$$

Step 2. Annual fee ÷ Days in year = $ per day
$250   ÷   360   = $.69445

Step 3. $ per day × Days due = Proration
$.69445   ×   105   = $72.92 debit buyer/credit seller

Now you try one.

The annual homeowners' association dues of $360 were paid in January. How much will the buyer be charged for a July 28 closing using a regular calendar year if prorations are calculated through the day of closing?

Step 1. July   = _____ days
Closing – _____   A   S   O   N   D
_____ + __ + __ + __ + __ + __ = _____ days due

Step 2. Annual fee ÷ Days in year = $ per day
$_____ ÷ _____ = $_____

Step 3. $ per day × Days due = Proration
$_____ × _____ = $_____ debit buyer/credit seller

Check your answers:

Step 1. July   _____31__ days
Closing –   __28__ A   S   O   N   D
__3 + 31 + 30 + 31 + 30 + 31 = 156__ days due

Step 2. Annual fee ÷ Days in year = $ per day
$360   ÷   365   = $.98630

Step 3. $ per day × Days due = Proration
$.98630   ×   156   = $153.86 debit buyer/credit seller

PRORATING MISCELLANEOUS ITEMS

For items such as propane gas or heating oil, calculate the value of the product remaining in the tank, then debit the buyer and credit the seller.

EXAMPLE: Thirty gallons of heating oil remain in the tank at closing. If the seller paid $1.10 per gallon when he filled the tank, the buyer would owe the seller 30 times $1.10 or $33 for the oil that he receives.

PROBLEMS FOR ADDITIONAL PRACTICE

Caution: In many state licensing exams, questions are designed to determine whether the examinee can carefully read and follow instructions. When reading a proration problem, be alert as to whether the calculation is to be *to* or *through* the day of closing and whether you are to base the calculation on a *banker's* or a *calendar* year. Practice in these matters will vary widely in different states. Your instructor may wish to assign only those problems that reflect local practice in your jurisdiction.

When you have finished these problems, check your answers at the end of the chapter. If you miss any of the problems, review this chapter before going on to Chapter 14.

1. A home with a market value of $175,000 was assessed at 82% of its value. The tax rate was $4.20 per $100. Figure the tax proration through the day of closing using a banker's year for a closing on June 1.

   a. $2,493.36
   b. $2,486.54
   c. $2,527.99
   d. $2,025.74

2. The previous year's taxes on Steve Seller's home were paid in full on December 31 and amounted to $2,753. Steve sold his home to Bill Buyer and closed the sale on May 4. What was the prorated tax amount using a regular calendar year and prorating to the day of closing? Was the proration a credit to the buyer or the seller?

   a. $935.27 credit buyer
   b. $948.26 credit buyer
   c. $935.27 credit seller
   d. $948.26 credit seller

3. The annual taxes on Sarah Williamson's house are $1,837.50. For a closing date of May 21, what will be the prorated amount using a banker's year? (The seller will pay for the day of closing.)

   a. $720.29
   b. $718.56
   c. $713.82
   d. $719.69

4. Cheryl Carter is purchasing the Landis house, which has been assessed at a value of $71,400 for tax purposes. If the tax rate is $2.17 per $100 and the sale will close on September 12 in a leap year, what will be the tax proration using a calendar year and prorating to the day of closing?

   a. $1,078.17
   b. $1,082.44
   c. $1,079.49
   d. $1,097.48

5. Annual taxes for a property that is set to close on July 16 are as follows: $350 for school tax, $280 for city tax and $177 for county tax. What is the tax proration using a regular calendar year and prorating through the day of closing?

   a. $441.61
   b. $435.56

   c. $434.37
   d. $433.35

6. After the monthly payment due on January 1 was made, $66,600 is the unpaid balance of a seller's 8% assumable mortgage. The purchaser assumed the seller's mortgage and the closing was set for January 16. Find the amount of accrued interest using a statutory year and prorating to the day of closing.

   a. $233.56
   b. $218.96

   c. $222.00
   d. $232.92

7. Using an interest rate of 8.5% on an outstanding mortgage balance of $102,743.50, calculate the proration on an assumption with a closing date of June 21. The June 1 payment has been made and the principal reduction is reflected in the above balance. Use a regular calendar year to calculate the proration through the day of closing.

   a. $502.46
   b. $501.09

   c. $478.53
   d. $455.74

8. After an October 1 monthly payment of $765.42 was made, the loan balance was $36,569.20. The assumable mortgage has an interest rate of 9%. Compute the proration using a regular calendar year if the day of closing is October 18. (The seller will pay through the day of closing.)

   a. $164.56
   b. $155.42

   c. $161.86
   d. $162.31

9. After the August 1 payment was made, Susie Seller's mortgage balance was $120,853. Her monthly payment of $1,160 includes principal and interest only on a $7\frac{3}{4}$% per annum loan. The sale of her home is to close on August 29. What will be the proration through closing using a banker's year?

   a. $742.12
   b. $728.48

   c. $744.16
   d. $754.49

10. The premium of $673 was paid in full for a one-year insurance policy that expires on May 21. The house sale is scheduled to close on February 1. Compute the proration through the day of closing using a statutory year.

   a. $203.77 debit buyer/credit seller
   b. $203.77 debit seller/credit buyer
   c. $469.23 debit seller/credit buyer
   d. $469.23 debit buyer/credit seller

11. The total annual premium for a $40,000 fire insurance policy is $615. This premium was paid on January 5. What will be the proration using a banker's year if the policy is transferred to the buyer at a closing on September 5. (The earnest money contract calls for the prorations to be calculated through the day of closing.)

   a. $200.51
   b. $201.63

   c. $203.29
   d. $205.00

12. Frank Fulton purchased a one-year homeowner's policy on January 12 and paid the $730 premium in full. He sold the home and closed on October 23. How much was Mr. Fulton's credit at closing using a regular calendar year if the buyer assumed the policy and the policy was prorated to the day of closing?

    a. $162.00
    b. $568.00

    c. $164.25
    d. $565.75

13. Ray Thomas paid the $844 insurance premium for a one-year policy on March 18. He will sell his home and close the sale on November 26. When the buyer assumes the policy, how much will the prorated amount be using a regular calendar year if Mr. Thomas pays through the day of closing?

    a. $253.66
    b. $256.67

    c. $260.23
    d. $254.36

14. The sale of Mrs. Gaston's home will close on September 28. Included in the sale is a garage apartment that is rented to Cindy Hart for $525 per month. Ms. Hart paid the security deposit of two months' rent when she leased the apartment and has paid the September rent. What is the rent proration?

    a. $35
    b. $1,085

    c. $490
    d. $1,540

15. An apartment complex contains 100 units, of which 50 units are one-bedrooms and rent for $600 per month; 30 units are two-bedrooms and rent for $825 per month; 20 units are three-bedrooms and rent for $1,100 per month. Prorate the rent for a closing in a leap year on February 18, assuming all units are occupied and have paid the rent for February.

    a. $30,151.79
    b. $29,112.07

    c. $27,410.71
    d. $26,465.52

ANSWER KEY

SOLUTIONS: WARM-UP EXERCISES

1. (c): $22,450.40 × .11 ÷ 365 = $6.765874 × 21 = $142.08

2. (d): June   J   A   S   O   N   D
       30 − 18 = 12 + 30 + 30 + 30 + 30 + 30 + 13 = 175
       $959 ÷ 360 = $2.6638889 × 175 = $466.18

3. (a): $187,650 ÷ 100 × $2.28 = $4,278.42
       J   F   M   A   M   J   J   A
       31 + 29 + 31 + 30 + 31 + 30 + 31 + 14 = 227
       $4,278.42 ÷ 366 = $11.689672 × 227 = $2,653.56

4. (b): 30 − 18 = 12
       $465 ÷ 30 = $15.50
       $15.50 × 12 = $186

5. (b): January–July = 7 months
       7 × 30 = 210
       210 + 8 = 218
       $3,212 ÷ 360 = $8.922222 × 218 = $1,945.04

SOLUTIONS: CHAPTER PROBLEMS

1. J F M A M J J A S O N
$31 + 28 + 31 + 30 + 31 + 30 + 31 + 31 + 30 + 31 + 30 = 334$
$\$2,840 \div 365 = \$7.7808219$
$\$7.7808219 \times 334 = \$2,598.79$ debit seller/credit buyer

2. $\$189,400 \div 100 \times \$3.34 = \$6,325.96$
J F M A M
$30 + 30 + 30 + 30 + 22 = 142$
$\$6,325.96 \div 360 = \$17.57211$
$\$17.57211 \times 142 = \$2,495.24$ debit seller/credit buyer

3. $\$92,355 \times .06875 \div 365 = \$17.39563$
$\$17.39563 \times 16 = \$278.33$ debit seller/credit Murphy

4. $\$43,560 \times .085 \div 360 = \$10.285$
$\$10.285 \times 16 = \$164.56$ debit seller/credit buyer

5.   J F M A
December $31 - 19 = 12 + 31 + 29 + 31 + 4 = 107$
$\$684 \div 366 = \$1.8688525$
$\$1.8688525 \times 107 = \$199.97$ debit buyer/credit Hughes

6. April $30 - 15 = 15$
$15 + 14 = 29$
$\$650 \div 360 = \$1.80556$
$\$1.80556 \times 29 = \$52.36$ debit buyer/credit Daubenspeck

7. August $31 - 11 = 20$
$\$1,250 + 1,650 = \$2,900$
$\$2,900 \div 31 = \$93.54839$
$\$93.54839 \times 20 = \$1,870.97$ debit Cezeaux/credit Duram

8. February $29 - 16 = 13$
$\$500 \div 29 = \$17.24138$
$\$17.24138 \times 13 = \$224.14$ debit seller/credit buyer

SOLUTIONS: PROBLEMS FOR ADDITIONAL PRACTICE

1. (c): $\$175,000 \times .82 \div 100 \times \$4.20 = \$6,027$
J F M A M J
$30 + 30 + 30 + 30 + 30 + 1 = 151$
$\$6,027 \div 360 = \$16.74167$
$\$16.74167 \times 151 = \$2,527.99$ debit seller/
credit buyer

2. (a): J F M A M
$31 + 28 + 31 + 30 + 4 = 124$
$\$2,753 \div 365 = \$7.54247$
$\$7.54247 \times 124 = \$935.27$ debit seller/
credit buyer

3. (d): J F M A M
$30 + 30 + 30 + 30 + 21 = 141$
$\$1,837.50 \div 360 = \$5.104667$
$\$5.104667 \times 141 = \$719.69$ debit Williamson/
credit buyer

4. (c): $\$71,400 \div 100 \times \$2.17 = \$1,549.38$
J F M A M J J A S
$31 + 29 + 31 + 30 + 31 + 30 + 31 + 31 + 11 = 255$
$\$1,549.38 \div 366 = \$4.23328$
$\$4.23328 \times 255 = \$1,079.49$ debit Landis/
credit Carter

5. (b): $350 + $280 + $177 = $807
       J   F   M   A   M   J   J
       31 + 28 + 31 + 30 + 31 + 30 + 16 = 197
       $807 ÷ 365 × 197 = $435.56 debit seller/credit buyer

6. (c): $66,600 × .08 ÷ 360 = $14.80
       $14.80 × 15 = $222 debit seller/credit buyer

7. (a): $102,743.50 × .085 ÷ 365 = $23.92657
       $23.92657 × 21 = $502.46 debit seller/credit buyer

8. (d): $36,569.20 × .09 ÷ 365 = $9.01706
       $9.01706 × 18 = $162.31 debit seller/credit buyer

9. (d): $120,853 × .0775 ÷ 360 = $26.01697
       $26.01697 × 29 = $754.49 debit seller/credit buyer

10. (a):   M   A   M
       February 30 − 1 = 29 + 30 + 30 + 20 = 109
             $673 ÷ 360 = $1.86944
             $1.86944 × 109 = $203.77 debit buyer/credit seller

11. (c):   O   N   D   J
       September 30 − 5 = 25 + 30 + 30 + 30 + 4 = 119
             $615 ÷ 360 = $1.70833
             $1.70833 × 119 = $203.29 debit buyer/credit seller

12. (a):   N   D   J
       October 31 − 23 = 8 + 30 + 31 + 12 = 81
             $730 ÷ 365 = $2
             $2 × 81 = $162 debit buyer/credit Fulton

13. (b):   D   J   F   M
       November 30 − 26 = 4 + 31 + 31 + 28 + 17 = 111
             $844 ÷ 365 = $2.31233
             $2.31233 × 111 = $256.67 debit buyer/credit Thomas

14. (a): September 30 − 28 = 2
       $525 ÷ 30 = $17.50
       $17.50 × 2 = $35 debit Gaston/credit buyer

15. (b):   50 × $ 600 = $30,000
           30 × $ 825 = $24,750
          _20 × $1,100 = $22,000_
       100           $76,750
       February 29 − 18 = 11
       $76,750 ÷ 29 = $2,646.5517
       $2,646.5517 × 11 = $29,112.07 debit seller/credit buyer

CHAPTER

Closing Statements

The real estate professional can use the information in this chapter in two practical ways: (1) Closing statements are usually prepared by those who actually close the transaction, but the real estate broker or salesperson should always check the statements for accuracy before closing. (2) Real estate licensees routinely use something called *net sheets* in every listing appointment, preparation of an offer from a buyer and presentation of an offer to a seller. Prospective sellers are obviously very interested in the amount they will *net* from the proposed sale and prospective buyers likewise are interested in their *net* due at closing. The generation of these figures involves the preparation of a document similar to a closing statement.

A closing statement is used in closing a real estate transaction. It is the document on which you will record the prorations that you learned to calculate in Chapter 13. It is, basically, a balance sheet on which debits and credits to the buyer and seller are recorded and, from the totals, the amount owed by the buyer is determined as well as the net amount that the seller will receive or must pay.

In this chapter, you will calculate prorations and learn to enter them on a closing statement. The examples used are generalities because many of the expenses are negotiable and can be paid by either the buyer or the seller. Also, the methods of closing a real estate transaction vary greatly across the nation and even within states. For example, depending on the area, brokers, attorneys, title insurance companies or escrow companies may routinely close real estate transactions. In this text, title or escrow companies will be considered to be the closers and the examples and problems are treated accordingly, even though this may not be the practice in your area.

The closing statement is the most important financial computation of a real estate transaction and there is no quick way to determine whether you know how to complete one. Therefore, we provide no warm-up exercises for this material. All students are advised to work through the entire chapter.

CLOSING STATEMENT FORMS

Every real estate transaction involving the transfer of property requires the preparation of a written form called a *closing* or *settlement statement*.

The closing statement is used to "balance the books." It is a way of calculating how much money is owed or due, taking all factors into account. Instead of exchanging money for each part of the transaction, the amounts are entered separately on the closing statement. The entire statement is then balanced to determine the total amount owed. This way, there is only one exchange of money and the closing statement serves as a summary of the receipts and disbursements of the transaction. For instance, if the sellers have 40 gallons of fuel left in their tank on the day of closing, they could siphon it out or ask the buyer for its value in cash. Instead, the value is entered on the closing statement as a *credit* to the *seller* and as a *debit* or *charge* to the *buyer*, who owes the seller that amount.

The amounts charged to the buyer increase the buyer's acquisition cost for the property. Amounts that the seller owes the buyer are entered as credits to the buyer and reduce the seller's net from the sale. The overall equations for closing statements are as follows:

Buyer's charges − Buyer's credits = Cash buyer owes at closing
Seller's credits − Seller's charges = Cash seller will receive at closing

A *DEBIT* takes money *From*.
A *CREDIT* gives money *To*.

CREDITS

Let us consider who receives credit for certain items. Items credited to the *buyer* may include

- the earnest money deposit (treated as a partial payment);
- the existing loan balance, when assumed by the buyer;
- items—such as real estate taxes—that have accrued or are accruing, but are not yet due or paid and for which the seller is debited, or charged, at the closing (see Chapter 13);
- unearned revenues (revenues—such as rent—collected in advance, but not yet earned); and
- proceeds of a new loan to be taken out by the buyer.

Items credited to the *seller* may include

- the sales price and
- prepaid items (items paid in advance—such as a fire insurance policy premium paid for a term that has not fully expired or fuel on hand).

Notice that *accrued* items are credits to the buyer and *prepaid* items are credits to the seller.

1. On the following chart, check the items that would normally be credited to the buyer and those that would normally be credited to the seller.

		Credit to Buyer	Credit to Seller
a.	Sales price of property ($100,000)		
b.	Balance of existing loan, assumed by the buyer ($40,500)		
c.	Mortgage interest accrued, but not yet due on the loan assumed by the buyer ($300)		
d.	Property tax reserve account ($600)		
e.	Premium for unexpired portion of insurance policy ($320)		
f.	Accrued portion of real estate tax ($450)		
g.	Prepaid security service ($175)		
h.	Fuel oil in tank on closing day ($150)		
i.	Water bill proration earned, but not yet due ($100)		
j.	Rents collected, but unearned ($805)		
k.	Tenants' security deposits ($2,000)		

The chart in problem 2 lists the credits used in problem 1. For each of these credits, there must be a debit, or charge, to the other party, who must pay for the items. For example, the selling price is a credit to the seller and must be a debit to the buyer.

In this chapter, the term *debit* will be used to mean a charge, an expense or a cost to either the seller or the buyer.

2. Complete the following chart by entering the amount of each debit in the debit column of the buyer or seller.

		Buyer Debit	Buyer Credit	Seller Debit	Seller Credit
a.	Sales price				$100,000
b.	Assumed loan balance		$40,500		
c.	Accrued interest on assumed loan		300		
d.	Tax reserve account				600
e.	Insurance premium proration				320
f.	Accrued portion of real estate tax		450		
g.	Prepaid security service				175
h.	Fuel oil in tank				150
i.	Prorated accrued water bill		100		
j.	Unearned rents collected		805		
k.	Tenants' security deposits		2,000		

ENTRY OF FIGURES

Definite rules govern the entry of the figures in a four-column closing statement. In problem 2, you followed Rule 1:

> **Rule 1.** The sales price and all the prorations of accrued and prepaid items between buyer and seller are each entered as a *debit* to one party and a *credit* to the other party.

Three kinds of items are *entered only once.* These are debits or credits to one party without offsetting second entries. Such items are covered by Rule 2:

> **Rule 2.** ■ *Earnest money*—a credit to the buyer. This money is deposited by the buyer and is usually held by the broker until the closing, when it is applied toward the purchase price. This money is not directly credited to the seller, but becomes part of the balance due the seller at closing.
>
> ■ *Seller's expenses*—debits to the seller. These are personal expenses of the seller—such as broker's commission, transfer tax stamps and so on—that do not involve the buyer.
>
> ■ *Buyer's expenses*—debits to the buyer. These are third-party expenses of the buyer—such as the fee for recording the seller's deed and the lender's fee for the buyer's assumption of the seller's loan balance—that do not affect the seller.

3. Using the following form, indicate which items are entered once and which are entered twice. Also mark how items are entered.

	Entered Once	Entered Twice	How Entered			
		Debit and Credit	Credit Seller	Debit Seller	Credit Buyer	Debit Buyer
Sales price						
Earnest money deposit						
Assumed loan balance						
Interest on assumed loan						
Real estate tax proration*						
Fuel oil in tank						
Recording fee for seller's deed						
Seller's commission to broker						
Buyer's title examination cost						

*Taxes have not been paid as of the closing date.

Types of Entries

The following list shows all entries included in the preparation of a four-column closing statement, grouped by type of entry and how each is typically debited or credited. Local practices may differ.

1. *Purchase price*—debited to the buyer and credited to the seller.
2. *Earnest money*—credited only to the buyer.
3. *Balance of assumed loan and accrued interest*—debited to the seller and credited to the buyer. (The proceeds of a *new mortgage* obtained by the buyer, however, are credited to the buyer *without* a corresponding debit to the seller because the buyer receives this money from the lender. The seller's existing mortgage must then be paid off by a debit to the seller.)
4. *Purchase-money loan*—credited to the buyer, who assumes an obligation for future payments; also debited to the seller, who accepts the note in lieu of cash.
5. *Prorations*—debited to one party *and* credited to the other.

   Items debited to buyer and credited to seller:

   - Prepaid insurance premiums
   - Prepaid real estate taxes, when applicable
   - Insurance and tax reserve impound account balance
   - Coal or fuel oil on hand
   - Prepaid utilities
   - Personal property purchased by buyer

   Items debited to seller and credited to buyer:

   - Principal of loan assumed by buyer
   - Accrued interest on existing assumed loan not yet payable
   - Accrued portion of real estate tax not yet due
   - Unearned portion of rent collected in advance
   - Accrued salaries of personnel (such as janitor or manager)
   - Tenants' security deposits

   Other items may be included, depending on the customs of your area.

6. *Expenses charged (debited) to seller or buyer*—to be disbursed by the closer.

   Debits to seller:

   - Broker's commission
   - Legal fee for drawing the deed
   - Title expenses required by the sales contract
   - Loan discount points
   - Repairs (as required by the sales contract)
   - Loan payoff fees
   - Filing fee for release of lien
   - Loan discount fees (if required by lender and as negotiated in the sales contract)

   Debits to buyer:

   - Assumption or transfer fee (when buyer assumes an existing loan)
   - Survey (if required by lender)

- Recording fees for deed and mortgage
- Loan origination fee
- Certified copies of deed restrictions
- Credit report
- Photos of property
- Prepaid taxes, insurance and interest
- Mortgage insurance premium (PMI or MIP, when required by lender)
- Flood insurance premium/homeowner's insurance premium
- Appraisal fee
- Termite, structural, mechanical and environmental inspections (Termite inspection is a charge to the seller in transactions with a VA-guaranteed loan.)

Debits to party responsible or shared by seller and buyer:

- Transfer tax
- Cost of title insurance or title examination
- Legal fees
- Escrow fee
- Inspection fees

Other items may be included, depending on the customs of your area and the provisions of the sales contract.

The preparation of a four-column closing statement is similar to the preparation of separate closing statements for the seller and buyer. These statements consist of debits and credits. *A debit is a charge*—a debit or an amount that the party being debited owes and must pay out of the closing proceeds. *A credit is an amount entered in a party's favor,* which the party being credited has already paid or promises to pay, in the form of a note for a loan, or for which the party must be reimbursed. When the buyer's debits have been entered and totaled, the buyer's credits are totaled and subtracted from the debits. This will determine the net amount of cash the buyer must pay to close the purchase. The difference between the seller's total credits and debits represents the amount due to the seller at the closing.

4. Examine the following situation, then enter the items on the form provided and determine (1) the amount the buyer will owe at closing and (2) the amount the seller will receive at closing.

   A house has been sold for $240,000 and the buyer has placed an earnest money deposit of $20,000 with the seller's real estate broker. The seller has agreed to pay the broker a 7% commission on the sales price.

	Buyer		Seller	
	Debit	Credit	Debit	Credit
Sales price				
Earnest money				
Broker's commission				
Subtotals				
Due from buyer at closing				
Due to seller at closing				
Totals				

5. Now prepare a complete closing statement by computing the prorations and entering the other necessary figures for the real estate transaction itemized below. Base prorations on a banker's year and prorate through the day of closing. Use the blank form on page 221, then compare your statement to the one in the answer key at the end of the chapter.

Sellers are Lester N. Smith and Mary B. Smith, 216 West Park, Pleasantown. They are selling the property located at that address.

Sellers' broker is Homestead Realty.

Buyers are Mark T. Haney and Liza A. Haney, 1313 Grove Avenue, Pleasantown.

Contract of sale is dated June 28.

Closing date is July 14.

Sales price is $135,000.

Earnest money is $6,000.

Buyers are to assume sellers' mortgage, including the 9% interest. The principal balance of the loan after the July 1 monthly payment is $87,500.

Annual real estate taxes are $2,648.

Tax reserve account of $1,986 is held by the mortgage lender.

Sellers paid $1,440 for a one-year fire insurance policy, which expires April 8 next year and which buyers will assume.

Buyers will be charged a 1-point transfer fee by the mortgage lender—the cost of changing records to show their assumption of sellers' mortgage loan.

Buyers must pay the county recorder $25 to record sellers' deed.

Sales commission is 5.75% of gross sales price.

Fee of $1,350 for sellers' title search and owner's title policy paid by sellers.

Transfer tax in this example is based on a rate of $.50 for each $500 or fraction thereof of the sales price in excess of the assumed mortgage.

Remember, the two "buyer's" columns must always balance, as must the two "seller's" columns. There is no need to compare the totals of both statements.

Important: For this problem, compute prorations on a 360-day year. When calculating the number of days, use the actual number of days in the month of closing to or through the closing date. However, local custom may vary.

Use the following space for your computations.

SETTLEMENT STATEMENT WORKSHEET

Settlement date _____	Buyer's Statement		Seller's Statement	
	Debit	Credit	Debit	Credit
Purchase price				
Earnest money				
Assumed loan balance				
Interest on assumed loan				
Real estate taxes through date				
Tax reserve				
Insurance premium proration				
Buyer's expenses:				
Assumption fee				
Recording fee				
Seller's expenses:				
Title search				
Broker's commission				
Transfer tax				
Subtotals				
Due from buyer				
Due to seller				
Totals				

RECONCILIATION

The four-column statement yields complete and accurate figures of the net amounts that the buyer must pay after deducting the buyer's expenses and that the seller will receive after paying the broker's commission and all other seller's expenses.

In order for the closer to be sure that all entries on the statement are properly handled and that more funds are not paid out than are received, a cash reconciliation or recapitulation should always be prepared.

6. Using information from problem 5, fill in the figures in the following chart for (1) the balance due from the buyer, (2) the paid amount due the seller and (3) the totals.

CLOSER'S RECONCILIATION STATEMENT

Items	Receipts	Disbursements
Earnest money	$6,000.00	
Due from buyer at closing		
Seller's expenses paid:		$9,160.00
Buyer's expenses paid:		$ 900.00
Amount paid to seller at closing		
Totals		

For instructional purposes, we have used simple forms in this chapter, but in actual practice, each person or company performing a closing will use its own printed forms. An exception to this practice occurs any time a buyer obtains a new loan that is connected to the U.S. government in any way. In such a case, a specific Department of Housing and Urban Development form is required, as a result of legislation known as the Real Estate Settlement Procedures Act, or RESPA. A copy of this two-page form is shown in Figure 14.1. Page 2 of the HUD form must be completed first because page 1 summarizes the detailed items there. Also, the term *debit* is not used; the RESPA form merely says "paid from borrower's/seller's funds." In this chapter, you learned that in real estate settlement language, *debit* means "charged to" or a "cost to" the buyer or the seller.

Figure 14.2 is an actual disbursement sheet from a closing office and is identical to the closer's reconciliation that you have worked with in this chapter. Both are designed to show that money received equals money disbursed, or paid out.

FIGURE 14.1

Transaction Information

Buyer's Debits

Buyer's Credits

Reconciliation

Signatures

Seller's Credits

Seller's Debits

Reconciliation

A. **Settlement Statement**

U.S. Department of Housing and Urban Development

OMB No. 2502-0265

B. Type of Loan

1. ☐ FHA   2. ☐ FmHA   3. ☐ Conv. Unins.
4. ☐ VA   5. ☐ Conv. Ins.

6. File Number | 7. Loan Number | 8. Mortgage Insurance Case Number

C. **Note:** This form is furnished to give you a statement of actual settlement costs. Amounts paid to and by the settlement agent are shown. Items marked "(p o c.)" were paid outside the closing; they are shown here for informational purposes and are not included in the totals.

D. Name and Address of Borrower | E. Name and Address of Seller Tax I.D. No. | F. Name and Address of Lender

G. Property Location | H. Settlement Agent and Agent Identification Number

Place of Settlement | I. Settlement Date

J. Summary of Borrower's Transaction		K. Summary of Seller's Transaction	
100. Gross Amount Due From Borrower		**400. Gross Amount Due To Seller**	
101. Contract sales price		401. Contract sales price	
102. Personal property		402. Personal property	
103. Settlement charges to borrower (line 1400)		403.	
104.		404.	
105.		405.	
Adjustments for items paid by seller in advance		**Adjustments for items paid by seller in advance**	
106. City/town taxes to		406. City/town taxes to	
107. County taxes to		407. County taxes to	
108. Assessments to		408. Assessments to	
109.		409.	
110.		410.	
111.		411.	
112.		412.	
120. Gross Amount Due From Borrower		**420. Gross Amount Due To Seller**	
200. Amounts Paid By Or In Behalf Of Borrower		**500. Reductions In Amount Due To Seller**	
201. Deposit or earnest money		501. Excess deposit (see instructions)	
202. Principal amount of new loan(s)		502. Settlement charges to seller (line 1400)	
203. Existing loan(s) taken subject to		503. Existing loan(s) taken subject to	
204.		504. Payoff of first mortgage loan	
205.		505. Payoff of second mortgage loan	
206.		506.	
207.		507.	
208.		508.	
209.		509.	
Adjustments for items unpaid by seller		**Adjustments for items unpaid by seller**	
210. City/town taxes to		510. City/town taxes to	
211. County taxes to		511. County taxes to	
212. Assessments to		512. Assessments to	
213.		513.	
214.		514.	
215.		515.	
216.		516.	
217.		517.	
218.		518.	
219.		519.	
220. Total Paid By/For Borrower		**520. Total Reduction Amount Due Seller**	
300. Cash At Settlement From/To Borrower		**600. Cash At Settlement To/From Seller**	
301. Gross Amount due from borrower (line 120)		601. Gross amount due to seller (line 420)	
302. Less amounts paid by/for borrower (line 220)	( )	602. Less reductions in amt. due seller (line 520)	( )
303. Cash ☐ From ☐ To Borrower		**603. Cash** ☐ To ☐ From Seller	

SOLICITATION

You are required by law to provide _____ with your correct taxpayer identification number. If you do not provide _____ with your correct taxpayer identification number, you may be subject to civil or criminal penalties imposed by

CERTIFICATION

Under penalties of perjury, I certify that the number shown on this statement is my correct taxpayer identification number.

Seller's Signature _____ Seller's Signature _____ Seller's Signature _____

SUBSTITUTE FORM 1099 SELLER STATEMENT

The information contained in Blocks E, G, H and I and on line 401 (or, if line 401 is asterisked, lines 403 and 404) is important tax information and is being furnished to the Internal Revenue Service. If you are required to file a return, a negligence penalty or other sanction will be imposed on you if this item is required to be reported and the IRS determines that it has not been reported.

SELLER INSTRUCTIONS

If this real estate was your principal residence, file Form 2119, Sale or Exchange of Principal Residence, for any gain, with your income tax return; for other transactions, complete the applicable parts of Form 4797, Form 6252 and/or Schedule D (Form 1040).

FIGURE 14.1 Continued

L. Settlement Charges

		Paid From Borrower's Funds at Settlement	Paid From Seller's Funds at Settlement
700. Total Sales/Broker's Commission based on price $ @ % =			
Division of Commission (line 700) as follows:			
701. $ to			
702. $ to			
703. Commission paid at Settlement			
704.			

Broker Fees (section 700)

800. Items Payable In Connection With Loan

		Paid From Borrower's	Paid From Seller's
801. Loan Origination Fee %			
802. Loan Discount %			
803. Appraisal Fee to			
804. Credit Report to			
805. Lender's Inspection Fee			
806. Mortgage Insurance Application Fee to			
807. Assumption Fee			
808.			
809.			
810.			
811.			

Loan Expenses (section 800)

900. Items Required By Lender To Be Paid In Advance

901. Interest from to @$ /day			
902. Mortgage Insurance Premium for months to			
903. Hazard Insurance Premium for years to			
904. years to			
905.			

Prepaids Required by Lender (section 900)

1000. Reserves Deposited With Lender

1001. Hazard Insurance months @ $ per month			
1002. Mortgage Insurance months @ $ per month			
1003. City property taxes months @ $ per month			
1004. County property taxes months @ $ per month			
1005. Annual assessments months @ $ per month			
1006. months @ $ per month			
1007. months @ $ per month			
1008. months @ $ per month			

Reserve Impounds (section 1000)

1100. Title Charges

1101. Settlement or closing fee to			
1102. Abstract or title search to			
1103. Title examination to			
1104. Title insurance binder to			
1105. Document preparation to			
1106. Notary fees to			
1107. Attorney's fees to			
(includes above items numbers:			
1108. Title insurance to First American Title Insurance Company of Texas			
(includes above items numbers:			
1109. Lender's coverage $			
1110. Owner's coverage $			
1111. Escrow Fee to First American Title Insurance Company of Texas			
1112. Restrictions to First American Title Insurance Company of Texas			
1113. Messenger to First American Title Insurance Company of Texas			

Title and Legal Exp. (section 1100)

1200. Government Recording and Transfer Charges

1201. Recording fees: Deed $; Mortgage $;Releases $			
1202. City/county tax/stamps: Deed $; Mortgage $			
1203. State tax/stamps: Deed $; Mortgage $			
1204.			
1205.			

Government Charges (section 1200)

1300. Additional Settlement Charges

1301. Survey to			
1302. Pest inspection to			
1303.			
1304.			
1305.			

Miscellaneous Closing Costs (section 1300)

1400. Total Settlement Charges (enter on lines 103, Section J and 502, Section K)

I have carefully reviewed the HUD-I Settlement Statement and to the best of my knowledge and belief, it is a true and accurate statement of all receipts and disbursements made on my account or by me in this transaction. I further certify that I have received a copy of the HUD-I Settlement Statement.

_____   _____

Borrowers   Sellers

The HUD-I Settlement Statement which I have prepared is a true and accurate account of this transaction. I have caused or will cause the funds to be disbursed in accordance with this statement.

_____   _____

Settlement Agent   Date

Seller's and Purchaser's signature hereon acknowledges his/their approval of tax prorations, and signifies their understanding that prorations were based on figures for the preceding year, or estimates for current year, and in event of any change for the current year, all necessary adjustments must be made between Seller and Purchaser direct; likewise any DEFICIT in delinquent taxes will be reimbursed to Title Company by the Seller.

Warning: It is a crime to knowingly make false statements to the United States on this or any other similar form. Penalties upon conviction can include a fine and imprisonment. For details see: Title 18 U.S. Code Section 1001 and Section 1010.

FIGURE 14.2

BUYER/BORROWER		SELLER		GF#_____ PROPERTY

RECEIPTS

DATE	RECEIPT NO.	FROM		AMOUNT
			$	
			TOTAL	$

DISBURSEMENTS

DATE	CHECK NO.	CHECK TO	AMOUNT

STEWART TITLE GUARANTY COMPANY

MESSENGER	RESTRICTIONS
OWNER'S POLICY	RECORDING
MORTGAGEE'S POLICY	TAX CERTIFICATES
ESCROW	

ESCROW OFFICER

TOTAL $

AN ADDITIONAL PRACTICE PROBLEM

Work the following closing statement problem and enter the figures on the form on page 227.

John P. Smith and Kristie A. Smith, husband and wife, of 2419 Monroe Street, Rockford, told their broker that they wanted to net $90,500 on the sale of their building after paying the broker's commission of $6\frac{1}{2}\%$. ABC Realtors agreed to take the listing of the two-family apartment building. The present loan had a principal balance of $37,000 after the June 1 monthly payment was credited. The monthly mortgage payment, due the first day of each month, is $396 and includes the $9\frac{1}{2}\%$ interest for the previous month.

Frank P. Jones and Linda K. Jones, of 1010 Lincoln Drive, Rockford, signed a purchase contract for the Smith building on May 15, which the sellers accepted and signed. The agreed purchase price is $96,000. The buyers will assume the sellers' loan and the sellers will take back a $10,000 purchase-money mortgage note to be paid on or before five years from closing, with 10% annual interest paid monthly.

On the closing date, which has been set for June 16, the sellers will be considered the owners of the property, which means that you must prorate *through* the date of closing. The buyers have already given the broker a 10% earnest money deposit and have yet to pay a $50 title insurance charge. The sellers' title charge is $960. The real estate tax bill for the year of $1,420 has not been paid and will become due on December 31. The buyers have also agreed to purchase 56 gallons of fuel oil remaining in the tank at closing, at a cost of $.75 per gallon.

The buyers will obtain a new insurance policy before closing and pay the premium directly to the insurance company.

On June 1, the sellers made their last regular monthly payment on the mortgage. The upper apartment is rented at $300 per month; the sellers occupy the lower apartment. The sellers have collected the June 1 rent and hold a security deposit equivalent to a month's rent. The sellers will pay for the transfer tax stamps on their deed. These cost $.50 per $500 or any fraction thereof of the next taxable consideration after deducting the assumed loan. The buyers have agreed to pay the recording fee of $25, the survey fee of $250 and the cost of preparing the seller-second loan documents, which is $150. The sellers' expenses include preparing the deed, at a cost of $130, and termite inspection, which costs $75. The broker is to disburse all of these expenses on the day of closing.

Compute the necessary prorations and prepare the four-column closing statement for this sale. Use a statutory year to calculate all prorations *through* the day of closing.

Read the following instructions before you begin.

To use the worksheet most efficiently, follow these steps:

1. As you read through the information given for the problem, list the types of expenses included in the transaction in the left-hand column of the worksheet.
2. Go through the list of expenses and consider those expenses related to the buyer; make any necessary proration computations and record each buyer-related expense as either a debit or a credit to the buyer.

    Debits to the buyer *increase the amount the buyer owes* at closing. They include the purchase price of the property, all prorations of prepaid items and third-party expenses of the buyer, such as the fee for recording the seller's deed. Credits to the buyer, on the other hand, *decrease the amount the buyer owes*. They include the earnest money deposit, the balance of the assumed loan and all prorations of accrued items.
3. Next go through the list of expenses and consider those expenses related to the seller; make any necessary proration computations and record each seller-related expense as either a debit or a credit to the seller.

    Debits to the seller *decrease the amount due* the seller at closing. They include the balance of the assumed loan, all prorations of accrued items and third-party expenses of the seller, such as the broker's commission and transfer tax stamps, that do not involve the buyer. Credits to the seller *increase the amount due* the seller. They include the selling price of the property and all prorations of prepaid items.

4. Total the buyer's debit and credit columns and subtract the lesser from the greater total to determine what amount the buyer must pay at the closing (if debits exceed credits).
5. Total the seller's debit and credit columns and subtract the lesser from the greater total to determine what amount the seller will pay at the closing (if debits exceed credits) or what amount the seller will be paid at the closing (if credits exceed debits).
6. Prepare the closer's reconciliation statement to verify that all items are entered in the proper columns.

Use the space below for your computations.

SETTLEMENT STATEMENT WORKSHEET

Property _____

Seller _____

Buyer _____

Settlement Date _____

	Buyer's Statement		Seller's Statement	
	Debit	Credit	Debit	Credit
Purchase Price				
Earnest money				
Assumed loan balance				
Interest on assumed loan				
Purchase-money mortgage				
Real estate taxes				
Oil in tank				
Rent proration				
Security damage deposit				
Broker's commission				
Transfer tax				
Title insurance				
Recording fees				
Survey				
Preparation of purchase-money mortgage				
Preparation of deed				
Termite inspection				
Subtotals				
Due from buyer at closing				
Due to seller at closing				
Totals				

CLOSER'S RECONCILIATION STATEMENT

Items	Receipts	Disbursements
Earnest money		
Due from buyer at closing		
Seller's expenses paid		
Buyer's expenses paid		
Amount due seller at closing		
Totals		

ANSWER KEY

SOLUTIONS: CHAPTER PROBLEMS

1. a. The *seller* receives credit for the total selling price of the property, which the buyer has agreed to pay.

 b. The *buyer* receives credit for assuming the seller's existing loan. The balance due on the assumed note is an offset to the selling price.

 c. The *buyer* receives credit for the interest incurred to date by the seller, which the buyer must pay at the next mortgage payment date.

 d. When the buyer assumes the seller's mortgage, the *seller* receives credit for any money held in a tax reserve account with the mortgage lender that will be transferred to the buyer.

 e. The *seller* receives credit for the unused amount of a prepaid insurance premium that the buyer assumes.

 f. The *buyer* receives a credit for the seller's share of the accrued real estate tax up to the closing date because the buyer must pay the *total* tax when it becomes due.

 g. The *seller* receives credit for money he or she has paid in advance for services that will benefit the buyer after the closing.

 h. The *seller* receives credit for fuel on hand that has already been paid for but that the buyer will use.

 i. The *buyer* receives credit for the water that the seller has used before closing because the buyer will have to pay for the total billing period when the bill becomes due.

 j. The *buyer* receives credit for rent collected in advance by the seller, which represents rent for that part of the month during which the buyer will own the building.

 k. The *buyer* receives credit for each security deposit held by the seller but that the buyer, as the new landlord, must return if a tenant decides not to renew his or her lease.

2.

		Buyer		Seller	
		Debit	Credit	Debit	Credit
a.	Sales price	$100,000			$100,000
b.	Assumed loan balance		$40,500	$40,500	
c.	Accrued interest on assumed loan		300	300	
d.	Tax reserve account	600			600
e.	Insurance premium proration	320			320
f.	Accrued portion of real estate tax		450	450	
g.	Prepaid security service	175			175
h.	Fuel oil in tank	150			150
i.	Prorated accrued water bill		100	100	
j.	Unearned rents collected		805	805	
k.	Tenants' security deposits		2,000	2,000	

3.

	Entered Once	Entered Twice	How Entered			
		Debit and Credit	Credit Seller	Debit Seller	Credit Buyer	Debit Buyer
Sales price		X	X			X
Earnest money deposit	X				X	
Assumed loan balance		X		X	X	
Interest on assumed loan		X		X	X	
Real estate tax proration*		X		X	X	
Fuel oil in tank		X	X			X
Recording fee for seller's deed	X					X
Seller's commission to broker	X			X		
Buyer's title examination cost	X					X

*Taxes have not been paid as of the closing date.

4.

	Buyer		Seller	
	Debit	Credit	Debit	Credit
Sales price	$240,000			$240,000
Earnest money		$ 20,000		
Broker's commission			$ 16,800	
Subtotals	240,000	20,000	16,800	240,000
Due from buyer at closing		220,000		
Due to seller at closing			223,200	
Totals	**$240,000**	**$240,000**	**$240,000**	**$240,000**

5. Interest proration:

$$\$87,500 \times .09 \div 360 \times 14 = \$306.25$$

Tax proration:

J   F   M   A   M   J   J

$$30 + 30 + 30 + 30 + 30 + 30 + 14 = 194 \text{ days}$$

$$\$2,648 \div 360 \times 194 = \$1,426.98$$

Insurance proration:

A   S   O   N   D   J   F   M   A

July $30 - 14 = 16 + 30 + 30 + 30 + 30 + 30 + 30 + 30 + 30 + 7 = 263$

$$\$1,440 \div 360 \times 263 = \$1,052$$

Transfer fee:

$$\$87,500 \times .01 = \$875$$

Broker's fee:

$$\$135,000 \times .0575 = \$7,762.50$$

Transfer tax stamps:

$$\$135,000 - \$87,500 = \$47,500$$

$$\$47,500 \div \$500 \times \$.50 = \$47.50$$

SETTLEMENT STATEMENT WORKSHEET

Settlement date _____ July 14 _____

	Buyer's Statement		Seller's Statement	
	Debit	Credit	Debit	Credit
Purchase price	$135,000.00			$135,000.00
Earnest money		$ 6,000.00		
Assumed loan balance		87,500.00	$ 87,500.00	
Interest on assumed loan		306.25	306.25	
Real estate taxes through date		1,426.98	1,426.98	
Tax reserve	1,986.00			1,986.00
Insurance premium proration	1,052.00			1,052.00
Buyer's expenses:				
Assumption fee	875.00			
Recording fee	25.00			
Seller's expenses:				
Title search			1,350.00	
Broker's commission			7,762.50	
Transfer tax			47.50	
Subtotals	138,938.00	95,233.23	98,393.23	138,038.00
Due from buyer		43,704.77		
Due to seller			39,644.77	
Totals	**$138,938.00**	**$138,938.00**	**$138,038.00**	**$138,038.00**

6.

CLOSER'S RECONCILIATION STATEMENT

Items	Receipts	Disbursements
Earnest money	$ 6,000.00	
Due from buyer at closing	43,704.77	
Seller's expenses paid		$ 9,160.00
Buyer's expenses paid		900.00
Amount paid to seller at closing		39,644.77
Totals	**$49,704.77**	**$49,704.77**

SOLUTION: AN ADDITIONAL PRACTICE PROBLEM

Earnest money deposit:
   $96,000 \times .10 = $9,600$
Interest proration:
   $37,000 \times .095 \div 360 \times 16 = 156.22
Tax proration:
   January – June 16 = 165 days due
   $1,420 \div 360 \times 165 = 650.83
Oil proration:
   56 gallons $\times$ $.75 = 42
Rent proration:
   June 30 – 16 days = 14 days due
   $300 \div 30 \times 14 = 140
Broker's fee:
   $96,000 \times .065 = $6,240$
Transfer tax stamps:
   $96,000 – $37,000 = $59,000$
   $59,000 \div $500 \times $.50 = 59

SETTLEMENT STATEMENT WORKSHEET

Property 2419 Monroe Street, Rockford

Seller John P. Smith and Kristie A. Smith

Buyer Frank P. Jones and Linda K. Jones

Settlement date June 16

	Buyer's statement		Seller's statement	
	Debit	Credit	Debit	Credit
Purchase price	$96,000.00			$96,000.00
Earnest money		$ 9,600.00		
Assumed loan balance		37,000.00	$37,000.00	
Interest on assumed loan		156.22	156.22	
Purchase-money mortgage		10,000.00	10,000.00	
Real estate taxes		650.83	650.83	
Oil in tank	42.00			42.00
Rent proration		140.00	140.00	
Security damage deposit		300.00	300.00	
Broker's commission			6,240.00	
Transfer tax			59.00	
Title insurance	50.00		960.00	
Recording fees	25.00			
Survey	250.00			
Preparation of purchase-money mortgage	150.00			
Preparation of deed			130.00	
Termite inspection			75.00	
Subtotals	96,517.00	57,847.05	55,711.05	96,042.00
Due from buyer at closing		38,669.95		
Due to seller at closing			40,330.95	
Totals	**$96,517.00**	**$96,517.00**	**$96,042.00**	**$96,042.00**

CLOSER'S RECONCILIATION STATEMENT

Items	Receipts	Disbursements
Earnest money	$ 9,600.00	
Due from buyer at closing	38,669.95	
Seller's expenses paid		$ 7,464.00
Buyer's expenses paid		475.00
Amount due seller at closing		40,330.95
Totals	**$48,269.95**	**$48,269.95**

Lease Calculations

Commercial leases generally run for three or more years and contain clauses that permit periodic increases of rent.

Retail leases may call for a base rental amount plus a percentage of gross sales in excess of an amount established in the lease. Leases for office space may call for rental escalations based on increases in one of the U.S. government consumer price indexes (CPIs) for a given geographic area. Other commercial and industrial leases may pass through some or all of the operating expenses to the tenant.

At the conclusion of your work in this chapter, you will be able to calculate

- the rent for a given number of square feet when rent is expressed as gross rent per square foot;
- the total rent due under a percentage lease; and
- a rental increase called for in a lease with a CPI escalation clause.

WARM-UP EXERCISES

Because readers will have varying amounts of knowledge and experience, the problems that follow will allow you to determine your familiarity with the material to be covered. Try all of the problems before checking your answers against the answer key at the end of the chapter.

1. What is the monthly rent for a 3,680-square-foot space if the annual rent being charged is $18.50 per square foot?

   a. $68,080.00   c. $6,808.00
   b. $4,836.24   d. $5,673.33

2. A lease calls for base rent of $12,000 per year plus 4% of gross sales in excess of $100,000. What is your total rent in a year in which your business generates $86,000 in gross sales?

   a. $12,000   c. $16,000
   b. $4,128   d. $18,270

3. Hosby's Salon has a lease that provides for the tenant to pay $375 minimum rent per month plus 4.5% of gross sales in excess of $100,000 per year. The gross sales last year were $250,000. What was Hosby's annual rent?

   a. $6,750

   b. $11,250

   c. $4,500

   d. $10,500

4. Two years ago, Hosby's rent came to $8,100 (see problem 3). What were the gross sales for that year?

   a. $180,000

   b. $75,000

   c. $80,000

   d. $81,000

5. Your office rent is $2,460 per month. Your lease calls for you to pay increased rent based on the upturns in the CPI tracked by the U.S. government. What is your rent this year if the CPI stood at 332 when you signed your lease and has increased by 50 points this year?

   a. $2,149.26

   b. $2,380.48

   c. $2,830.48

   d. $2,684.14

RENT PER SQUARE FOOT

Rent can also be quoted as being so many dollars per square foot on an annual or monthly basis.

EXAMPLE: If the rental rate in a new office building is $12.10 per square foot, what is the *monthly* rent on a space having 1,800 square feet?

First find the total annual rent:

1,800 square feet × $12.10 per square foot = $21,780

Then convert the annual rent to monthly rent:

$21,780 annual rent ÷ 12 months = $1,815

Or the rent might be stated on a monthly basis and then converted to an annual rate per square foot for comparison. If the monthly rent is $2,000 for a 2,220-square-foot space, what is the annual rate per square foot?

First find the total annual rent:

$$\$2,000 \times 12 \text{ months} = \$24,000$$

Then find the rent per square foot:

$$\$24,000 \text{ annual rent} \div 2,200 \text{ square feet} = \$10.91 \text{ per square foot}$$
$$\text{(rounded)}$$

PERCENTAGE LEASE

Under a percentage lease, the annual rent is a percentage of the gross sales, usually subject to a minimum monthly payment. The tenant generally pays a minimum monthly rent *plus* a percentage of gross sales income if it exceeds the stipulated minimum amount. Or some leases may provide for a minimum (base) rent plus a percentage of all gross sales income.

EXAMPLE: A percentage lease calls for a minimum monthly rental fee of $500, plus 6% of gross annual sales in excess of $100,000 per year. Based on gross annual sales of $250,000, compute the total rent for the year.

First find the minimum annual rent:

$$\$500 \text{ per month} \times 12 \text{ months} = \$6,000$$

Then find the percentage of gross sales to add to the minimum:

$$
\begin{array}{ll}
\$250,000 & \text{actual gross sales} \\
\underline{-100,000} & \text{sales covered by minimum rent} \\
\$150,000 & \text{sales subject to percentage rent}
\end{array}
$$

$$\$150,000 \times .06 = \$9,000 \text{ additional rent due}$$

The total annual rent is the minimum plus the additional rent due:

$$\$6,000 + \$9,000 = \$15,000$$

Minimum or Base Rental

EXAMPLE: Mr. Muncie pays 2% of his total gross sales for rent, with a minimum base rental of $1,000 per month. In the past year, his sales volume was $400,000. How much rent did he pay? At what sales volume will Mr. Muncie effectively begin to pay percentage rent?

$1,000 base monthly rental × 12 months = $12,000 minimum annual rent
$400,000 sales volume × .02 = $8,000 percentage rent

Mr. Muncie paid the minimum rent, $12,000, because it was greater than the percentage rent.

$12,000 ÷ .02 = $600,000 total gross sales to reach minimum rent

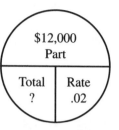

When Mr. Muncie exceeds $600,000 in total gross sales, his percentage rent will be greater than the minimum rent and he will pay that rather than the minimum rent.

1. If a percentage lease requires a tenant to pay $400 monthly minimum rent plus 4% of gross annual sales in excess of $120,000, what was the total rent paid for a year in which gross sales amounted to $360,000?

2. A lease provides for the tenant to pay $450 monthly minimum rent plus 4% of gross sales in excess of $135,000 per year. What were the gross sales last year if the lessee paid a total rent of $12,420?

3. Flowerland, Inc., has operated a flower shop for several years in a highly desirable, active shopping center. The company has a lease requiring a $500-per-month base rental plus a percentage of gross sales in excess of $75,000 per year. If gross sales for the year totaled $141,250 and rent paid amounted to $11,300, what percentage rate was contained in the lease?

4. Burrow's Delicatessen pays a monthly rental of $330 plus 4% of annual gross sales exceeding $99,000. Last year, the gross sales were $300,000. What was one month's rent for the delicatessen?

5. The Ski and See Shop had a three-year lease that required a $600-per-month rental guarantee plus an escalating percentage of annual gross sales in excess of $180,000. Complete the schedule that follows by determining how much rent was paid each year:

Year	Percentage of Gross Sales	Actual Gross Sales	Annual Rent
1	4	$200,000	
2	4.5	160,000	
3	5	250,000	

6. Mrs. Young collects rent from four stores in the Yardley shopping center. Last year, she collected $12,500 from Mr. Tompson, $14,000 from Mr. Berry and $9,000 from Miss Huerta. She also collected rent from Mr. Miller, who was to pay 5% of all gross sales, with a minimum payment of $375 per month. His gross sales last year were $75,000. On the average, how much rent did Mrs. Young collect for one month last year?

INDEX LEASE CALCULATIONS

Every month, the U.S. government, through the Bureau of Labor Statistics, publishes data that reflect the costs of goods and services. These costs are shown as percentages of change over the past year and the past month. The percentages are then used to adjust the CPI. In general, *index numbers* indicate the change in the size of something over time, by comparison to its size at some specified time. Specifically, the CPI compares the number of dollars needed to buy a certain bundle of goods each year to the number of dollars needed to buy those goods in 1967. Thus, 1967 is the *base year* for the CPI. The CPI for 1967 is 100 and for 1995 it is 384. Thus, a bundle of goods that would have cost a consumer $100 in 1967 would have cost a consumer $384 in 1995.

A landlord can use the CPI to help him or her decide on the size of annual rent adjustments. By tying the adjustments to this index, the landlord is better able to offset the effects of inflation on property management expenses. Other indexes are used for lease adjustments, however, for simplicity of illustration, only the CPI will be used in this book. The math for using another index is the same as the math involved in using the CPI.

First divide the current index by the previous year's index to obtain the adjustment factor:

$$\frac{308 \text{ (1997 index)}}{299 \text{ (1996 index)}} = 1.030 \text{ (rounded)}$$

Then multiply the rent by the adjustment factor to calculate the adjusted rent:

$$\$600 \text{ (for example)} \times 1.030 = \$618$$

7. When a new warehouse leases for $4,000 per month and the CPI is 300, what will the adjusted rent be in each of the next three years if the indexes at each adjustment time are 305, 309 and 315, respectively?

PROBLEMS FOR ADDITIONAL PRACTICE

When you have finished these problems, check your answers at the end of the chapter. If you miss any of the problems, review this chapter.

1. Ms. Harper pays $300 monthly minimum rent plus 4.5% of gross sales in excess of $80,000 per year. If gross sales last year were $125,000, how much monthly rent did Ms. Harper pay?

a. $168.75

b. $468.75

c. $313.50

d. $600.00

2. Jake Jones's lease requires that he pay $250 monthly minimum rent plus 5% of gross sales exceeding $60,000. Mr. Jones paid $10,500 in rent last year. What were his gross sales?

a. $750,000

b. $210,000

c. $60,000

d. $150,000

3. The Yard Goods Shop pays $600 monthly minimum rent plus a percentage of gross sales in excess of $144,000 per year. Last year, gross sales totaled $350,000 and the rent paid amounted to $17,500. What percentage of gross sales is required by this lease?

a. .02 or 2%

b. .055 or 5.5%

c. .05 or 5%

d. .0528 or 5.28%

4. A store lease provides for the tenant to pay a minimum monthly rental of $416.67 plus 6% of gross annual sales exceeding $100,000. What were gross annual sales last year if the tenant paid a total of $7,820 in rent?

a. $130,334

b. $100,000

c. $146,999

d. $136,725

5. A tenant's store lease requires a minimum monthly rental of $600 plus a percentage of gross annual sales in excess of $180,000. If gross sales for last year were $264,000 and the tenant's rent was $13,080, what is the percentage rate stated in the lease?

a. 6%

b. 6.5%

c. 7%

d. 7.5%

6. A store lease provides for minimum monthly rental payments of $425 plus a percentage rent of 8% of gross annual sales exceeding $160,000. Last year, when gross annual sales were $229,500, what was the tenant's gross rent bill for the year?

a. $27,100.00
b. $10,660.00

c. $13,787.50
d. $28,686.25

7. A store tenant's lease called for $600 per month guaranteed rental plus 4.5% of gross annual sales exceeding $180,000. When gross annual sales were $164,000, what was the amount of the tenant's gross annual rent?

a. $8,100
b. $7,200

c. $7,380
d. $7,500

8. A store lease required a tenant to pay a minimum monthly rent plus 6% of gross annual sales in excess of $80,000. When total gross annual sales were $120,000 and gross annual rent was $6,400, what was the monthly minimum rent?

a. $400
b. $350

c. $333
d. $325

9. A tenant's lease requires a payment of $2,000 per month. If the lease provides for an adjustment based on the CPI, which was 300 a year ago and is now 306, what will the new payment be?

a. $2,040
b. $2,120

c. $2,200
d. $2,250

10. If the rent on a 1,750-square-foot office is $14.50 per square foot, what is the monthly rent?

a. $3,192.51
b. $23,375.00

c. $2,114.58
d. $2,022.44

ANSWER KEY

SOLUTIONS: WARM-UP EXERCISES

1. (d): 3,680 square feet × $18.50 ÷ 12 = $5,673.33 (rounded)

2. (a): $12,000

3. (b): $250,000 − $100,000 = $150,000
$150,000 × .045 = $6,750
$375 × 12 = $4,500
$4,500 + $6,750 = $11,250

4. (a): $8,100 − $4,500 = $3,600
$3,600 ÷ .045 = $80,000
$80,000 + $100,000 = $180,000

5. (c): $332 + 50 = 382$
$382 \div 332 = 1.15060$
$1.15060 \times \$2,460 = \$2,830.48$

SOLUTIONS: CHAPTER PROBLEMS

1. $\$360,000 - \$120,000 = \$240,000$
$\$240,000 \times .04 = \$9,600$
$\$400 \times 12 = \$4,800$
$\$4,800 + \$9,600 = \$14,400$

2. $\$450 \times 12 = \$5,400$
$\$12,420 - \$5,400 = \$7,020$
$\$7,020 \div .04 = \$175,500$
$\$175,500 + \$135,000 = \$310,500$

3. $\$500 \times 12 = \$6,000$
$\$11,300 - \$6,000 = \$5,300$
$\$141,250 - \$75,000 = \$66,250$
$\$5,300 \div \$66,250 = .08$ or 8%

4. $\$300,000 - \$99,000 = \$201,000$
$\$201,000 \times .04 = \$8,040$
$\$8,040 \div 12 = \$670$
$\$670 + \$330 = \$1,000$

5. 1. $\$600 \times 12 = \$7,200$
$\$200,000 - \$180,000 = \$20,000$
$\$20,000 \times .04 = \$800$
$\$800 + \$7,200 = \$8,000$
2. Because \$160,000 is less than \$180,000, only base rent of \$7,200 is due.
3. $\$250,000 - \$180,000 = \$70,000$
$\$70,000 \times .05 = \$3,500$
$\$3,500 + \$7,200 = \$10,700$

6. $\$75,000 \times .05 = \$3,750$ or $\$375 \times 12 = \$4,500$, whichever is greater
$\$12,500 + \$14,000 + \$9,000 + \$4,500 = \$40,000$
$\$40,000 \div 12 = \$3,333.33$ (rounded)

7. 1. $305 \div 300 \times \$4,000 = \$4,066.67$ (rounded)
2. $309 \div 300 \times \$4,000 = \$4,120.00$
3. $315 \div 300 \times \$4,000 = \$4,200.00$

SOLUTIONS: PROBLEMS FOR ADDITIONAL PRACTICE

1. (b): $\$125,000 - \$80,000 = \$45,000$
$\$45,000 \times .045 \div 12 = \$168.75$
$\$168.75 + \$300 = \$468.75$

2. (b): $250 \times 12 = \$3,000$
$10,500 - \$3,000 = \$7,500$
$7,500 \div .05 = \$150,000$
$150,000 + \$60,000 = \$210,000$

3. (c): $350,000 - \$144,000 = \$206,000$
$17,500 - (\$600 \times 12) = \$10,300$
$10,300 \div \$206,000 = .05$ or 5%

4. (c): $416.67 \times 12 = \$5,000.04$
$7,820 - \$5,000.04 = \$2,819.96$
$2,819.96 \div .06 = \$46,999$ (rounded)
$46,999 + \$100,000 = \$146,999$

5. (c): $264,000 - \$180,000 = \$84,000$
$13,080 - (\$600 \times 12) = \$5,880$
$5,880 \div \$84,000 = .07$ or 7%

6. (b): $425 \times 12 = \$5,100$
$229,500 - \$160,000 = \$69,500$
$69,500 \times .08 = \$5,560$
$5,560 + \$5,100 = \$10,660$

7. (b): $600 \times 12 = \$7,200$

8. (c): $120,000 - \$80,000 = \$40,000$
$40,000 \times .06 = \$2,400$
$6,400 - \$2,400 = \$4,000$
$4,000 \div 12 = \$333$ (rounded)

9. (a): $306 \div 300 \times \$2,000 = \$2,040$

10. (c): 1,750 square feet $\times \$14.50 = \$25,375$
$25,375 \div 12 = \$2,114.58$ (rounded)

Review Exam I (Chapters 2–8)

1. If a property is purchased for $300,000 and later sold for $345,000, what percentage of profit is earned?

    a. 115%

    b. 14%

    c. 15%

    d. 110%

2. A property was listed at $200,000 and sold for 80% of the list price. For how much did it sell?

    a. $160,000

    b. $250,000

    c. $180,000

    d. $170,000

3. Zena Jones listed her home at $100,000 and later sold it for 90% of the list price to Ted Johnson. Ted sold the property six months later for $100,000. What percentage of profit did Mr. Johnson realize?

    a. 10%

    b. 15%

    c. 12%

    d. 11.1%

4. The assessed value of a home is $132,500, which is 53% of market value. What is the market value of this home?

    a. $202,725

    b. $250,000

    c. $205,000

    d. $250,725

5. A broker charged Andrea 6% of the sales price to sell her home. The listing broker split the fee and gave 40% of the total fee to a selling broker, who split the fee equally with the salesperson who sold the property. What sales price was paid if the salesperson received a commission check for $1,200?

    a. $40,000

    b. $100,000

    c. $80,000

    d. $92,500

6. If a seller is charged 6% commission on the first $100,000 of the sales price, 5% on the second $100,000 and 3.5% on the balance of the sales price, what will he pay in commission if his home sells for $486,500?

    a. $29,190.00

    b. $10,027.50

    c. $6,000.00

    d. $21,027.50

7. Salesperson Sam received a commission check for $18,000 for selling the Snyder house. If he received 60% of the total commission and the house sold for $300,000, what rate of commission was charged?

   a. 6%
   b. 7%
   c. 10%
   d. 5%

8. A property is listed for $1.4 million and sells for $1.2 million. If the broker charges an 8% commission, gives the listing salesperson 10% of the total commission and splits the balance equally with the selling salesperson, what would the salesperson earn for both listing and selling this property?

   a. $120,000
   b. $60,000
   c. $52,800
   d. $72,000

9. A seller received $56,400 after paying her broker a 6% brokerage fee. What was the selling price of home?

   a. $60,000
   b. $56,400
   c. $59,784
   d. $65,400

10. You purchase a lot measuring 75 feet by 125 feet for $4.80 per square foot. During your ownership, the street is paved and a paving lien of $2.50 per front foot is placed against the property. What must the property's sales price be if you wish to realize a 15% net profit after you pay off the paving lien, pay $1,860 in closing costs and pay your broker a 7% brokerage fee?

    a. $53,797.50
    b. $51,750.00
    c. $57,563.33
    d. $57,846.77

11. If you purchased a property for $80,000 and sold it for $96,000, what percentage of profit would you realize?

    a. 10%
    b. 18%
    c. 20%
    d. 25%

12. A property sold for $240,000 that was 80% of the list price. What was the list price?

    a. $300,000
    b. $288,000
    c. $282,353
    d. $295,000

13. If you purchased a property for the list price less 20% and sold it for the list price plus 10%, what percentage of profit would you realize?

    a. 25%
    b. 37.5%
    c. 20%
    d. 80%

14. The area of a rectangle 75 feet by 150 feet is

    a. 9,375 square feet.
    b. 416.67 square yards.
    c. 1,250 square yards.
    d. 600 linear feet.

15. You have purchased a tract of land that measures 800 feet by 545 feet. You plan to develop it into building lots measuring 60 feet by 100 feet. If you set aside a strip of land 800 feet by 20 feet for a road, how many building lots can you create?

    a. 72.67

    b. 65.00

    c. 60.50

    d. 70.00

16. What will it cost to purchase three-fifths of a six-acre tract at $2.25 per square foot?

    a. $352,836

    b. $156,816

    c. $261,360

    d. $294,030

17. Calculate the cost to build a 3 inch thick patio measuring 48 feet by 18 feet if concrete will cost $60 per cubic yard and the workers will charge $3.75 per square foot for finish work.

    a. $4,680

    b. $3,720

    c. $3,240

    d. $5,160

18. You purchase a property for $185,000 of which 25% is land value. What is the per annum depreciation if depreciated over 40 years?

    a. $3,468.75

    b. $4,625.00

    c. $1,156.25

    d. $5,550.00

19. A property was purchased for $235,000. At the time of purchase, the land was worth 22% of the total property value. The purchaser held the property for seven years, during which time the land appreciated 6% per year straight-line and the building depreciated 2.5% per year straight-line. What is the value of the property at the end of the seven years?

    a. $233,623.29

    b. $243,225.00

    c. $224,636.50

    d. $232,081.46

20. If $50,000 in cash is paid down on a $250,000 property having land value of $60,000, how much can be depreciated over the useful life of the property?

    a. $60,000

    b. $250,000

    c. $200,000

    d. $190,000

21. The four units in a four-plex rent at $250 each per month. If the property generates $7,200 in annual operating expenses and maintains an occupancy rate of 95%, what is the property's indicated value to an investor seeking a 9% annual rate of return?

    a. $43,200.00

    b. $46,666.67

    c. $53,333.33

    d. $58,967.43

22. Using the cost approach, calculate the indicated value of a property with a 2,300 square-foot building sitting on an $18,000 plot of land if construction costs are $74 per square foot. (The building's effective age is eight years and it appears to have a remaining useful life of 42 years.)

    a. $160,968

    b. $142,968

    c. $155,781

    d. $188,200

23. Billy Banker collected $8,400 in principal and interest at the end of six months on a term loan of $8,000. What rate of interest did the borrower pay?

a. 20%

b. 10%

c. 12%

d. 15%

24. How long will it take for $15,000 to yield $2,250 at 10% annual simple interest?

a. 12 months

b. 9 months

c. 2 years

d. 1.5 years

25. If an interest payment of $300 is made every three months on a $10,000 loan, what annual rate of interest is being charged?

a. 12%

b. 10%

c. 15%

d. 18%

REVIEW EXAM I ANSWER KEY

1. (c): $345,000 − $300,000 = $45,000
$45,000 ÷ $300,000 = .15 or 15%

2. (a): $200,000 × .80 = $160,000

3. (d): $100,000 × .90 = $90,000
$100,000 − $90,000 = $10,000
$10,000 ÷ $90,000 = .111 (rounded) or 11.1%

4. (b): $132,500 ÷ .53 = $250,000

5. (b): $1,200 ÷ .50 = $2,400
$2,400 ÷ .40 = $6,000
$6,000 ÷ .06 = $100,000

6. (d): $100,000 × .06 = $6,000
$100,000 × .05 = $5,000
$486,500 − $200,000 = $286,500
$286,500 × .035 = $10,027.50
$10,027.50 + $6,000 + $5,000 = $21,027.50

7. (c): $18,000 ÷ .60 = $30,000
$30,000 ÷ $300,000 = .10 or 10%

8. (c): 100% − 10% = 90%
90% × .50 = 45%
10% + 45% = 55%
$1,200,000 × .08 = $96,000
$96,000 × .55 = $52,800

9. (a): $100\% - 6\% = 94\%$
$56,400 \div .94 = \$60,000$

10. (d): $75' \times 125' = 9,375$ square feet
9,375 square feet $\times \$4.80 = \$45,000$
$75' \times \$2.50 = \$187.50$
$\$45,000 \times 1.15 = \$51,750$
$\$51,750 + \$187.50 + \$1,860 = \$53,797.50$
$\$53,797.50 = 93\%$ of sales price
$\$53,797.50 \div .93 = \$57,846.77$ (rounded)

11. (c): $\$96,000 - \$80,000 = \$16,000$
$\$16,000 \div \$80,000 = .20$ or 20%

12. (a): $\$240,000 \div .80 = \$300,000$

13. (b): $100\% - 20\% = 80\%$
$100\% \times 1.10 = 110\%$
$110\% \div 80\% = 1.375$
$1.375 - 1 = .375$ or 37.5%

14. (c): $75' \times 150' = 11,250$ square feet
11,250 square feet $\div 9 = 1,250$ square yards

15. (d): $800' \times 545' = 436,000$ square feet
$800' \times 20' = 16,000$ square feet
436,000 square feet $- 16,000$ square feet $= 420,000$ square feet
$60' \times 100' = 6,000$ square feet
420,000 square feet $\div 6,000$ square feet $= 70$

16. (a): 6 acres $\times 43,560$ square feet $= 261,360$ square feet
$\dfrac{3}{5} = .60$
$.60 \times 261,360$ square feet $= 156,816$ square feet
156,816 square feet $\times \$2.25 = \$352,836$

17. (b): $48' \times 18' \times .25' = 216$ cubic feet
216 cubic feet $\div 27 = 8$ cubic yards
8 cubic yards $\times \$60 = \$480$
$48' \times 18' = 864$ square feet
864 square feet $\times \$3.75 = \$3,240$
$\$3,240 + \$480 = \$3,720$

18. (a): $\$185,000 \times .75 = \$138,750$
$\$138,750 \div 40 = \$3,468.75$

19. (c): $235,000 × .22 = $51,700

$235,000 − $51,700 = $183,300

$7 × 6\% = 42\%$

$100\% + 42\% = 142\%$

$7 × 2.5\% = 17.5\%$

$100\% − 17.5\% = 82.5\%$

$51,700 × 1.42 = $73,414

$183,300 × .825 = $151,222.50

$151,222.50 + $73,414 = $224,636.50

20. (d): $250,000 − $60,000 = $190,000

21. (b): $250 × 4 × 12 = $12,000

$12,000 × .95 = $11,400

$11,400 − $7,200 = $4,200

$4,200 ÷ .09 = $46,666.67 (rounded)

22. (a): 2,300 square feet × $74 = $170,200

$8 + 42 = 50$

$170,200 ÷ 50 × 42 = $142,968

$142,968 + $18,000 = $160,968

23. (b): $8,400 − $8,000 = $400

$400 ÷ 6 × 12 = $800 (rounded)

$800 ÷ $8,000 = .10 or 10\%

24. (d): $15,000 × .10 = $1,500

$1,500 ÷ 12 = $125

$2,250 ÷ $125 = 18 months or 1.5 years

25. (a): $300 ÷ 3 × 12 = $1,200

$1,200 ÷ $10,000 = .12 or 12\%

Review Exam II (Chapters 9–15)

1. Bob and Judy Jones want to purchase a home for $270,000 with a 90% conventional loan. If the lender uses qualifying ratios of 28/36, how much verifiable income must they show to qualify for a 30-year loan that requires monthly principal and interest payments of $10.14 per $1,000? (The annual taxes are $3,600 and the annual insurance premium will be $1,800.)

   a. $10,407.21
   b. $8,800.00

   c. $6,844.44
   d. $8,094.44

2. If you are required to pay 1.5 discount points, a 1-point loan origination fee, a .75 point private mortgage insurance premium and $3,800 for other closing costs and prepaids, how much cash will you need to close the 90% conventional loan on your new $148,500 home? (You have previously deposited $8,000 in earnest money with the escrow officer.)

   a. $14,993.63
   b. $18,143.63

   c. $13,943.63
   d. $8,143.63

3. Sydney can obtain a 95% conventional loan on a home selling for $68,800. His required down payment will be

   a. $6,880.
   b. $3,440.

   c. $10,320.
   d. $688.

4. Mr. Shrum can obtain a 30-year, 90% conventional loan at 8.75% interest that will require monthly principal and interest payments of $7.87 per $1,000. If his annual gross income is $62,500 and the lender will permit him to devote 25% of his gross monthly income to his monthly principal and interest payment, how much loan can he obtain?

   a. $183,832.18
   b. $174,963.94

   c. $157,329.00
   d. $165,448.54

5. A property has a market value of $348,000 in an area where a 53% assessment ratio is used. What is the annual tax bill if taxes are charged at $4.25 per $100 of assessed value?

   a. $14,790.00
   b. $783.87

   c. $7,838.70
   d. $1,479.00

6. A property is assessed at $175,000. If the tax rate is 23 mills, what is the amount of the annual tax bill?

    a. $230.00   c. $4,025.00

    b. $402.50   d. $3,450.00

7. A home is valued at $150,000 and assessed for 60% of its value. If the tax bill is $2,700, what is the tax rate per $100 of valuation?

    a. $3   c. $8

    b. $27   d. $6

8. Your new home has a market value of $152,000. The taxes in the area are levied on 66% of market value at a rate of $2.50 per $100 of assessed value. What will be the amount of your first annual tax bill?

    a. $1,672   c. $2,508

    b. $3,800   d. $1,003

9. The Johnsons are selling their home to the Cain family for $108,000. The Cains will assume the present loan balance of $28,000; the Johnsons will carry back a second loan for $40,000; and the Cains will pay the difference in cash. What will be the amount of the transfer tax if the state requires $.50 per $500 or fraction thereof and exempts assumed loans?

    a. $120   c. $104

    b. $80   d. $160

10. How many acres are in the N $\frac{1}{4}$ of the SW $\frac{1}{4}$ of the NE $\frac{1}{4}$ of section 32?

    a. 480   c. 60

    b. 10   d. 7.5

11. John James sold the N $\frac{1}{2}$ of the SW $\frac{1}{4}$ of the NW $\frac{1}{4}$ of section 10 and all of section 9 to James Johns for $1,200 per acre. How much did Mr. Johns pay Mr. James for this land?

    a. $768,000   c. $840,000

    b. $792,000   d. $780,000

12. Prorate the annual taxes of $3,600 for an August 28 closing using a statutory year to the day of closing. (Taxes are paid in arrears.)

    a. $2,370.00 debit seller

    b. $2,370.00 credit buyer

    c. $2,347.40 debit seller

    d. $2,347.40 debit buyer

13. A loan with an outstanding balance of $148,600 is being assumed. The loan was taken at 9% annual interest and is current in its payments as of June 1. What credit will the buyer receive from the seller at closing on June 16 for interest if the proration is calculated using a regular calendar year through the day of closing?

    a. $594.40   c. $512.98

    b. $520.10   d. $586.26

14. Peter Petersham is purchasing a four-plex and closing on February 16 of a leap year. Each unit rents for $680, with unit 3 vacant as of February 1. How much rent will be credited to the buyer at closing?

a. $1,500.69

b. $1,165.71

c. $914.48

d. $1,262.86

15. Using a banker's year, prorate the insurance premium for a policy that was purchased on October 16 at a cost of $450. (The closing will take place August 20 and the contract calls for all prorations to be calculated to the day of closing.)

a. $70 charge buyer/credit seller

b. $380 credit buyer/charge seller

c. $380 charge buyer/credit seller

d. $70 credit buyer/charge seller

In problems 16 through 19, identify how each would be entered on a closing statement in the most typical transaction.

16. Earnest money

a. Credit to the seller only

b. Credit to the buyer/debit to the seller

c. Credit to the buyer only

d. Debit to the buyer/credit to the seller

17. Tax proration, when taxes are paid in arrears

a. Debit to the seller only

b. Debit to the seller/credit to the tax collector

c. Credit to the seller/debit to the buyer

d. Credit to the buyer/debit to the seller

18. Loan balance being assumed

a. Credit to the buyer/debit to the seller

b. Debit to the buyer/credit to the seller

c. Debit to the buyer only

d. Credit to the buyer only

19. Proceeds of a new loan

a. Debit to the buyer only

b. Credit to the buyer only

c. Debit to the buyer/credit to the seller

d. Credit to the seller only

20. Another name for HUD Form 1 is the

a. Transaction Balance Sheet.

b. Standardized Closing Form.

c. RESPA Disbursement Form.

d. Uniform Settlement Statement.

21. Hilda's Hair Salon pays minimum rent of $650 per month plus 5% of annual gross sales in excess of $125,000. What monthly rent total will Hilda pay in a year in which her gross sales are $155,000?

   a. $775.00   c. $645.83
   b. $125.00   d. $1,295.83

22. Another tenant in the center where Hilda's salon is located (see problem 21) has a lease that requires a minimum monthly rental of $1,200 plus a percentage of gross annual sales in excess of $360,000. If gross sales were $528,000 and the tenant paid a total of $26,160 in rent, what percentage is stated in the lease?

   a. 6%   c. 7%
   b. 6.5%   d. 7.5%

23. Joanie Shot earns $78,000 annually. A lender will permit her to devote 24% of her gross monthly income to a principal and interest payment. How much can she spend each month for this payment if she can get a 15-year, 95% conventional loan that requires monthly payments of $8.23 per $1,000? (The loan is offered with 9.25% annual interest.)

   a. $487.87   c. $1,560.00
   b. $609.84   d. $641.94

24. Prorate the taxes for an April 4 closing using a regular calendar year and prorating through the day of closing. If the tax rate is $3.80 per $100 of valuation on a home with an assessed value of $203,000, the credit to the buyer is

   a. $1,986.62.   c. $1,992.78.
   b. $2,014.21.   d. $1,965.48.

25. What is the down payment on a home that sells for $398,000 if the buyer gets a 90% conventional loan for 30 years at 8.5% interest? (The transaction will close on December 6. The appraiser estimates the market value of the home to be $389,000.)

   a. $38,900   c. $39,800
   b. $79,600   d. $47,900

REVIEW EXAM II ANSWER KEY

1. (a): $270,000 × .90 = $243,000
        $243,000 ÷ $1,000 × $10.14 = $2,464.02
        $3,600 + $1,800 = $5,400
        $5,400 ÷ 12 = $450
        $450 + $2,464.02 = $2,914.02
        $2,914.02 ÷ .28 = $10,407.21

2. (a): $148,500 \times .90 = \$133,650$
$148,500 \times .10 = \$14,850$
$1.5 + 1 + .75 = 3.25$
$.0325 \times \$133,650 = \$4,343.63$ (rounded)
$4,343.63 + \$3,800 = \$8,143.63$
$8,143.63 + \$14,850 - \$8,000 = \$14,993.63$

3. (b): $100\% - 95\% = 5\%$
$68,800 \times .05 = \$3,440$

4. (d): $62,500 \div 12 \times .25 = \$1,302.08$ (rounded)
$1,302.08 \div \$7.87 \times \$1,000 = \$165,448.54$

5. (c): $348,000 \times .53 = \$184,440$
$184,440 \div 100 \times \$4.25 = \$7,838.70$

6. (c): $23 \div 1,000 = .023$
$175,000 \times .023 = \$4,025$

7. (a): $150,000 \times .60 = \$90,000$
$90,000 \div \$100 = 900$
$2,700 \div 900 = \$3$

8. (c): $152,000 \times .66 = \$100,320$
$100,320 \div \$100 \times \$2.50 = \$2,508$

9. (b): $108,000 - \$28,000 = \$80,000$
$80,000 \div \$500 \times \$.50 = \$80$

10. (b): $640 \times .25 \times .25 \times .25 = 10$ acres

11. (b): $640 \times .50 \times .25 \times .25 = 20$ acres
20 acres $+ 640$ acres $= 660$ acres
660 acres $\times \$1,200 = \$792,000$

12. (a): January – July = 7 months $\times$ 30 days = 210 days + 27 days = 237
$3,600 \div 360 \times 237$ days due $= \$2,370$ debit seller

13. (d): $148,600 \times .09 \div 365 \times 16 = \$586.26$ (rounded)

14. (c): $29 - 16 = 13$
$680 \times 3 = \$2,040$
$2,040 \div 29 \times 13 = \$914.48$ (rounded)

15. (a): Closing: August 20   September   Expires: October 16
$30 - 20 = 10 +$ 30 $+$ 16 $= 56$
$450 \div 360 \times 56 = \$70$ charge buyer/credit seller

16. (c): Credit to the buyer only

17. (d): Credit to the buyer/debit to the seller

18. (a): Credit to the buyer/debit to the seller

19. (b): Credit to the buyer only

20. (d): Uniform Settlement Statement

21. (a): $155,000 − $125,000 = $30,000
$30,000 × .05 = $1,500
$1,500 ÷ 12 = $125
$650 + $125 = $775

22. (c): $1,200 × 12 = $14,400
$528,000 − $360,000 = $168,000
$26,160 − $14,400 = $11,760
$11,760 (part) ÷ $168,000 (total) = .07 or 7% (rate)

23. (c): $78,000 ÷ 12 × .24 = $1,560

24. (a): $203,000 ÷ $100 × $3.80 = $7,714

   J   F   M   A
31 + 28 + 31 + 4 = 94

$7,714 ÷ 365 × 94 = $1,986.62 (rounded)

25. (c): $398,000 × .90 = $358,200
$398,000 − $358,200 = $39,800

TABLES OF MEASURE

Measures of Length

1 foot (ft.) = 12 inches (in.)
1 yard (yd.) = 3 feet (ft.)
1 rod (rd.) = 5.5 yards
1 rod = 16.5 feet
1 mile (mi.) = 5,280 ft.
1 mile = 320 rods (rd.)
1 chain = 66 feet
1 chain = 4 rods
4 rods = 100 links
1 link = 7.92 inches
1 vara = 33.333 inches (Texas)

Measures of Surface (Square Measure)

1 square foot (sq. ft.) = 144 square inches (sq. in.)
1 square yard (sq. yd.) = 9 square feet (sq. ft.)
1 square rod (sq. rd.) = 30.25 square yards (sq. yd.)
1 township = 36 sections
1 section = 1 square mile (sq. mi.)
1 square mile = 640 acres
1 acre = 43,560 square feet
1 acre = 10 square chains

Circular Measure

$$\text{area} = 3.14 \times \text{radius} \times \text{radius}$$
$$360 \text{ degrees } (°) = 1 \text{ circle}$$
$$90 \text{ degrees } (°) = \tfrac{1}{4} \text{ circle}$$
$$1 \text{ degree } (°) = 60 \text{ minutes } (')$$
$$1 \text{ minute } (') = 60 \text{ seconds } ('')$$

FORMULAS

Percentages

$$\text{Total} = \frac{\text{Part}}{\text{Rate}}$$

$$\text{Rate} = \frac{\text{Part}}{\text{Total}}$$

$$\text{Part} = \text{Total} \times \text{Rate}$$

Simple Interest

$$\text{Principal} \times \text{Rate} \times \text{Time} = \text{Interest}$$

$$PRT = I \qquad \frac{I}{RT} = P$$

$$\frac{I}{PT} = R \qquad \frac{I}{PR} = T$$

Area and Volume

Area of a rectangle = Length × Width
Area of a triangle = $\tfrac{1}{2}$ (base × height)
Volume of a rectangular prism = Length × Width × Height
Volume of a triangular prism = $\tfrac{1}{2}$ (base × height × width)

Income Approach to Appraising

$$\frac{\text{Net income}}{\text{Rate of return}} = \text{Value}$$

$$\frac{I}{R} = V \qquad \frac{I}{V} = R \qquad V \times R = I$$

Cost Approach Method of Appraising

Building replacement cost − Depreciation + Land value = Estimated property value

Straight-Line Method of Computing Depreciation

$$\frac{\text{Replacement cost}}{\text{Years of useful life}} = \text{Annual depreciation charge} \qquad \text{or} \qquad \frac{100\%}{\text{Years of useful life}} = \text{Depreciation rate}$$

Percentage of depreciation × Building replacement cost = Total depreciation

INDEX